The Digital Document

The Digital Document

A Reference for Architects, Engineers and Design Professionals

Bruce Duyshart

Routledge
Taylor & Francis Group

LONDON AND NEW YORK

Architectural Press is an imprint of Routledge
2 Park Square, Milton Park, Abingdon, Oxon OX14 4RN
711 Third Avenue, New York, NY 10017, USA

Routledge is an imprint of the Taylor & Francis Group, an informa business

First published 1997

British Library Cataloguing in Publication Data
A catalogue record for this book is available from the British Library

ISBN 0 7506 3602 5

Library of Congress Cataloguing in Publication Data
A catalogue record for this book is available from the British Library

Transferred to digital print on demand, 2005

CONTENTS

Chapter 1 A New Medium for Documents 1

Chapter 2 The Document 7
The Document Defined 7
Use of Paper as a Document Substrate 13
Use of Digital Documents 19

Chapter 3 Document Use in the Construction Industry 23
Architects in the Construction Industry 23
The Scope of Architectural Services 26
Office Document Types 28
The Volume of Project-Related Documents 33
Known Problems with the Use of Documents 35
Other Influences on Document Use 37
Performance Criteria for Documents 40

Chapter 4 The Digital Document Environment 43
The Integrated Computing Environment 43
Computing Fundamentals 44
Computer Hardware 45
Networks 53
Operating Systems 65
Applications 69

Chapter 5 Digital Data Types 81
Basic Principles 81
Numerical Data 82
Text Data 83
Graphical Data 88
Audio Data 98
Digital Ink Data 99
Compression of Data 101
Data Retrieval 106

Chapter 6 Digital Document Types 109
An Overview of Digital Documents 109
Classification of Digital Documents 112
Proprietary Application-Based Documents 113
Output Documents 115
Interchange Documents 117
Messaging Documents 125

Dynamic Compound Documents 135
Processable Compound Documents 136
Electronic Reference and Hypermedia Documents........................... 143
Viewer Documents.. 153
Multimedia Documents 160
A Comparison of Digital Documents... 165
Summary 167

Chapter 7 Applying Digital Documents... 173
Selecting Digital Document Technologies... 173
Distribution Methods.. 175
Document Management 177
Document Security 182
Document Storage 191

Chapter 8 Professional Opportunities.. 199
Benefits of Digital Documents... 199
Implications for Professional Practice.. 200
Recommendations for the Industry.. 201

Abbreviations 203
Internet Resources... 207
Index 211
Colophon 218

FIGURES

Figure 2.1   The relationship between an author and reader via a document............8
Figure 2.2   The components of a document 9
Figure 2.3   The distinction between actual and virtual documents. 10
Figure 2.4   Examples of structural and procedural mark-up 12
Figure 2.5   Some common formatting properties..13
Figure 2.6   The comparative storage capacity of paper vs. digital media 16
Figure 2.7   The consumption of paper products 1981-95 17
Figure 2.8   Comparative methods of document delivery 19
Figure 3.1   The participants in the design process *circa* 1939 24
Figure 3.2   The participants in the design process *circa* 1986 24
Figure 3.3   Potential construction industry participants and lines
              of communication 25
Figure 3.4   The scope of architectural services identified by the RAIA...................27
Figure 3.5   The relationship between main groups of documents 28
Figure 3.6   Information volume (number of 'documents') by project value...........34
Figure 3.7   A representation of the reuse of information during a project 38
Figure 3.8   Some key documents in a quality management system 39
Figure 4.1   Schematic diagram of a computer...44
Figure 4.2   The construction of a typical pen-based display device........................46
Figure 4.3   A proposed architectural input and display device................................52
Figure 4.4   A proposed augmented reality hard hat for use on a construction site .53
Figure 4.5   A representation of the extent of the Internet as of June 1996.............54
Figure 4.6   A representation of private and virtual private networks......................55
Figure 4.7   Use of video conferencing to discuss a design between remote users ..57
Figure 4.8   An example of a simple local area network (LAN)................................57
Figure 4.9   The progress of network communication methods 58
Figure 4.10   The OSI reference model 59
Figure 4.11   Basic Unix file permissions..62
Figure 4.12   A typical firewall set-up 63
Figure 4.13   File locking of documents to prevent simultaneous editing.................64
Figure 4.14   Sample user interfaces 67
Figure 4.15   A typical suite of software tools used by a designer 69
Figure 4.16   Use of multiple applications to create a single document 70
Figure 4.17   The capabilities of various text-based document creation systems 71
Figure 4.18   The concept of a document-centric approach to editing documents....72
Figure 4.19   The Java Environment 75
Figure 5.1   A comparison between decimal and binary numbers............................81
Figure 5.2   A representation of the flow of data...82
Figure 5.3   Numerical input and output of data 83
Figure 5.4   Examples of some sample fonts and typeface characteristics................87
Figure 5.5   A representation of physical vs logical pixels 90
Figure 5.6   A bitmap image..92
Figure 5.7   A range of grey scale tones 92

Figure 5.8   Some entities created using vector coordinates 95
Figure 5.9   An analogue signal replicated digitally with increasing
              precision levels 99
Figure 5.10   Ink data and its conversion on an Apple Newton PDA 100
Figure 5.11   Some typical pen gestures as used in the Newton OS.........................101
Figure 6.1   Documents in context with the general computing environment 109
Figure 6.2   The concept of application-specific document formats 114
Figure 6.3   A page description language used to support multiple devices 116
Figure 6.4   A PostScript program and printed output...117
Figure 6.5   Methods of exchanging native document formats 118
Figure 6.6   The effect of using a document interchange file 119
Figure 6.7   The effect of ASCII text interchange from a formatted source 119
Figure 6.8   The effect of delimited ASCII interchange 120
Figure 6.9   An example of the RTF interchange format...121
Figure 6.10   A section of a DXF file..124
Figure 6.11   A typical email header, message body and signature 127
Figure 6.12   The delivery of mail over the Internet using the SMTP protocol 128
Figure 6.13   A paper-based purchase order and its EDIFACT EDI equivalent 131
Figure 6.14   A Web form used to upload a file and notify other users 134
Figure 6.15   A representation of the structure of an SGML DTD............................139
Figure 6.16   A typical SGML document instance 140
Figure 6.17   An SGML authoring and parsing process...141
Figure 6.18   A series of hyperlinked documents...143
Figure 6.19   Artist's impression of The Memex (1945)...144
Figure 6.20   The hyperlinking of documents 145
Figure 6.21   The Netscape browser displaying information from a Web site.........147
Figure 6.22   HTML source code and its appearance in a Web browser...................148
Figure 6.23   The BCAider software interface 151
Figure 6.24   The creation and distribution of a viewer document 154
Figure 6.25   The Adobe Acrobat Exchange application interface 156
Figure 6.26   Comparative distribution times for a report..159
Figure 6.27   Media types used in multimedia and print documents. 160
Figure 6.28   A VRML world with navigation controls..162
Figure 6.29   Design sources for a multimedia document...163
Figure 6.30   A CD-ROM based multimedia product catalogue 164
Figure 6.31   An example of a multimedia reference encyclopaedia.........................165
Figure 7.1   The relative complexity and file size of various document types........176
Figure 7.2   The basic document life cycle in a document management system ...180
Figure 7.3   The Lotus Domino.Doc document management system...................181
Figure 7.4   The private-key encryption method 184
Figure 7.5   The public-key encryption method 186
Figure 7.6   The digital signature process of verified message exchange...............187
Figure 7.7   A sample PGP signature 188
Figure 7.8   The Digital Notary system..190
Figure 7.9   A sample Digital Notary signature file...190
Figure 7.10   The CALS phase 1 environment 195

TABLES

Table 2.1	Usage of paper by Commonwealth Departments and selected agencies in 1988-89	15
Table 3.1	A range of typical quality management documents	29
Table 3.2	A range of typical general office documents	30
Table 3.3	A range of typical archival documents	30
Table 3.4	A range of typical pre-design documents	30
Table 3.5	A range of design documents	31
Table 3.6	A range of typical contract documentation documents	31
Table 3.7	A range of typical contract administration documents	32
Table 3.8	A range of typical trading documents	32
Table 3.9	A range of typical reference documents	32
Table 3.10	A range of typical communication documents	33
Table 3.11	Information volume (number of 'documents') by project value ($A)	33
Table 4.1	Potential applications of network technologies in the AEC industry	56
Table 4.2	A range of typical software tools	70
Table 5.1	ASCII codes for printable characters	84
Table 5.2	Examples of some common uses of ASCII text data	85
Table 5.3	Primary scripts currently supported by UNICODE	86
Table 5.4	Examples of some common font types	88
Table 5.5	Examples of some common bitmap file types	93
Table 5.6	Examples of some common vector file types	95
Table 5.7	Examples of some common metafile file types	97
Table 5.8	Examples of some common animation file types	97
Table 5.9	Examples of some common multimedia file formats	98
Table 5.10	Examples of some typical audio file types	99
Table 5.11	Some popular digital archive standards	105
Table 5.12	Effectiveness of compression techniques upon data types	106
Table 6.1	Examples of some common native document formats	115
Table 6.2	Examples of some output and page description languages	116
Table 6.3	Examples of some common document interchange standards	121
Table 6.4	Examples of some IAC and dynamic compound document standards	136
Table 6.5	Examples of some common compound document processing models	137
Table 6.6	Methods of searching reference documents	146
Table 6.7	Examples of some common viewer document formats	153
Table 6.8	Cost savings from the use of PDF documents	158
Table 6.9	Examples of some multimedia document products	161
Table 6.10	A summary of the main digital document groups	166
Table 6.11	Some common features of digital documents	167
Table 7.1	Examples of some common document distribution methods	177
Table 7.2	Expected lifetimes and predicted obsolescence of storage media	192

PREFACE

In an increasingly digital world, architects, engineers and design professionals are rapidly approaching a work environment in which information will be created, delivered, managed and stored, using vastly different methods to traditional paper-based systems.

Documents such as drawings, memos, and specifications, form an essential role in the design and construction industry. From conception to completion of a project hundreds, even thousands, of documents can be used. Each of these documents forms a node in a complex web of data that conveys information from the germination of a design idea, through to its final built form. In many ways, therefore, the success of a design or construction-based practice relies upon an understanding of the use of documents, and the technologies and techniques that are used to create them.

In today's computer-based work environment, digital documents are generally regarded as having far greater functionality and usability features than their traditional paper predecessors. Digital documents are capable of being easily reused for different purposes, searched by title and content, managed in customised work environments, delivered over vast distances almost instantaneously, and accumulated in valuable information repositories. Yet, despite these advantages, few users are accustomed to the broad range of capabilities and use of this relatively new medium. This may be partly attributable to the bewildering array of alternative technologies on offer.

The Digital Document provides an extensive background to the issues and technologies surrounding this very important topic. This book explores the role of documents in the design and construction industry and examines the components, capabilities, viability, and application of various digital document technologies.

In any industry, the transition between two mediums is always a difficult process. Not only are there many new technologies to comprehend but, more importantly, there are many new work practices that need to be built upon an understanding of these technologies. It is hoped that the information in this book will begin to demystify a number of the technologies involved, and ultimately, assist this process of change.

Bruce Duyshart
Sydney, 1997

Bruce_Duyshart@lendlease.com.au

ACKNOWLEDGEMENTS

In the preparation, research, and production of this book I am grateful to many people for their assistance.

The original research was carried out for my Master of Architecture degree received from the Faculty of Architecture, Building and Planning at the University of Melbourne. They have also generously assisted me in getting this publication to print.

My employer, Lend Lease, is now one of the largest property investment, development and management companies in the world, and it has been my fortune to become a part of an organisation where I have been able to test and apply many of the principals and technologies covered in this publication. Their support for this work as part of their own vision for the integrated digital workplace of the future, has been exemplary.

Over ten years ago my father had his own vision of how a design practice could better handle the creation and management of digital documents. In many respects his quest for 'finding a better way', and the early development work I did with him, has led me to the field where I am now. Thanks Dad. Thanks Mum for your support on the way.

In between relocating to a new city, starting new jobs, and contending with the writing and preparation of this book, my wife Nicola was the best pit support crew one could hope for. Tyre changes, fresh coffee, meal breaks and an update board telling me how many laps were left to go, were only some of the things she helped me with. As any driver will tell you, without a good support crew you rarely go well in the race. Thanks Nic.

I would like to thank the following companies/organisations for their support during the writing of this book and their support of the concepts behind it:

 Lend Lease Corporation

 The Royal Australian Institute of Architects

 The University of Melbourne
Faculty of Architecture, Building & Planning

Chapter 1
A New Medium for Documents

INTRODUCTION

> As one industry after another looks at itself in the mirror and asks about its
> future in a digital world, that future is driven almost 100 per cent by the
> ability of that company's product or service to be rendered in digital form.[1]

In an era where technology is now an implicit part of almost all professional activities,
the role of the document as a container of information, is becoming increasingly
important. The Internet is now recognised as the fastest growing medium in history,
and its prolific use is now exposing millions of users to a whole range of new and
exciting document types that have very powerful capabilities. In order to take best
advantage of those capabilities, it is important for business professionals to acquire an
understanding of how information can be used in multiple formats using a wide
range of sources. This book explores a number of issues related to the application of
digital documents, and examines how they can be used by architects, engineers and
design professionals in the construction industry.

Traditionally, it has been argued that societies have been shaped more by the nature
of the media by which people communicate, than by the actual content of the
communication.[2] However, it has also been recognised that it is usually the content of
any medium which blinds people to the real character of the medium they are using.[3]

Paper is a typical example. Rarely is thought given to how effective paper is as a
means of delivering the information in a document. This is because it is generally
perceived that a document does not exist until it is in a paper form. In this book a
new medium is examined for the packaging of information. That medium is digital
rather than analogue, made of bits rather than atoms, and is incorporeal rather than
tangible. One of the aims of *The Digital Document* is to explore the benefits that can be
gained from shifting to this new media type in the use of documents.

A change in media types would represent a paradigm shift in the way that documents
are used. Thomas Kuhn introduced the notion of a paradigm shift as being a change
in 'an accepted model or pattern'.[4] It is commonly recognised that the accepted model

of a document is one that is based upon the use of paper. This book sets out to challenge that view, and to demonstrate that there are a sufficient number of valid alternatives to the 'paper document paradigm'.

Throughout history there has always been a propensity for each new medium to build upon its predecessors and to redefine them in the process.[5] Negroponte argues that one way to look at the future of digital environments, is to ask if the quality of one medium can be transposed to another.[1] In this book it will be demonstrated that digital documents offer not only similar qualities to their paper counterparts, but also certain functionalities that are far superior.

Documents such as drawings, memos, and specifications, form an essential component of the architectural and engineering practices. From conception to completion of a project, hundreds or even thousands of documents are used. Each document forms a node in a complex web of data that conveys information from the germination of a design idea, through to its final built form.[6,7] Without using documents, the communication between the different groups in the design and construction process can become incomplete or ambiguous.[8,9] In many ways, therefore, the success of the architectural practice relies upon an understanding of the use of documents, and the technologies and techniques used to create them.

When an architect or engineer is confronted with a design problem, the process of resolution usually involves a visualisation, or graphic preview, of a range of possible solutions. In the 1930s, Le Corbusier explained that for him, architectural form and space was first a concept of the brain, and that paper was the only means of transmitting these ideas back to the designer and to others.[10] Today however, there are a multitude of alternative digital and electronic approaches that can be taken to achieve this aim.

Over the centuries, architects and engineers have not only used a diverse range of document types, but have also utilised an array of substrates from clay to tracing paper on which to produce them. In Egypt, evidence of simply drawn and roughly scaled plans have been found on ancient papyrus fragments and flakes of limestone.[10] The Greeks and Romans are known to have used full-sized templates and mock-ups of designs on site.[11] In the Middle Ages, designers used specially prepared plaster screed floors next to the building site to convey their ideas to the master masons.[10] By the time of Alberti, in the mid fifteenth century, documents had become inexpensive and portable enough that the work of the designer could be removed in time and space from the construction site.[12]

Over the last 600 years paper has been the dominating medium for the transfer of written information. Paper has stood the test of time. It has high contrast display characteristics, is relatively light, highly portable, easy to reproduce, easy to browse through, and is familiar to every user. On the surface these characteristics seem incredibly difficult to compete with.

However, despite the conveniences of paper, there are a multitude of disadvantages associated with its use in today's modern work environment. The main issues relate to problems of superfluous reproduction, poor accessibility, poor searchability of content, physically large storage requirements, expensive consumption of resources and inefficient handling and delivery procedures.

As society has made the transition from an industrial economy to one based on information, the role of documents in business has also changed.[13] Computers have completely transformed the concept of what information is, and how it can be interacted with and manipulated. Documents are no longer merely used for record-keeping or the temporary transfer of ideas. Users are beginning to realise that the data contained within their office documents are one of the most valuable assets that a company can possess. Once documents are in a digital form they are capable of being used and reused in a number of powerful and different ways.

Today, digital documents are generally regarded as having far greater functionality and usability features than their paper predecessors. Digital documents are capable of being easily reused for different purposes, searched by title and content, managed in customised work environments, delivered over vast distances almost instantaneously, and accumulated in valuable information repositories. Yet despite these advantages, few users seem accustomed to the capabilities and use of this relatively new medium.

One of the major reasons behind this perception, has been the metamorphic and dynamic state of the computer industry. From an industry that was initially predicted by the founder of IBM, Thomas J. Watson, to grow to no more than eleven computers world-wide, the industry has experienced an explosive and extensive growth. For example, by 1992, the computer equipment and services sector in the US had become larger than the automotive, steel, mining, petrochemical, and natural gas sectors combined.[13] The effect of this phenomenal growth and the changes it has brought, has left many users in a state of confusion and industry standards in disarray.

The lack of standards and the inability to easily integrate computing solutions, is one of the biggest problems associated with the growth of the computer industry today. In the early days of computing, plain text files were the standard means of creating, distributing and interchanging documents. Then, as documents became more complex with the inclusion of computer graphics, image processing, and advanced text applications, a portability problem began to arise. Competing market forces introduced a multitude of different applications and a diverse range of associated file formats. Not surprisingly, this led to large-scale incompatibilities between many systems, and resulted in what are known as islands of technology.[13]

Only since the early 1990s, coinciding with the extensive popularity of the Internet, has there been any true efforts to promote the development and standardisation of document types to meet the needs of common work practices. United by an extensive and comprehensive communication medium, the Internet now offers many new challenges for users to understand the use of documents in a digital environment. In the ensuing chapters, many related issues will be examined.

The transition from paper-based to digital-based systems will represent, for most designers, a fundamental shift in their current method of practice. It has often been acknowledged that the building and construction sector has been slower than most others in embracing information technology. Therefore, given the speed at which IT is developing, it is becoming increasingly important for architects and engineers to keep up to date with new technologies, if they are to remain competitive in the industry. In the context of this book, it will mean that architects and engineers will need to understand the capabilities of a wide range of digital document types, and to develop new approaches to their use. This book provides additional information to facilitate this process, and a catalyst which will open up the debate on the suitability of this approach.

In the adoption of new technologies, it seems that architects have always wanted to shroud in mystery the methods and techniques they have used. In the Italian Renaissance, Filipo Brunelleschi avoided questioning on his method of perspective projection in a public demonstration in 1417. Even by the late eighteenth century, Gaspard Monge's method of orthographic projection had become classified as 'top secret' by the French Government.[10] It is almost ironical therefore, that approximately 200 years after Monge, a similar air of mystery is still prevalent in the construction industry over the use of computers for CAD and other digital methods of producing documents.

The timing of this book is important given the developments that are occurring in the construction industry and information technology. Traditional work practices in most offices are now being constantly challenged through the application of IT. New business models based upon the use of quality assurance, process re-engineering and workgroup computing are being continually advocated. Most of these changes are based upon the need for increased access to information and improvements in efficiency. The gains can be significant. For example, it has been shown that attaining only a ten per cent improvement in the efficiency of the construction industry, would result in an increase in the Australian GDP of 2.5 per cent.[14] In this book, it will be shown how improved efficiency is just one of many benefits that can be gained from the use of digital documents.

In the analysis of new technologies, one of the fundamental errors is to view them through the lens of existing processes.[15] By trying to adapt technologies to the confines of an existing sphere of knowledge there is a danger of missing out on new opportunities. A more pragmatic approach is usually required. *The Digital Document* should be analysed with a view to finding new approaches to and a better understanding of the use of documents, and a realisation that paper may not be the ultimate solution.

REFERENCES

1.   Negroponte, N. (1995), *Being Digital*, Rydalmere: Hodder and Stoughton.

2.   McLuhan, M. and Fiore, Q. (1967), *The Medium is the Massage*, Harmondsworth: Penguin.

3.   McLuhan, M. (1964), *Understanding Media*, London: Abacus.

4. Kuhn, T. S. (1970), *The Structure of Scientific Revolutions*, 2nd edn, International Encyclopedia of Unified Science, vol. 2, no. 2, Chicago: University of Chicago.

5. Schrage, M. (1995), *No More Teams! Mastering the dynamics of creative collaboration*, New York: Doubleday.

6. Porter, T. (1993), *Architectural Drawing Master Class: Graphic Techniques from the World's Leading Architect's*, London: Studio Vista.

7. Schmitt, G. (1988), *Microcomputer Aided Design for Architects and Designers*, New York: Jon Wiley and Sons.

8. NPWC (1993), *Integration of Documents: Quality Management of Documentation for Construction*, Procurement Management Series, Canberra: National Public Works Council.

9. Schilling, T. G. and Schilling, P. M. (1987), *Intelligent Drawings: Managing CAD and Information Systems in the Design Office*, New York: McGraw-Hill.

10. Porter, T. (1990), *Graphic Design Techniques for Architectural Drawing*, London: Hamlyn.

11. Haselberger, L. (1995), 'Deciphering a Roman blueprint', *Scientific American*, vol. 272, no. 6, pp. 56–61.

12. Mitchell, W. J. and McCullough, M. (1995), *Digital Design Media*, New York: Van Nostrand Reinhold.

13. Tapscott, D. and Caston, A. (1993), *Paradigm Shift – The New Promise of Information Technology*, New York: McGraw-Hill.

14. DIST (1994), *Strategy for Information Management in the Building and Construction Industry*, Department of Industry, Science and Technology, Melbourne.

15. Hammer, M. and Champy, J. (1994), *Reengineering the Corporation: a Manifesto for Business Revolution*, St Leonards: Allen and Unwin.

Chapter 2
The Document

THE DOCUMENT DEFINED

It is estimated that 60 per cent of an average business person's time is spent processing documents. World-wide, this equates to an average production of over 92 billion originals and 400 billion photocopies a year.[1] Thought is rarely given to how each of the documents has been conceived, written, produced, or even distributed. The only important fact for many people is that there is a tangible mechanism for the exchange of information.

Documents not only convey many different messages, they also use different methods of encoding those messages. For example, consider the range and complexity of different document types that can be found in architectural and engineering offices. Plans, schedules, specifications, product catalogues, information brochures, instruction manuals and legal pro formas can all be readily recognised by the user, but they are usually created using different encoding, syntactic and presentation methods.

Documents are of a paramount importance to architects and engineers, and are used extensively in the confluence of information between the various parties involved in the design and construction process. Their existence, in most cases, not only forms a legal requirement, but is an indispensable means of processing vast quantities of diverse information. In fact, one of the reasons that documents exist at all is the limitation of the human brain to abstract large amounts of information. Modern psychology acknowledges that the human information-processing capacity is limited to being able to handle only seven (plus or minus two) items of information at once.[2] Documents therefore, become a necessary means for architects and engineers to accurately and effectively record and convey design intent to clients, consultants, contractors, and other participants in the building process.

What is a Document ?
So far, the definition of the term *document* has been implied. In using this term there are a multitude of definitions and interpretations that could suffice. These definitions will usually depend on the interpretations formed by a person's own experiences.

Lawyers for example would use the term in reference to legal evidence, architects in reference to specifications and drawings, and musicians in reference to musical scores. Each of these definitions are as valid as each other, but they are only instances of the term. Underlying each of these examples, is a universal definition that is perhaps not as well recognised.

Computer scientists, typographers, linguists and psychologists have each taken their own view of what a document is and what it should contain. The difficulty in providing a universal definition, is that there is no comprehensive theory of documents that provides a coherent picture into which the detailed insights developed in these various fields of research can be fitted.[3] Another difficulty, is that new methods of document creation and distribution have evolved in the last few decades which have added to the number of known document types.

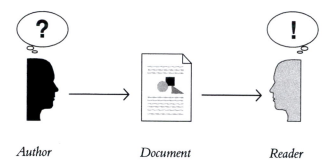

Author   *Document*   *Reader*

Figure 2.1 The relationship between an author and reader via a document

Despite the enormous range of document types in existence, they all have one important feature in common, *conveying information*. Therefore, a fairly simple description of a document could be:

> A document is something written or inscribed that furnishes evidence or information on any subject.[4]

alternatively;

> A document is the commonly accepted medium for distributing and acquiring information.[5]

or more comprehensively;

> A document is a series of marks on a substrate which acts as a vehicle by means of which messages can be conveyed from an author to communities of readers who are separated from the author in space and time.[3]

A more universal definition therefore, is that:

> A document is a container of information used to convey messages between an author and a reader.

The Components of a Document

The key components of a document can be divided into three parts: the marks, the substrate and the container as illustrated in Figure 2.2.

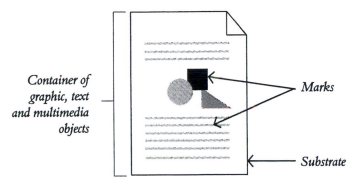

Figure 2.2 The components of a document

The Marks

The marks can be defined as the inks, dyes, or pixels which form the graphic and textual objects upon a substrate e.g. ink, graphite, charcoal, crayon, ball-point, water-colour, paint, pixels.

The Substrate

The substrate can be defined as a fixed or portable 'surface' upon which the marks of a document are made.

A *portable* substrate, therefore, is one which can be taken away from the device or place where it was made e.g. vellum, trace, butter paper, blueprint, dyeline, photocopy, cartridge, cloth, mylar, board, film, acetate.

A *fixed* substrate is one which requires the reader to come to the document to read it, e.g. a computer screen, signage.

The Container

The container can be considered as the 'receptacle' that forms the marks and substrate, e.g. plans, contracts, specifications, brochures, pro formas, a computer file.

Beyond this definition of a document, the next stages to consider are the mechanisms and structures by which documents convey the messages they carry.

Types of Documents

Documents can be categorised into two main types: *actual documents* and *virtual documents*.[3] The distinction is necessary in order to introduce further concepts relating to the technologies of digital documents, and the way that they can be created, exchanged, and displayed in a digital environment.

Actual Documents

The term *actual document* is used to denote the physical objects that readers see and use. In other words, an actual document is the assembly of marks that appear on a substrate. These marks can be either simple or complex, but every perceptible feature will play some part in forming the reader's understanding of a particular document. For example this is why it is very important that legal documents are precisely worded, and that an architect's working drawings are accurately drafted.

When the author of a document is absent, it is common that the reader must rely solely upon the information that can be physically viewed on an actual document itself. For example, a builder remotely located on a building site will usually rely on the information that can be interpreted from the drawings and specifications that have been created by the architect. In this case, the drawings have enabled the architect to be removed in space and time from the building site.

The following definition of an actual document can therefore be used:

> An actual document is the physical presentation of an assembly of marks on a substrate.

Virtual Documents

The term *virtual document* is used to describe the specification for an actual document that a system is about to produce.[3] This is term is primarily used in conjunction with computers, whereby a virtual document exists as data structures, constructed according to the rules of a particular production system (such as a word-processor or CAD software application). In order for a document to be produced, the instructions contained in the specification have to be further interpreted by a marking device such as a printer or computer screen. (Interestingly, the term virtual document, can also be used to describe the imprinting surface used in traditional lithographic, gravure, offset, letterpress and screen printing processes).

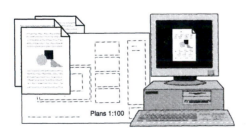

```
<Heading> Building Specification <Heading>
<Subtitle> 1.0 Introduction</Subtitle>
<body>
These are the general specifications of
works to be carried out and materials to
be used in the construction of a building
as shown and dimensioned on the
accompanying drawings as listed in
<bold>Appendix A</bold> - <emph>Schedule
of Drawings </emph>.
</body>
```

Actual documents   *A virtual document*

Figure 2.3 The distinction between actual and virtual documents.

A virtual document can therefore be defined as follows:

> A virtual document is the structural data specification of the content
> a document.

An illustration demonstrating the distinction between an actual and virtual document is shown in Figure 2.3.

Document Structures

Throughout this book, a document has been defined as being a container of information. This implies therefore, that it has a *content*. When a document is in a digital form this content can be manipulated in a number of different ways that are not possible when using a paper substrate alone.

Before the advent of computers, there was little that could be done to increase the usability of a paper-based document beyond its ability to be read, categorised and filed away. In a library system for example, the 'Classified Sequence' of categorisation uses a Dewey decimal code, author, title, year, place of publication, physical description, notes, International Standard Book Number (ISBN) or International Standard Serial Number (ISSN), and a limited number of keywords.[6] When using searches across library indexes using this system, it is usually only possible to find the titles of documents rather than any information in the content of the referenced item.

A similar situation is also common in architectural and engineering offices, where drawings and specifications are usually categorised and stored according to a job number, title, and/or client name. With no easy means of cataloguing the content of paper documents, there is usually no way of quickly searching for specific details or specifications across previous (or even current) project files. Instead, the alternative is to make a painstaking manual search which usually requires the knowledge of people who are known to have worked on those projects.

With the use of computers, there is an increased interest in the way that documents can be structured to overcome these problems. In a digital form, documents become far easier to locate, because searches can be made based on their title, information content, or any number of other associated attributes. For example, it is now possible to search through digital documents using techniques such as hypertext links, full-text searches, graphical browsing, keyword searching, object recognition and live tables of contents.

In its virtual form, the digital document can also contain large amounts of information about itself. This can include information about a documents origin and identity, the date and time of revision levels, annotation notes, security levels, as well as executable code that specifies how it might manipulate and present itself to a user.[7]

In their digital form, documents are also inherently richer than their paper counterparts. It is now quite common to include multimedia objects such as rendered images, video and audio in the structure of a document.

There are also a number of other esoteric features of document's structure which can be identified, such as the complex criteria which can be used to describe the graphic encoding scheme of the content of a document.[3] For example, it is possible to encode documents to four separate (and relatively complex) levels such as verbal content encoding, semantic attribute encoding, syntactic structure encoding and content structure encoding. In essence, these mechanisms allow an author to encode the messages within a document in a number of different ways, such as the use of use punctuation, positioning and differentiation.

Document Presentation and Rendering

The final property of a document to be considered, is the way in which its graphical objects (such as the text and images) can be specified for rendering to a computer screen or output (marking) device. The term *rendering,* is used to describe the way in which a document is displayed or presented to a user on a given substrate.

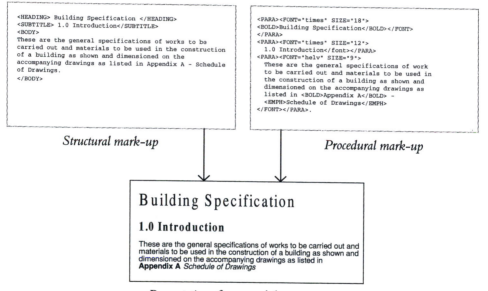

Figure 2.4 Examples of structural and procedural mark-up

In its virtual form, a digital document can be encoded using a number of different mark-up tags to specify how it is organised and intended to be presented to readers. This usually refers to two different forms of mark-up, *structural* and *procedural*. Structural mark-up refers to the way in which a document can be marked up into various organisational elements such as headings, paragraphs, sections, lists, bullet points etc. Procedural mark-up is used to describe characteristics such as font, point size, metric properties of the text, and various other aspects of a document's layout. Figure 2.4 illustrates a simplified example of these principles.

Collectively, structural and procedural mark-up are generally referred to as *formatting* a document. Formatting is a very important aspect of the way a document can communicate its message. For example, in an architect's working drawings, there are certain graphical conventions which can be used for the presentation of information, such as the placement of the title block and labelling of graphics.[8] There are also certain conventions used in the layout, organisation and appearance of building specifications. Figure 2.5 illustrates some common formatting properties of text. (Interestingly, these conventions almost break down completely in the formatting of documents used for design competitions. In these cases, freedom of expression is a desired attribute that often distinguishes one architect's work from another).

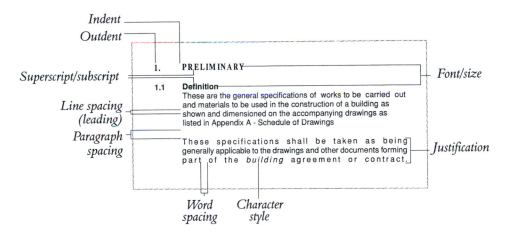

Figure 2.5 Some common formatting properties

To display a document on a computer screen, the formatting codes are usually handled by the software application. But in order to print a document, a device independent page description language (PDL) is usually required. When a document has to be printed, the encoding and mark-up within the document usually has to be translated into a PDL which is known to the output device. An example of a common PDL used by many printers, is the PostScript language. Within this PDL there a set of image operators such as 'fill' to mark areas, 'stroke' to generate lines, 'image' to paint raster (bitmap) images, and 'show' to create text. Also contained within this description will be a number of operators which describe the position of various objects on the page, and to set other attributes such as font, line width, fill colour, fill pattern etc.

USE OF PAPER AS A DOCUMENT SUBSTRATE

One of the most contentious issues in the use of documents is the choice of paper versus digital substrates. The most familiar and portable of these substrates is paper.

Over a period of centuries, paper has become the most widely used medium for the publishing, printing, distribution and archiving of documents. This is mainly because it is highly portable, easy to use, relatively inexpensive to produce, provides high definition and contrast, is relatively maintenance free, requires no complex machinery to interpret, takes advantage of established conventions regarding data structure and formatting, and can be easily annotated by hand.

Despite these advantages, however, there are an incredible number of inefficiencies associated with its use. The main disadvantages relate to problems in reproduction, storage methods, consumption of resources and management issues.

Reproduction of Paper

Since the 1800s there has been a steady development of a number of extraordinarily efficient tools for the production and reproduction of paper-based documents. These tools range from Linotype and Monotype, to today's computers and photocopiers. As a result, it has often been argued that the use of computers to achieve the 'paperless office' is not an unrealised goal; it is just unrealistic.[9] Even after almost forty years of computing, the paperless office has yet to appear. In fact, in a typical office today, document handling still continues in a style that has changed little since the turn of the century. For example, it is still estimated that 92 per cent of all information is in manila folders, and that 80 per cent of all technical information is on paper or microfilm.[10]

In the business world, an estimated 252 million original documents are created, every day. These documents go through various processes of reproduction, with the average office document being copied nineteen times.[1] Throughout this reproduction process, documents often deteriorate in quality, and the original documents get lost in a sea of paper duplicates. In the US alone, an average of 1.1 billion photocopies are made every day, which is an amount so large that it could form a stack of copying paper 110 km high. Over the course of a year, this stack would reach a height of over 40,000 km, or enough to encircle the Equator over three times.[1]

Not only is the volume of paper documents large, there is also a considerable weight problem associated with their use. An often quoted fact in the defence industry, is that an average US frigate carries about 26 tonnes of documentation and would visibly rise out of the water if it was removed.[11] Architects and engineers should also consider the effects that similar loads of paper would create in a multi-storey building.

Volume and weight are also a consideration in the delivery and management of paper documents. For example, up to 45 per cent of the final cost of a book goes towards the cost of inventory, shipping, and returns.[12] Couriers also charge according to the physical attributes and distance that a document has to travel.

To give a better appreciation of the amounts of paper that can potentially be consumed by an organisation, Table 2.1 lists the usage of paper and paper products by Commonwealth Departments in Australia over a period of one year.

The duplication of documents not only creates unnecessary waste, it also adds to the problems of document management and quality control. For example, the copying of original documents often leads to an enormous amount of confusion over the date and revision level of an original, and its copies. This has often been a major problem in the construction industry where there have been a number of expensive litigation cases resulting from construction faults caused by the use of out-of-date documents.

Table 2.1 Usage of paper by Commonwealth Departments and selected agencies in 1988-89[13]

Product	Usage	Quantity	Value in $m
Photocopy, cut fine, bulk bond	tonnes	3 188	5.912
Writing paper ruled stationery	tonnes	4 246	0.943
Scribbling pads, manila folders and backing sheets	tonnes folders	267 6 583	0.628
Envelopes	ctn. of 3 000	15 273	3.359
Paper for facsimile and electronic whiteboards	rolls	44 356	0.449
Paper rolls and page printers and telex	rolls	43 378	0.217
Printed forms	cartons	5 900	7.100
Pamphlets	rolls	1 600	0.470
Computer paper/continuous	tonnes	1 460	2.813
Word-processing (laser) stationery	tonnes	10	0.493
Total			$A22.384

A further problem that results from the reproduction of documents is that of security. Often documents contain sensitive information such as tender figures, client budgets or proposed plans. If these types of documents are duplicated and distributed, they can cause situations ranging anywhere from embarrassment to political turmoil. (In the then Soviet Union until as late as the mid 1980s, the problem of the replication of sensitive documents, was dealt with by keeping Xerox photocopy machines under lock and key.[14])

Storage of Paper

There are a number of problems associated with storage of paper. The two main problems relate to their physical volume and the methods required to retain them.

One of the largest problems with the use of paper, is the space it consumes when stored. Despite the fact that only one in five of the documents that are produced end up being filed, there are still an estimated 200 million pieces of paper a day that have to be stored.[1] In 1994 it was estimated that there were 2 trillion documents and 8 billion drawings world-wide, which are still stored in standard files. Xerox estimates that these figures will double every 3.5 years.[10] The ramifications of these figures as a space requirement are enormous, considering that an average four-drawer filing cabinet is capable of storing only about 10,000 documents.

As a means of comparison to digital storage capacity, the same 10,000 documents, can be stored on only *one* 640Mb standard CD-ROM disk, as illustrated in Figure 2.6. This same capacity CD-ROM could also be used to store two years worth of the *Wall Street Journal* or 100 classic novels. (Assuming someone can read two novels a week, this would represent five years worth of reading.[12]) The more advanced DVD (Digital

Versatile Disk) CD-ROM standard is capable of storing between 4.7Gb and 17Gb of data. Consequently, many publishers and software manufacturers are using CD-ROM as a publishing medium, and a method of replacing bulky manuals.

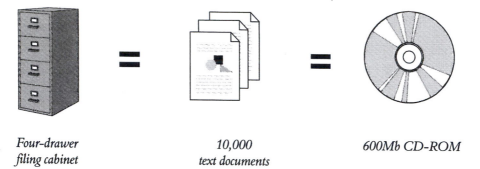

Four-drawer   10,000   600Mb CD-ROM
filing cabinet   text documents

Figure 2.6 The comparative storage capacity of paper vs. digital media

In architectural practice, the recommendation from professional bodies, such as the RAIA, is that all documents which come into existence during the course of an architect's engagement in a project, should be retained for at least twenty years.[15,16] These documents are required for the purposes of income tax assessment, bankruptcy law, environmental law, technical precedent, facilitation of alterations, additions and repairs, and for the purposes of other forms of potential litigation. The RAIA recommend that the following document types are retained.

- Sketches and preliminary drawings.
- Documents lodged for application or tendering purposes.
- Original and copies of drawings and schedules.
- Bills of quantities.
- Documents submitted for building approval or statutory approval or consent.
- Construction contract documents.
- As-built drawings.
- Correspondence, records of telephone conversations and notes or minutes of meetings.

Considering these requirements, the actual numbers and volume of documents required to be retained are enormous. A common recommendation to overcome such storage issues is to use microfilm. A drawback to this system however, is that documents which have been stored on microfilm are not admissible in every jurisdiction unless there is an accompanying affidavit to establish their validity as copies of the originals.[15] Given the complexity of this requirement, the usual result is that many project documents which are regarded as being 'non-essential' by the architect or engineer, end up being destroyed well before the prescribed period.

Consumption of Resources

A commonly expressed concern with the use of paper documents is the amount of resources that are consumed. Every year a vast number of non-renewable resources are used in the manufacture, processing, transport, printing, compilation, distribution, filing and disposing of printed material. Across the world it is estimated that every second, 2.3 tonnes of paper are consumed and that for every ton of paper, seventeen trees are required.[1] Research has also shown that two-thirds of the fibre in fine printing papers comes from native forests, and that only one-third of the fibre comes from plantations, on imported or recycled paper. By the year 2000, the projected world demand for paper and paperboard is expected to be 310 million tonnes.[1]

Not only is the consumption of paper high, there is also a considerable amount of wastage. For example, it is estimated that the average office worker throws away about a quarter of a kilogram of paper a day. In a financial institution this figure climbs to 0.9 kg per person, and in a law office employing more than sixty attorneys an estimated 18 kg a day per attorney is common.[1] Based on the previous figures, this would mean that the average office worker throws away about the equivalent of one tree per year in waste paper. The construction industry is also renowned for the vast quantities of paper it consumes throughout the design and documentation process.

The figures for the consumption of paper for printings and writings in Australia is shown in Figure 2.7. As can be seen from this graph, there is an increasing trend for the consumption of paper-based documents, while the consumption of newsprint has remained reasonably consistent.

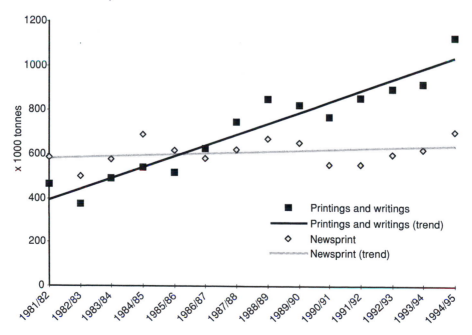

Figure 2.7 The consumption of paper products 1981-95 [17]

Included in the problem of storage is the vast number, cost and space requirements of additional stationary items needed to maintain the use of paper. Common to almost every office are large numbers of staplers, paper clips, binders, hole punches, hanging files, labels, manila folders, filing cabinets, envelopes, scissors, glue, white out, markers, pens and the like. These items require space in warehouses, stationary cupboards and drawers. There are also large amounts of valuable real estate being taken up for the warehousing of archives, extra printers, copiers, fax machines and filing cabinets. Each one of these items has an associated cost which could be considered a part of the overall cost of maintaining a printed document.

Management Issues

Another major problem associated with the use of paper-based documents is the process of filing.

In most offices it is usually left up to the individual to file the documents they use. Given the same document, there is tendency for it to be filed under different categories by different people, according to how descriptive or well designed the office filing system is. This system may be alphabetic, numeric, topical, or even *ad-hoc*. Anecdotal evidence suggests that whatever the system, it is often difficult to adhere to, unless there is some form of strict regulation regarding its use. Statistically, it is estimated that only 10 per cent of documents that are retrieved from files are returned to their correct place in a filing system.[18]

Even when documents are filed very carefully and systematically, there is usually no index or database that is maintained on the location of each paper document. More often than not, users are expected to hold the correlation between the various documents in their heads. This situation usually results in the person who originally filed the document having to be consulted.

Paper storage methods are also extraordinarily inefficient time wise. It is estimated that employees spend up to 60 per cent of their time processing documents, and that a significant proportion of that time is spent trying to locate documents which exist in a so-called 'document float.'[1] Document float is defined as the situation where used paper documents are waiting to be re-filed and cannot be accessed unless they are manually located among other 'lost documents'. For example, research has shown that one accounts receivable worker takes on average 12 minutes to process a document. Of this time, the majority of it (75 per cent) is devoted to locating and re-filing the document.[18]

Inefficient storage methods cost companies a considerable amount of money. Even though it only costs on average 30–70 cents to produce a page and half a cent to reproduce it, it can cost $150–$200 to recover one misfiled document from cold storage.[1,10] Consequently, this has made document management one of the single largest costs to a company.[10]

Paper documents ultimately have to be delivered. Currently, most paper-based document delivery methods are relatively inefficient. Usually, the more recipients there are, the more complex the delivery path is, and the longer the document float is.

Today paper documents are still largely delivered by hand in traditional, time-consuming and expensive ways, using a variety of different processes such as internal or external mail, facsimile machines and couriers. On average, it is estimated that it takes at least 50–60 per cent more time to get documents distributed when using paper.

Figure 2.8 shows some comparative methods of document delivery. From this illustration it can be seen how a computer network can be used to deliver single or multiple documents in an almost instantaneous manner rather than the multi-staged manual methods.

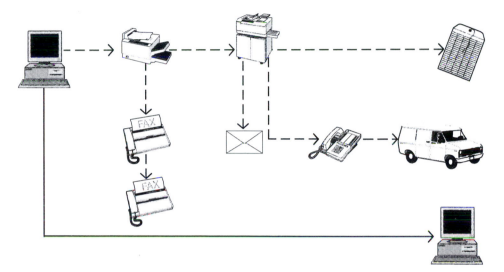

Figure 2.8 Comparative methods of document delivery

USE OF DIGITAL DOCUMENTS

In this chapter there have been a number of issues raised over the shortcomings of paper as a document substrate. Although actual examples of digital document technologies have yet to be introduced, it is worth briefly itemising some of the potential benefits that digital technologies might offer to address some of these issues. Some potential benefits for digital technologies include the ability:

- To easily *reuse* the information contained within, or externally referenced from, digital documents, thus avoiding the unnecessary, time-consuming and error prone replication of information by hand.
- To easily *manage* and *co-ordinate* documents using a computer-based document management system.
- To easily *search* for a range of document titles or document content which might be of relevance to a particular project.

- To easily *integrate* and *exchange* information contained within digital documents, with other participants involved in the building process.
- To quickly and easily *deliver* documents to geographically remote locations using computer networks.
- To *retain* documents in an efficient and compact manner for legal and reference purposes.
- To increase the *efficiencies* of various work practices. This could lead to reduced production costs and increased availability of time to work on other activities.
- To create a valuable *information repository* based upon the documents retained in a document management system.

Each of these potential benefits will be examined in more detail in the following chapters.

REFERENCES

1.   Ames, P. (1993), *Beyond Paper: the Official Guide to Adobe Acrobat*, Mountain View, CA: Adobe Press.

2.   Heath, T. (1991), *What, if Anything, is an Architect ?*, Port Melbourne: Architecture Media Australia.

3.   Southall, R. (1988), *Visual Structure and the Transmission of Meaning*, Document Manipulation and Typography: Proceedings of the International Conference on Electronic Publishing, van Vleit, J.C. (ed.), Cambridge: Cambridge University Press.

4.   Downing, D. and Covington, M. (1989), *Dictionary of Computer Terms*, New York: Barron's.

5.   Wood, J. M. (1995), *Desktop Magic: Electronic Publishing, Document Management, and Workgroups*, New York: Van Nostrand Reinhold.

6.   AGPS (1994), *Style Manual for Authors, Editors and Printers*, Canberra: Australian Government Publishing Service.

7.   Reinhardt, A. (1994), 'Managing the new document', *BYTE*, vol. 19, no. 8, p. 90.

8.   SAA (1975), *Metric Handbook: Metric Data for Building Designers*, North Sydney: Standards Association of Australia.

9.   Miller, M. (1994), 'The less paper office', *Australian Personal Computer*, vol. 15, no. 8, p. 158.

10. Stover, R. N. (1994), 'Document Management Overview', *EDM '94*, Washington DC.

11. Upton, P. (1993), 'Status of CALS in Australian industry', *CALS Australia '93*, Melbourne, EDICA.

12. Negroponte, N. (1995), *Being Digital*, Rydalmere: Hodder and Stoughton.

13. DAS (1990), *A Guide to the Use of Recycled Paper*, Canberra: Department of Administrative Services.

14. Murdoch, R. (1994), John Boynthon lecture, *Herald Sun*, 21 October, p. 13.

15. RAIA (1980), *Retention of Documents*, RAIA Practice Note 44A. Sydney: Royal Australian Institute of Architects Practice Division.

16. RAIA (1993), *Keep Copies of Documents*, RAIA Cautionary Note 86. Sydney: Royal Australian Institute of Architects Practice Division.

17. PPMFA (1997), *Consumption of Pulp and Paper Products*, The Pulp and Paper Manufacturers Federation of Australia.

18. Nicolls, S. (1994), 'Crushing the paper monster', *Desktop*, April, no. 79, p. 50–55.

Chapter 3
Document Use in the Construction Industry

ARCHITECTS IN THE CONSTRUCTION INDUSTRY

One of the key considerations of this book is the important role that documents play as a communication mechanism in the design and construction process. Although there are usually a large number of disciplines on a construction project, it has traditionally been the architectural profession that is assigned the role of document co-ordination. This chapter therefore, focuses upon the role of architects and the documents they produce. The document types that are identified are applicable to the entire construction industry.

Changing Architectural Practice

As the complexity of building types has increased throughout history, the actual role of the architect has changed considerably. Traditionally, architects have assumed a leadership role, but today the architectural profession is being subjected to increasing pressure from other building participants to surrender this position.[1,2]

The start of the diversification in the building industry has been traced back to the period after the Great Fire of London in 1666. During that time, huge amounts of rebuilding had to be carried out, individual craftsmen began to emerge as entrepreneurs, and architects began to assume the role of centralised design controllers and co-ordinators.[3]

By the end of the nineteenth century, a network of specialist consultants, quantity surveyors, contractors, and subcontractors had emerged, forming the basis of today's modern design and construction process. As the complexity of building types further increased in the next century, and the number of participants continued to rise, the diminishing importance of the architect was already being predicted. An edition of the *Architects' Journal* in 1964 voiced these feelings:

> Modern building contracts necessitate an increasingly complex organisation of labour and materials. Effective means of communication, management and control will become yet more important with the development of industrialised techniques. Unless the architect is willing to accept the

challenge of technological progress and adapt himself to the new situation, he may find that he is losing his position as leader of the building team.[4]

Further evidence to back these claims is illustrated in Figures 3.1 and 3.2 where it can be seen how the numbers of participants in the design process have increased over time. These figures have been derived from the proportion of fees distributed to participants during the design process.

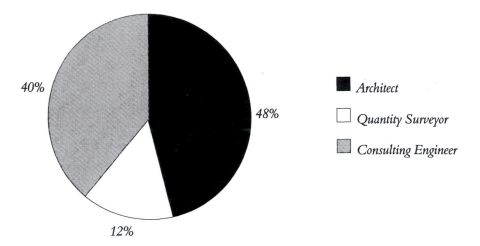

Figure 3.1 The participants in the design process *circa* 1939[5]

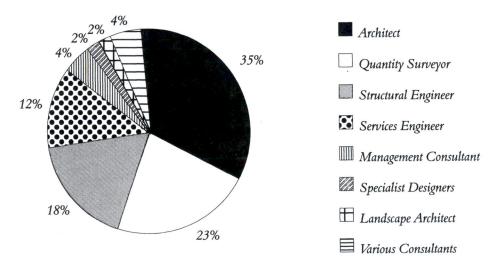

Figure 3.2 The participants in the design process *circa* 1986[5]

A Model of the Construction Industry

Today, it is now widely recognised that the construction industry has a larger number and more diverse types of participants than many other business sectors.[6] A number of studies on the construction industry[7] have revealed that:

- the AEC (Architecture, Engineering, Construction) industry is comprised of a large number of small (often less than five persons) businesses;
- projects are often an *ad hoc* combination of several firms (typically three to five, but often ten or more) that exist only for the duration of the project;
- projects comprise a large number of specialist disciplines, with widely differing needs for information;
- co-ordination and integration of the design (information) is the responsibility of a team leader (often an architect);
- building technology is dramatically increasing in complexity;
- clients are seeking much improved levels of quality control;
- the industry is not only a national enterprise, but has a potential and need to be able to operate in a competitive international context.

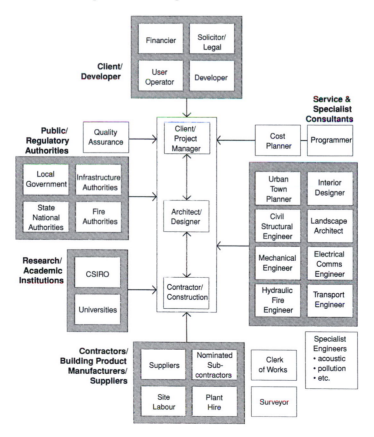

Figure 3.3 Potential construction industry participants and lines of communication[6]

In Figure 3.3 a portrayal of the diverse types of participants in the construction industry and their various lines of communication are illustrated. From this illustration and the previous portrayals, it is apparent that architects are expected to co-ordinate and communicate information in an industry which is in a continuous state of flux.

From this model it can be seen how each new construction project has the potential to introduce a new set of communication standards and procedures. When computers are involved, an additional layer of standards adds to this complexity. Therefore, if digital documents are to be widely adopted, there will be a potentially large number of performance and standards criteria that need to be established.

THE SCOPE OF ARCHITECTURAL SERVICES

To better understand the actual types of documents that are used in the construction industry, it is relevant to show the range of services for which these documents are required. Each of these document types will usually have a specific function in the conveyance of information between individual parties.

In the architectural profession, the responsibilities of an architect are traditionally broken down into four basic stages:

1. The *pre-design phase* in which a programme of requirements is established and agreed upon.
2. The *design phase* in which a number of design alternatives are examined and a final design agreed upon.
3. The *contract documentation phase* in which the design is developed further and a set of working drawings and specifications are produced. Tenders are then usually called, based on this documentation, and the contract awarded to the successful bidder.
4. The *contract administration phase,* in which the actual building process occurs.

These phases can be further broken down as illustrated in Figure 3.4. From this range of services, there are four basic groups of documents which can be identified.

Project Documents
Documents required for the organisation, specification and management of an individual project (for which there will usually be a number of projects under way at any one time).

Office Management Documents
Documents pertaining to the day to day management and operation of an office.

Communication Documents
Documents concerned with the communication of information in an office environment or among the participants of a design and construction process.

Reference Documents
Documents which are used in the design and decision-making process such as legal regulations, manufacturers catalogues and instructions, pricing guides, and the like.

Pre-Design Phase

1. PRE-DESIGN SERVICES
e.g. brief preparation, space schematics

Design Phase

2. SITE ANALYSIS SERVICES
e.g. Selection, preparation and anlysis of site

3. SCHEMATIC DESIGN SERVICES
e.g. Preparation of schematics and costings

4. DESIGN DEVELOPMENT SERVICES
e.g. further development of schematic

Contract Documentation Phase

5. CONTRACT DOCUMENT SERVICES
e.g. create main set of architectural documents

6. TENDERING & NEGOTIATING SERVICES
e.g. preparation of tender documents

Contract AdministrationPhase

7. CONSTRUCTION SERVICES
e.g. provision of all contract administration

8. POST-CONSTRUCTION SERVICES
e.g. inspection of works, as built drawings

9. SUPPLEMENTARY/SPECIAL SERVICES
e.g. project programming, energy studies, interior architecture, project promotions etc.

Figure 3.4 The scope of architectural services identified by the RAIA

These groups are of course notional. There is a propensity for many documents to serve a number of different functions, and be referenced in a number of different contexts. A drawing, for example, can serve as a communication device between an architect and a builder, but is also a part of the project documentation. A drawing could also be stored for later retrieval as part of an office management system, and then used for reference purposes. Figure 3.5 illustrates this principle.

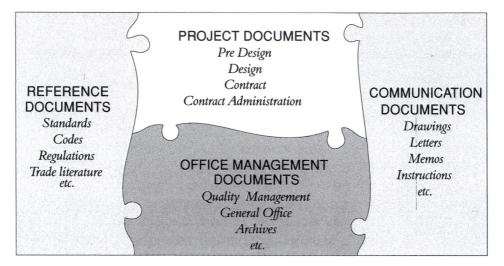

Figure 3.5 The relationship between main groups of documents

OFFICE DOCUMENT TYPES

Having established a portrayal of the industry and of the professional services for which documents are required, what remains to be identified are the actual *types* of documents that are in use. The range of document types listed in this section are indicative of those used by a wide range of disciplines.

Method of Classification

The document types in this section have been classified under the four main groups identified previously. Accordingly, some document types can be classified under a number of different groups, so only the most common instance is listed. For each identifiable document type, additional information is also provided regarding the main types of data which are used and any verification or authorisation levels which are required.

Data Types (Data)

Most documents are composed of text, but there are also documents which contain solely graphics or a combination of text and graphics. The following tags are used to indicate whether the document type is primarily text or graphics based.

T	Text	*Documents which are primarily text based*
G	Graphics	*Documents which are primarily graphics based*
C	Composite	*Combined text and graphics documents*

Verification Levels (Verify)

Some documents require the addition of verification marks to evidence their authenticity. These include the use of authorised marking devices such as signatures, stamps or seals, and the use of official stationary such as letterheads, pro formas, and other forms of company identification. The following verification levels are suggested.

1 Direct verification *Requires official stationary and an authorised mark*
2 Indirect verification *Requires some form of identification*
3 No verification *Requires no special authorisation*

Access Levels (Access)

In many offices, especially those smaller in size, documents are readily accessible to most members of that office. Due to the confidential nature of their content however, certain documents should be restricted to be accessible only by senior management or certain authorised personnel. The following levels are used to indicate required access to certain document types.

1 Restricted Access *Restricted or personal use only*
2 General access *For general office use*
3 Public access *For general distribution*

Office Management Documents

Office management documents are those which are used in day-to-day management and operation. Under this group, three main categories have been identified: quality management, general office and archival.

Quality Management Documents

These document types usually consist of a set of documentation which is required for the establishment and operation of a quality system. A quality system is the set of procedures, activities, organisational structures and personnel used to implement a company's objectives towards a level of quality.[1]

Table 3.1 A range of typical quality management documents

Document	Description	Data	Verify	Access
Quality policy manual	A document stating the company's overall objectives	T	2	2
Quality manual	A document of intent describing the company's quality policies, structure and outline procedures	T	2	2
Quality procedures	Office procedures, project procedures	T	2	2
Quality records	Certificates, checklists, minutes, test results, correspondence etc.	T	1	2
Company/Office standards	Document naming conventions, CAD layering standards etc.	T	2	3

General Office Documents

These documents are used as part of the professional management of an office.

Table 3.2 A range of typical general office documents

Document	Description	Data	Verify	Access
Company profile	Information profile used for marketing purposes	C	2	3
Curriculum vitae	Record of an employees work history	T	3	2
Strategy plan	A strategic direction of a company	T	2	1
Time sheets	Records of time spent on a particular project	T	1	2
Leave forms	Record of employee holiday or sick leave	T	1	1
Expense forms	Record of employee project related expenditure	T	1	1
Accounts report	A report of the companies financial position	T	1	1

Archival Documents

These are documents which are identified as having future relevance to a business but need to be archived due to limited storage capabilities within the office. Most of these documents are project related and tend to exist in the original format.

Table 3.3 A range of typical archival documents

Document	Description	Data	Verify	Access
As-built documentation	Post-occupancy drawings and other documentation describing a completed project	C	2	2
Administration records	Company administration-related documents	T	1	1
Financial records	Financial-related documents	T	1	1
Microfilms and fiches	Archival replicas of original project documents	C	1	2

Project Documents

Project documents may be organised under the four main stages of a project namely: pre-design, design, contract documentation, and contract administration. Additional support documents used for trading and reference purposes can also be included.

Pre-Design Documents

These documents are typical of those used in the preliminary stages of a project.

Table 3.4 A range of typical pre-design documents

Document	Description	Data	Verify	Access
Brief	Description of requirements	T	3	2
Instructions	Specific directions from participants	T	2	2
Space schematics	Sketches, bubble diagrams etc.	C	3	2
Reports	Marketing studies, various consultant reports	C	1	2
Presentation drawings	Concept drawings for client review	G	3	2
Tender documents	Documents for consultants to tender on	C	2	2

Design Documents

These documents are typical of those used throughout the design process.

Table 3.5 A range of design documents

Document	Description	Data	Verify	Access
Sketches	Conceptual drawings, usually artistic in nature	G	3	2
Drawings	Plans, elevations, sections and details	G	1	2
Renderings	Photo-realistic or conceptual studies of a design	G	3	2
Design review records	Official records of design changes	T	2	2
Design verification	Recording of design status	T	3	2
Illustrative sketches	Sketches used to verify details on site	G	3	2

Contract Documentation Documents

These documents contain essential information required for the construction documents.

Table 3.6 A range of typical contract documentation documents

Document	Description	Data	Verify	Access
Working drawings	Graphical, annotated, scaled and dimensioned instructions for the construction of a design	G	1	2
Schedules	Tabulated list of details for doors, finishes etc.	T	2	2
Specifications	A detailed description of construction, workmanship and materials	T	1	2
Inventories	A detailed list of goods and materials	T	2	2
Cost estimates	A report on the estimated cost of construction materials and goods	T	2	2
Calculations Computations	A report ascertained by mathematics and/or measurement, regarding quantities and performance requirements of materials	C	1	2

Contract Administration Documents

These documents primarily deal with design verification, to ensure that appropriate approvals are gained at critical stages of the design process. In the administration of the RAIA Building works contract, for example, there are potentially over 67 different document types (such as instructions, notices and certificates etc.) that can be used.[8]

Table 3.7 A range of typical contract administration documents

Document	Description	Data	Verify	Access
Contracts	Agreements between parties for the supply of goods or services at a specified price	T	1	2
Notices	Notifications of intent etc.	T	1	2
Instructions	A direction to perform an activity	T	1	2
Certificates	A formal document indicating a progress stage	T	1	2
Adjustments	Notification of changes to a contract	T	1	2
Field notes	Notations taken on site visits	T	1	2

Trading Documents

These are documents used as records for the exchange of goods or services.

Table 3.8 A range of typical trading documents

Document	Description	Data	Verify	Access
Purchase order	A request for the purchase of goods or services	T	1	2
Internal order	An internal office request for goods or services	T	1	2
Invoice	A itemised list of prices and charges for goods shipped or services performed	T	1	2
Quotation	An official cost estimate of goods or services	T	1	2

Reference Documents

These documents are used as reference sources in any stage of the design, construction or decision making process.

Table 3.9 A range of typical reference documents

Document	Description	Data	Verify	Access
Standards	Regulations and guides produced by standards associations to identify an exact level of quality	T	2	2
Planning Schemes	Regulations and guides issued by regulatory bodies and used in the planning process	C	2	2
Building Codes	Regulations on process or product description, such as building or local government codes	C	2	2
Trade Literature	Product descriptions and specifications	C	2	2
Pricing Guides	Guides used in the estimations of building cost	T	2	2
Directories	Lists of clients, consultants and contractors	T	2	2

Messaging Documents

These documents are primarily used as a method of communication between employees or the various participants in the design and construction process.

Table 3.10 A range of typical communication documents

Document	Description	Data	Verify	Access
Letter	An addressed document of legal or formal kind used for various communication purposes	T	1	2
Memorandum	An informal letter (usually without signature) used to record or notify of an event	T	2	2
Transmittal document	A document accompanying the transfer of other documents, confirming the date, time and authenticity of the documents being transferred	T	1	2
Minutes	A record of notes taken at a formal meeting	T	2	2
Records of verbal communication	A record of a conversation or informal meeting	T	2	2
Telephone record	A record of a phone conversation	T	2	2
Facsimile	A copy of a document created by the transmission of a signal from the scanning or encoding of a master document	C	2	2

THE VOLUME OF PROJECT-RELATED DOCUMENTS

A further important consideration related to the use of documents, is the number of documents that are produced. Understandably, the number of active communication paths between participants increases considerably, as the size of a project increases. Large projects can sometimes collapse under the weight of communication overheads, and hence must be properly organised to avoid this occurrence.[9] Table 3.11 lists a potential number of documents that can be produced from various sized projects, and Figure 3.6 illustrates them.

Table 3.11 Information volume (number of 'documents') by project value ($A) [12]

	$700m	$80m	$50m	$15m	$10m
Contracts	300	170	100	80	50
Tenders	1 200	700	400	300	200
Drawings	30 000	5 000	4 000	1 000	200
Drawings Issued	400 000	150 000	100 000	48 000	30 000
Variations	10 000	5 000	1 000	300	150
Site Instructions	30 000	6 000	3 000	1 000	600
Rooms/areas	3 000	100	50	11	7
Consultants	15	12	11	8	5
Cash flow/month	$144M	$2M	$1.5M	$0.6M	$0.5M
Approvals/week	70	26	20	18	13
Meetings/week	30	20	11	10	6

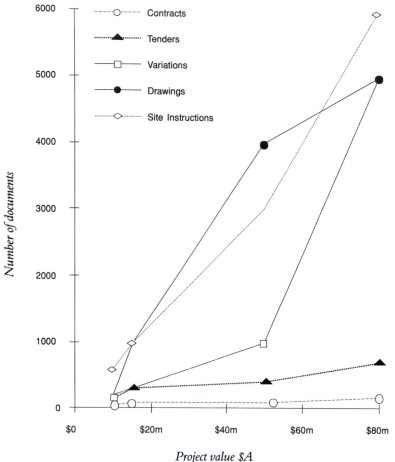

Figure 3.6 Information volume (number of 'documents') by project value

Additional research from the UK, as part of the BRICC (broadband integrated communications in construction) project, has found that on average there are about one thousand technical documents that can be expected to be issued for each million pounds of project turnover.[10]

As has been previously mentioned, there are an enormous number of inefficiencies associated with the use of such large volumes of paper-based documents. Given the previous figures, indications are that there is a demonstrable need, especially in large projects, for document management systems that can effectively and efficiently manage these large quantities of documents. There are a number of document management systems available on the market that are suitable for this task, but these systems are most suited to the use of documents that exist in a digital form.

From these figures, it can also be seen that there are at least thirteen times the number of drawings *issued* as there are actual drawings. This demonstrates that there is a large number of revisions for each drawing, and hence there is also a requirement for a secure method of control over the authorisation and revision levels of documents. Traditionally, the revision levels of documents have always been acknowledged as being a known problem in the construction industry.[11]

KNOWN PROBLEMS WITH THE USE OF DOCUMENTS

Research studies have shown that the principal causes of delays, disruptions, increased costs and poor workmanship are a direct result of problems with documents.[11] Some of these problems relate to:

- errors in documents;
- contradictions and ambiguities in documents;
- late supply of documents;
- outdated information;
- inconsistent formatting;
- unnecessary duplication of documents; and
- difficulties in combining document standards from different disciplines.

Many of these issues can be attributed to the fact that the majority of documents use paper as a substrate, and will naturally inherit many of the problems that were discussed in the previous chapter.

Other problems that occur with the use of documents in the construction industry are often the result of human error, when the resources available to produce and review documents are limited. These errors and faults tend to vary in significance, but there is always a chance that they could have a significant impact on a contract no matter how subtle they may appear.[11] Considering the increase in the number of documents that are used as the value of a project increases, there is also a possibility that the number of errors will also grow.

From this evidence it can be seen that documents need to be managed with an effective use of time and resources through the use of in-built mechanisms for easy review. Given the large numbers of inadequacies that have been associated with existing paper-based management systems, this evidence forms a strong case for the adoption of computer-based document management systems.

Security and Privacy Issues

The security and privacy of information contained within documents is also an issue to be considered. Documents not only carry a considerable contractual significance to a number of different parties, but should also represent a long-term asset to the originator.

As mentioned in the previous chapter, the data contained within documents can become an extraordinarily valuable asset to a company's knowledge base. In many instances the information can represent the development and investment of many thousands, even millions of hours of work, and is worthy of due consideration to its protection.

Security issues are relevant to both the external and internal access of documents. Externally, information contained within tender briefs, client budgets and proposed plans can be extremely sensitive. In the public arena, for example, it is quite common to hear of incidents where project details have been leaked through the unauthorised duplication of documents.

Within an architectural or engineering office, there are also certain document types which need to be protected from modification, either during or after the construction process. This protection is often necessary so that only people with the necessary expertise are able to modify certain details or calculations. This is particularly relevant on computer networks where it is often possible for a single document to be simultaneously opened and modified by a number of different people, unless there are in-built mechanisms to prevent this occurrence.

Authorisation of documents is another important issue. Many documents are required to be validated by authorised personnel such as the director of a company, or a representative of an authoritative body like a council building department. The traditional methods of authorisation include the use of signatures, stamps, or seals on a paper substrate. Usually, the characteristics of the authorisation mark (such as colour, texture, ink type, font metrics, and other graphic properties) make it distinguishable from the base document, and hence make it clearly identifiable.

While authorisation methods of paper documents are open to many different forms of forgery, digital documents face an even bigger challenge, that of proving *any* form of authenticity. Current methods of authenticating digital documents involve the use of highly complex mechanisms such as encryption algorithms, digital signatures, and the use of document management systems. In Chapter 7, various methods of document security are discussed in more detail.

Intellectual Property and Copyright

Because most documents in an office are freely accessible to almost all employees, there is a constant susceptibility to copyright infringement.

As previously mentioned, the collection of documents within a company represent a considerable investment in time and knowledge. It is for this reason, that almost all documents are restricted from general access to all other people outside the office, except those who are part of the immediate project team. This clearly brings up the issue of copyright.

Copyright is the exclusive right of an author or designer to protect their original work from reproduction by others. Architects, for example, usually retain copyright for both the plans and the building that has been erected in accordance with them. In most cases, this topic can be quite complex and there is usually a fine line between what constitutes an original work and a copy which has been influenced by that work.

Traditionally, the main method of indicating the copyright of a document, although often ineffectual, is to clearly mark its ownership and any conditions of copyright that might apply to it. Other methods include, restricting its general distribution, or by providing some form of authorisation or security mark that will distinguish the original from a plagiarised copy.

The use of these protection methods are particularly important when the document is in a digital form, where there is an even greater propensity for it to be copied.

OTHER INFLUENCES ON DOCUMENT USE

In the discussions so far, traditional methods of architectural and engineering practice have been assumed. There are, however, a number of other management and process factors which may affect the way in which documents can be used or are required to perform. From a management perspective, two main influences to be considered include process re-engineering principles and the use of quality management systems. From a process perspective, two main influences that could be considered, are the fast-track construction method, and the concurrent engineering method.

Process Re-engineering
In order to develop new methods of practice, there is a requirement to precede the with changes in methods of office and process management. The most radical approach to such changes, would involve a substantial reorganisation of the whole design and construction process, in order to take the greatest advantage of potential of computer-based solutions. This approach is now commonly referred to as process re-engineering.

Process re-engineering requires an organisation to think outside the accepted paradigms of business practice, in order to devise more efficient and cost-productive methods of production and management. For example, many large companies, such as the Ford Motors Company, have managed to dramatically increase their productivity by simply eliminating some of their commonly accepted, but often outmoded, business practices. A typical example of this approach, is to remove the use of invoicing procedures from the purchasing process, by adopting direct methods of payment on receipt of goods.[13]

In the construction industry there is also a case that can be made for the redundancy of certain document types. For example, in the electronic exchange of documents, transmittal forms would no longer be required. Instead, a document management system could be used to automatically verify and record details of the sender, recipient, transmission date and time in a project database.

If solutions to many of the current inefficient and costly processes in the industry are to be found, then process re-engineering principles will need to be adopted. This will be particularly important in the development of many new computer-based management solutions. For example, if it is accepted that there are a large number of inefficiencies in the use of paper-based systems, which could be described as 'slow and stupid', introducing a computer-based system to replicate it, will only create a system which could be considered 'fast and stupid'.[14]

Quality Management Systems

A further management principle that is usually required to precede other techniques such as concurrent engineering is the use of a quality management system. Since the early 1990's there has been increasing pressure for many organisations to operate quality management systems to the ISO 9000 set of standards. For the architect or engineer, the implementation of these systems enables the production of quality products related to the various services described in this chapter, as well as to the final built product.

Quality systems demand the extensive control of documents of all types, ranging from office standards to trade literature. In these systems there is an emphasis on the availability of the correct versions of all documents where they are needed, and on the prompt removal of obsolete ones. There is also an expectation that all technical data referred to will be accurate, current and informative. This information is crucial to the performance of professional services and is critical to the correct and complete specification of products.[15]

A good example of the use of a quality system, is in the preparation of building specifications. When source technical information is in a digital form it can greatly assist a range of disciplines in the preparation of quality building specifications. In a digital-based system, searches for product information can be made through large databases and then copied or linked into the specification or even linked to an associated object in a CAD drawing. There is also the ability to create multiple references from a single document without the need to duplicate the original. All of these features improve the quality and control of information. A typical system of reusable information sources is illustrated in Figure 3.7.

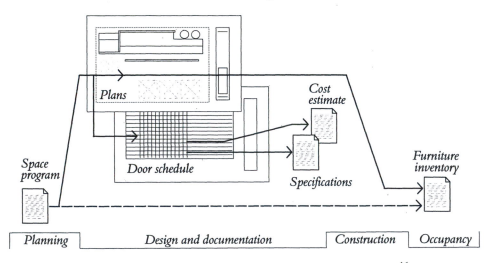

Figure 3.7 A representation of the reuse of information during a project[16]

With the development of a QMS (quality management system) there is also an additional set of documents that must be maintained. This documentation set consists of two parts: the corporate quality system, and the project quality system (as illustrated in Figure 3.8). While these additional document types add to the overall number of required documents in a professional practice, their purpose is to ensure that quality products are consistently delivered.

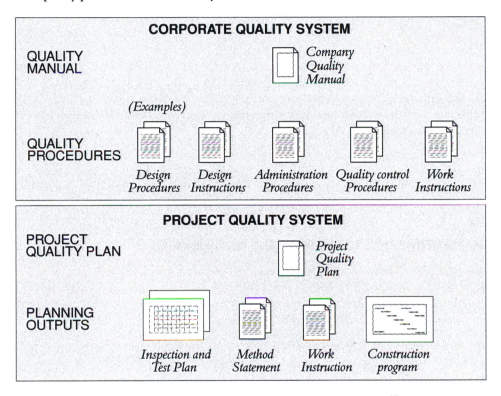

Figure 3.8 Some key documents in a quality management system[17]

Fast-Track Construction

A further influence in the use of documents is the popular design and construction method of fast-track construction. In this process certain building and documentation works can commence before the completion of a previous phase. In some circumstances, the ability to overlap activities can enable a significant shortening of the design and construction time, and a reduction in the overall cost of a project.

One of the main techniques for this method of construction is that the scheduling of the project is extremely well organised. This in turn, requires that documents should be easily and accurately produced, easily revised, quickly distributed, easily referenced and efficiently managed. The suitability of computers and the use of digital documents to fulfil these requirements is self-evident.

Concurrent Engineering

One of the newer techniques for implementing fast-track methods of construction, is the use of concurrent engineering principles. This process attempts to link all the people who might have an impact on the development of a design, such as the architects, engineers and other consultants, via a logical process or 3D computer model. Concurrent engineering enables a product to be completed faster and less expensively by improving communication channels and reducing the duplication of effort.

Concurrent engineering methods have been used extensively in the aerospace industry to great effect and are now being advocated for adoption by the building industry.[18,19] If this approach is adopted, there will be a dramatic shift from the traditional reliance upon paper documents to that of digital documents. In most cases digital documents will be generated from information derived from the computer-based design models.

From these examples, it can be seen that the future use of documents in the construction industry will be affected by a number of new computer and management-based techniques. Many of these approaches will ultimately involve the implementation of some form of process re-engineering.

PERFORMANCE CRITERIA FOR DOCUMENTS

Based on the evidence given in this chapter, it now becomes clear that there are a number of general performance criteria for the use of documents. These criteria are based upon their requirements for internal use within a practice, and their concurrent use among a large number of industry participants.

The technical requirements of documents may be summarised as follows:

- **Accessible**. A document must be able to be easily accessible by a number of different groups or individuals at different levels of authorised use.
- **Adaptable**. A document's presentation should be able to be modified so that it can be used for a number of different purposes.
- **Compact**. A document should be capable of being easily and efficiently stored for access as part of an office archive or reference system and to occupy as little storage space as possible.
- **Extensible**. A document should be able to be easily added to or modified by a range of authorised participants regardless of the system they use.
- **Interchangeable**. A document should be capable of being easily exchanged between a range of computing systems and software applications.
- **Portable**. A document should be able to be easily moved from one physical or logical location to another.
- **Reusable**. A document should have the capacity to be easily reused or referenced without being duplicated.

- **Securable**. A document should be capable of being protected or restricted to particular levels of use.
- **Verifiable**. A document should be capable of being verified for its authenticity, revision level, and relevance.

Some of the key issues that need to be ensured in the quality management of documents have been identified as follows[20]

- That documents receive sufficiently prompt attention.
- That only correct versions of documents are to be issued.
- That obsolete documents are removed from a system.
- That documents are adequately circulated to ensure availability of correct documents on a 'need-to-know' basis.
- That there is a clear statement of the current status of a document.
- That there is adequate storage appropriate to a document usage and status.
- That documents are able to be stored in theft-proof and fire-proof locations.
- That documents can be traced back to an original instruction or decision.

REFERENCES

1.   Crump, C. E., Llewellyn, R. and Renouf, A. (1992), *A Guide to Documenting Quality Systems for Architectural Practices*, Sydney: The Royal Australian Institute of Architects.

2.   Gutman, R. (1988), *Architectural Practice: a Critical View*, New York: Princeton Architectural Press.

3.   Mitchell, W. J. (1977), *Computer-Aided Architectural Design*, New York: Van Nostrand.

4.   Architects' Journal (1964), 'CBC: co-ordinated building communication: application of SfB to contract documentation', *Architects' Journal*, 25 March, p. 670.

5.   Reynolds, R. A. (1987), *Computing for Architects*, London: Butterworths.

6.   Mitchell, J. (1993), 'Networking Design', *Networking CAD*, Melbourne: CSIRO Division of Building, Construction and Engineering.

7.   Wix, J. and McLelland, C. (1986), *Data exchange between computer systems in the construction industry*, Berkshire: BSRIA.

8.   Di Conza, A. (1991), 'Processing and the JCC Contract', for , Faculty of Architecture, Building & Planning, The University of Melbourne.

9.   Mitchell, W. J. and McCullough, M. (1995), *Digital Design Media*, New York: Van Nostrand Reinhold.

10.   Crotty, R. (1995), 'Advanced Communications in Construction' – Broadband Integrated Communications for Construction. London: Bovis Construction Ltd.

11.   NPWC (1993), *Integration of Documents: Quality Management of Documentation for Construction*, Procurement Management Series, Canberra: National Public Works Council.

12.   Newton, P., Wilson, B., Crawford, J. and Tucker, S. (1993), 'Networking CAD in the AEC sector: an introduction', *Networking CAD*, Melbourne: CSIRO Division of Building, Construction and Engineering.

13.   Hammer, M. and Champy, J. (1994), *Reengineering the Corporation: a Manifesto for Business Revolution*, St Leonards: Allen and Unwin.

14.   May, T. (1994), 'Creative approaches to justifying document management', *EDM '94*, Washington DC.

15.   Hobbs, G. (1993), 'Technical information: quality product?', *Specifier*, vol. 2, no. 1, p. 12.

16.   Schilling, T. G. and Schilling, P. M. (1987), *Intelligent Drawings: Managing CAD and Information Systems in the Design Office*, New York: McGraw-Hill.

17.   AS/NZS-3905.2 (1993), *Quality System Guidelines*, Part 2: Guide to the Quality System Standards AS 3901/NZS 9001, AS 3902/NZS 9002 and AS 3903/NZS 9003 for Construction. Sydney: Standards Australia & Standards New Zealand.

18.   Barker, M. (1993), 'The benefits of concurrent engineering', *CALS Australia '93*, Melbourne: EDICA.

19.   Potter, C. D. (1993), 'Should architects adopt concurrent engineering?', *Cadence*, vol. 8, no. 6, p. 54.

20.   Maple, A. (1992), *The Architect's Guide to Quality Standard AS 3901*, Sydney: The Royal Australian Institute of Architects Practice Services.

Chapter 4
The Digital Document Environment

THE INTEGRATED COMPUTING ENVIRONMENT

Previously, it was determined that a document can be defined as a container of information. This particular view implies that a number of graphic, text and other multimedia objects can be integrated into a single document. However, due to differences in hardware and software this process of integration is rarely straightforward.

One of the principle aims in any computer-based architectural or engineering practice, should be to create a congruous environment in which all physical devices, software tools, and project data can easily communicate. Once these communications are established, it should be possible for all members of the design team to distribute, share and reuse information, irrespective of the hardware or software that is used. Design team members can then become more productive, and their work can be co-ordinated more effectively.

Although the consistent growth of the Internet is promoting a standardised framework for computer-based communication, the accomplishment of large-scale integrated hardware and software environments is still far from being easily and consistently realised. Despite the demands of most end-users for integrated solutions, and the best intentions of many developers, most computing technologies are still heavily market and profit driven.

For any type of hardware or software product, there are usually numerous competing interests, and numerous (often incompatible) standards in existence. Given the fact that the software industry is always in a state of flux, this situation is likely to remain unchanged for some time. Users, therefore, will still need to become familiar with a wide range of different standards and technologies on both a local and international scale.

COMPUTING FUNDAMENTALS

Without leading into a complex discussion of various exceptions to the case, a *computer* can be simply described as a machine capable of executing instructions on data to produce a desired result.

A computing procedure begins when an input device is used to import and encode data. The data is then stored in an internal memory called RAM (random access memory) where it is acted upon by a central processing unit (CPU). The CPU is controlled by a stored set of instructions, called programs (or software applications). The output from these processes are then stored in some form of additional storage space such as a hard disk, or to an output device such as a monitor or printer as illustrated in Figure 4.1.

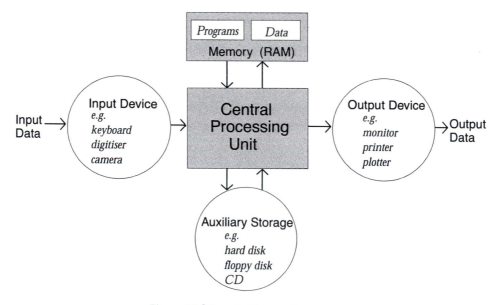

Figure 4.1 Schematic diagram of a computer

Digital vs Electronic

At this stage, a distinction should be made between the terms digital and electronic; since they are often mistakenly interchanged with each other.

Today, all modern general purpose computers are digital, as opposed to some earlier types which were analogue in nature. (Analogue devices use data that is measured through continuously variable physical quantities.) Before any text, graphics, audio, or video information can be processed by a computer, it must be reduced to a series of binary digits made up of 1s and 0s. Therefore, any data which is processed by a computer can be described as being in a *digital* form.

Anything described as being *electronic*, should correctly refer to the flow of electrons in the circuitry of a computer or any associated device. For example, this would include the electrical connections between the processor and any external hardware devices, or the connections from one computer to another.

In the context of this book, the distinction between digital and electronic is important. The term digital, is used to describe the nature of documents which exist in a form used by a computer. The term electronic is used in reference to the methods of distribution or communication of those documents.

COMPUTER HARDWARE

Today, computers exist in many different configurations and sizes, ranging from powerful mainframes to miniaturised devices that are incorporated into a number of common household appliances.

Generally speaking, most computers are assembled and marketed for different levels of functionality. For example, a graphic designer performing desktop publishing, will usually require a computer which has a much larger monitor, a more powerful processor, more RAM and a larger hard disk than a person who has relatively simple word-processing needs. Similarly, a designer using a CAD system will require a workstation with different requirements again, because they will have a specific need for high resolution vector graphics and rendering capabilities.

There are an enormous range of peripheral devices which can be used with computers. The quality, capability and cost of these devices will vary considerably according to the function for which they are intended. As with most computing equipment, the greater the capabilities of the device, the more expensive it usually is.

Some of the more common devices which can be used in the creation of digital documents are listed in the following sections.

Input Devices

Input devices are used to enter data into the computer for processing purposes. Because the inputting of data can be slow and time-consuming, it is often considered to be one of the most expensive aspects of computing. As a result, there have been a number of considerable advancements to counter this restriction.

Mouse and Keyboard

The mouse, which is now synonymous with most personal computers, exists in many different forms ranging from keyboard trackballs and trackpads found on laptop computers, to 3D spaceballs used in spatial visualisation applications such as VR (virtual reality) simulators. The mouse has also become synonymous with the use of icons and buttons, which are part of the GUI (graphical user interface) that is used by most Windows-based applications and operating systems.

The keyboard, which is used as the principal method of inputting text, has also undergone some re-design. A popular variant today is the split keyboard, in which the keys can be angled towards a more natural pose for the hands.

Pens

A common problem faced by many architects and engineers in the interaction with computers, is the relatively awkward nature of most input devices. Compared to the natural feel of traditional lightweight pens and pencils, most input devices seem relatively clumsy by comparison.

To address this problem, a number of computers can now use lightweight, cordless and pressure sensitive pens to enable the input of natural hand gestures. On some computers these pens are used as the primary pointing device and can be used to write directly on to a computer screen, as illustrated in Figure 4.2. The cursive handwriting or gestures made by the pen can then be automatically converted to text or interpreted as input commands.

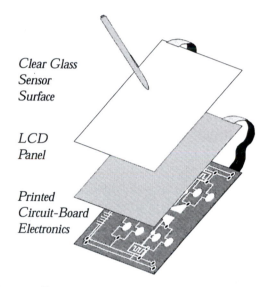

Clear Glass Sensor Surface

LCD Panel

Printed Circuit-Board Electronics

Figure 4.2 The construction of a typical pen-based display device

Multimedia Devices

With the increasing popularity of multimedia, there is also a growing demand for the use of input devices such as microphones, digital cameras and video cameras.

Many computers have sound input and output ports as part of their standard configuration. Some computers also come standard with a small video camera, which mounts on top of the monitor, and is used for video conferencing purposes.

A number of manufacturers also produce simple to use and relatively inexpensive digital cameras. These devices are capable of storing both high and low resolution images on to an internal storage disk, which bypasses the need for film and chemical processing.

A further, more specialised device is a video frame grabber. This device works by changing a signal from a video recorder into a digital image.

Scanners

Scanners are very versatile input devices, which can be used to:

- input text from paper documents;
- input line work from drawings; and
- input graphical images from photographs or artwork.

There are a wide range of scanners on the market and, like printers, vary widely in their capacity to deal with different format sizes, colour depths and resolutions. Depending on these attributes, and the accompanying software, they are capable of being used for three main functions: graphics scanning, text scanning and vectorisation.

For graphical sources such as photographs, simple hand-held or flatbed scanners can be used to capture artwork ranging from 72 to 1200 dpi (dots per inch), in black and white, greyscale or colour. Professional quality drum scanners, which rotate an image on a fast rotating cylinder, are capable of capturing true colour images (containing 16.7 million colours) in excess of 4800 dpi. Another alternative is to use a slide scanner, which can be used to scan standard 35 mm transparencies at resolutions in excess of 3600 dpi.

Line work, as used in graphical illustrations and drawings, can be scanned in and converted into discrete vectors. The vectorisation process converts a scanned image from a series of individual dots called a bitmap, into an image which is composed of geometrically specified lines, called vectors. This process allows existing drawings to be scanned in and processed, and produces output ready for further manipulation by a CAD or vector-based drawing package. Vectorisation is usually performed using large format scanners and special vectorising software.

Text can also be scanned in as a bitmapped image, but rather than being converted to vectors, can be converted into editable text. This process of conversion is known as optical character recognition or OCR. Optical character recognition is a software driven process that is more dependent upon the algorithms which are used upon the scanned images, rather than the physical capabilities of the scanner itself.

Usually, when a page contains both text and graphics, it can only be scanned for one or the other, and not both. There are, however, some software products which are capable of scanning both text and graphics in one scanning pass.

Some software also offers optical page recognition or OPR. In this process text and graphic elements can be scanned, OCR'd and composited on a page that is similar in layout to the original. Given the variations that are possible in any page layout, this can be an extremely complex process. Applications such as Adobe Capture which forms part of the Adobe Acrobat suite of software, offer this capability.

Depending on the quality of the hardware and software that is used, most scanners are only capable of converting text at a rate of 1–2 pages per minute. Some military specification scanners, however, are capable of converting up to 60 pages of text and graphics per minute. These scanners are typically used in the capture and conversion of large numbers of paper documents (referred to as legacy data).

Other Data Capture Devices

Data capture is not strictly limited to the input of information from existing paper documents. Some other methods of input relate to the capture of information from physical objects using a technique known as automatic identification (sometimes referred to as Auto-ID).[1]

The basis of automatic identification techniques, is to provide efficient and accurate tools for the capture of data which would normally be input by error-prone manual methods. A common scenario is a stocktake or inventory when items have to be individually counted and collated. Some of the data capture technologies that can be used include: bar coding, optical and magnetic character recognition, magnetic stripe, electronic/radio frequency (RF) tagging, vision and speech recognition systems. Each of these methods are capable of being implemented on a building site.

Bar Codes

Bar coding has now become a ubiquitous method of identifying and pricing items in retail shops. The system works by scanning a pattern of rectangular bars and spaces of various widths, using a light source. The encoded data on the bar code, represent data elements or characters in a particular symbology that follow certain rules defined by the symbology. Typically, the data in the bar code usually relates to corresponding information found in a database, which contains more detailed descriptions of the item's characteristics. A number of different bar code schemes exist such as the: Codabar, Code39, Code128, Code2of5, UPC, EAN, and PostNet standards. Each of these standards supports the encoding of different types of data for use in different industries.

Radio Frequency Tagging

Radio frequency systems can be used to store a wide variety of information in uniquely coded tags. When data needs to be collected, special readers can be used to interrogate, extract and modify this information by means of radio waves, before passing it on to a host computer.

Vision Systems

Vision systems are capable of automatically recognising the shape of certain objects. The system works by capturing a digital image of an object and then comparing its edges and special features against a known template. Current systems are commonly used on assembly lines in manufacturing plants, but they have yet to be effectively demonstrated for use in other areas, such as building sites, where recognition would have to be performed on widely varying sources in often unfamiliar surrounds.

Voice Recognition Systems

Voice recognition systems are now being used as add-ons to many different computer operating systems and specialist applications. Using these systems the computer can be taught new words to build up a specific user dictionary in addition to the factory provided glossaries.

Magnetic Stripe

Various types of information can also be recorded on to a strip of magnetic material bonded to a substrate of plastic, card or paper. The input of data from these sources is achieved by passing the stripe across a read/write head connected to a computer.

Smart Cards

Smart cards are similar in functionality to magnetic stripe cards but have much greater capacity to store information by virtue of a computer chip that is built into the plastic of the card.

Many of these Auto-ID systems are used in industries such as warehousing, retailing, transport, health, motor, security and defence.

As a means of inputting data, Auto-ID systems are highly suitable for use in conjunction with digital documents. For example, data captured on site could be directly imported into the fields of a database or into a pro forma report without the need for time-consuming and potentially inaccurate paper-based methods. In many cases, the collection of data using these methods can become highly automated and can lead to many improvements in accuracy and productivity. What they also enable, is a means of associating otherwise inanimate objects with the digital computing environment.

Output Devices

One of the significant factors against the development of the 'paperless office', has been the increased production of paper that has resulted from the use of computers. The construction industry is renowned for the vast quantities of paper they produce, and there is a large range of different printers and plotters to choose from for this purpose.

Printers

For most general purpose office documents, up to A3 in size, the laser printer has become the standard output device. Laser printers are capable of printing from 300 to 1200 dpi. They can also be used as a proofing tool for larger A1-sized drawings which generally require the use of a plotter.

For colour work, a number of technologies are currently in use including: thermal wax transfer, colour inkjet and dye sublimation. The latter process is capable of producing photograph quality output.

Plotters

A plotter used to be defined as a device which uses a pen as a method of marking a substrate. Today, however, the definition has been broadened to include all large format printing devices, which are able to produce outputs ranging from A3 to A0 in size. Most modern plotters are ink-jet based, whereby a nozzle jet is gently heated, or electrostatically charged, to cause a spray of ultra fine drops of ink on to a page. More expensive plotters use thermal transfer, electrostatic, and laser technologies.

Multifunction Devices

An increasingly common capability among some output devices, is multiple functions. Since many of the working parts of fax machines, photocopiers, laser printers and scanners are quite similar, there are quite a number of devices on the market which combine all or some of these functions into one device.

Display Devices

Previously, it was determined that a display device such as a computer monitor can be considered a document substrate. Even though over 50 per cent of most users needs can be met by simply viewing a document on a screen there tends to be a large number of limitations associated with this act.[2] These problems tend to be associated with the physical properties of the monitor and need to be considered when discussing the use of digital documents.

Most computer monitors today consist of an enclosed cathode ray tube (CRT) and a screen surface that is coated with a light-sensitive phosphor. An image is created on the screen when the phosphor briefly glows after being bombarded by a stream of electrons created by the computer.

There is a very large range of monitor types in existence. Each monitor type is usually designed to display different complexities of information, from monochrome text to high resolution multi-coloured images.

In the assessment of different types of monitors, there is a parallel that can be made between the characteristics of the computer monitor and that of paper documents. Usually, a monitor can be judged by the quality of its resolution (the granularity of the screen), colour (the number of displayable colours), refresh rate (the rate at which the screen can be updated), portability and display size. Similarly, a paper document substrate has measurable physical properties such as size, hue (colour) and reflectance.

Portability

Because all CRT monitors require a strong power source and have a relatively large depth compared to the surface area of the screen, they only offer a very limited degree of portability. As a result, cumbersome CRT monitors tend to restrict where digital documents can be used. Because a CRT monitor is a fixed substrate, the reader is required to come to the computer, rather than the document being taken to the reader in the manner in which paper is used. On a building site, for example, drawings and other types of documents often need to be shown to a range of different participants. Without a portable display device this process can become impractical to perform.

A part-way solution to overcoming this problem, has been the development of LCD (liquid crystal display) display devices, such as those used in portable laptop computers. These screens do not require the use of a CRT and are generally low cost, low weight, comparatively thin, and can operate from low power sources such as batteries.

Currently, LCD monitors come in two varieties: passive matrix and active matrix. Active matrix screens provide reasonably high-quality images because each of the pixels on the screen has its own transistor. This offers good control over the colour and brightness of images, similar to a CRT screen, and it enables the screen to be viewed in bright outdoor conditions. Passive screens, however, use a more economical plasma-like construction and are characterised by cruder display controls and poorer viewing angle display.

A current drawback with many LCD screens is that they are less capable of delivering the type of high-quality images that can be obtained from CRT monitors. In the display of certain types of documents, such as CAD drawings and renderings, this quality can be quite important. Portable display devices, however, are being rapidly improved for these purposes.

Resolution

Historically, computer monitors were only available as either raster or vector displays. Vector displays were specifically designed to show vector data and were quite often slow, clumsy devices which had been adapted from the oscilloscope industry.[3] Today, however, raster displays are by far the most popular kind available, and are capable of displaying all types of data, including vector and bitmap graphics.

On a raster display, the image is made up of a number of a matrix of dots called pixels. Behind the surface of the monitor an electron beam scans across the screen in a *raster* of parallel lines called scan lines. The image which is formed on the screen is then continuously refreshed at a rate somewhere between 50 and 200 kHz depending on the capabilities of the graphics card and monitor. The higher the frequency, the less tendency there is for a flickering effect.

Since the surface of the screen is made of individual dots, this will affect the resolution at which images can be displayed. With only a small number of dots available, the appearance of curved lines will often appear to have a staircase effect or what are known as *jaggies*. By increasing the number of dots on the surface of the screen, this effect can be dramatically reduced to the point where, on very high resolution monitors, the effect becomes almost unnoticeable.

Display Size

A further consideration in the assessment of monitors is that of size. Most computer screens are about 380 mm (15in.) across the diagonal, which is adequate for most general display purposes. A common problem when interacting with documents, however, is the fact that they have been designed to be printed, and therefore do not fit the proportions of a monitor. Consequently, for the user to gain the overall effect of the intended rendering of the document, low resolution page previews, or scrolling and zooming have to be used. To overcome this problem, the user will have to design the document purely for display on a monitor, or use a much larger and consequently more expensive monitor.

Future Developments

Future display devices are proposed to be as thin, flexible and portable as paper. The technology that makes this feasible is an electronic 'ink' made up of tiny spherical particles that are black on one side and white on the other. These particles flip over, depending on the electronic charge underneath them, making patterns similar to those on a paper page. A computer in the electronic book's spine would program these particles to 'set' the desired text, which would remain stable until reprogrammed. An electronic book that uses this technology will have the weight and feel of a traditional book of a few hundred pages.[4] These electronic display devices will also have the capacity to display documents that have been transmitted to them from a computer via infra-red or radio communication signals. This capability will enable the device to receive broadcasts of information and 'typeset' itself every day or week when required.[5]

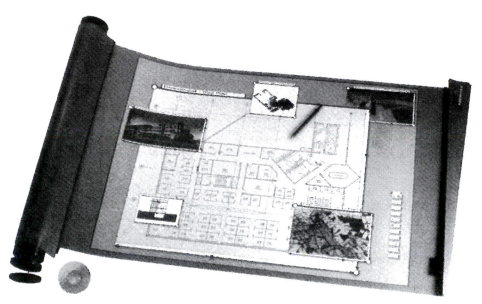

Figure 4.3 A proposed architectural input and display device[6]

A mock up of a similar device has been developed for the display of architectural working drawings (see Figure 4.3). It operates by rolling out a flexible screen from a drawing tube much like a roller-blind. In the tube itself is a computer and a CD-ROM drive that can store a large number of drawings. Once unrolled, the user is then able to interact with the drawings by means of a pen based input device.

These augmented reality systems have also been suggested for use in the construction industry. One device that has been proposed, is an 'intelligent' hard hat for use on a construction site. It incorporates the use of a camera, receiver, microphone, ear plugs, and tilt-down stereo display device as illustrated in Figure 4.4.

A further method of displaying documents that is being developed, particularly by the defence industry, is the use of heads-up display devices. This type of technology was initially developed to project critical flight information on to the surface of the pilot's cockpit screen or visor. While these systems are now commonly in use in most military fighter planes (and even by some car manufacturers) they are also being developed for use by mechanics. In these systems, augmented reality or telepresence technology is used to superimpose information from a repair manual on to a see-through visor worn by the mechanic. For example, when a mechanic is physically looking at a part, they can refer to the manual for an illustrated repair guide. They can then follow a step-by-step procedure for repairs while simultaneously viewing the problem at hand.

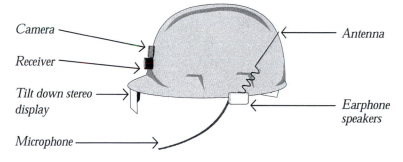

Figure 4.4 A proposed augmented reality hard hat for use on a construction site[7]

When display devices such as these eventually arrive in the mainstream, they will be destined to have an enormous impact on the portability and usability of digital documents outside of an office environment.

NETWORKS

In the last few decades, a number of paradigm shifts in computing have been identified. In the 1960s it was batch processing, in the 1970s it was time-sharing, and in the 1980s desktop systems were the main focus.[8,9] In the 1990s, the shift was towards network computing. In relation to digital documents, networks represent a significant proportion of the environment in which they exist. Networks are able to reduce the barriers of time and distance, and enable documents to be instantaneously transferred from one computer to another, anywhere in the world.

Using various forms of telecommunications technology, networks enable a number of computers to be connected together for the remote input and output of data. By allowing distant access to a number of different resources, the power of a computer can be dramatically increased beyond its capability as a standalone machine. The implications for the construction industry is that it allows key specialist personnel to remain in their preferred or necessitated work environment, yet still be able to provide critical input contributions in major projects involving a consortia of skills and expertise.[10]

Networks vary enormously in scale, capacity and complexity. The largest type of networks are known as WANs (wide area networks) and MANs (metropolitan area networks). Originally, WANs were based on a centralised approach to computing, where a number of dumb terminals were connected to a large mainframe computer. Individual users then shared time on the CPU. Today, however, the term WAN is used to describe the interconnection of computers over very long distances. The largest example of this type of network is the Internet which spreads across the world to over 40 million users as illustrated in Figure 4.5. At an intermediate level, MANs are designed for use in localised regions. On a smaller scale, LANs (local areas networks) allow an economical distribution of computers and peripheral devices within a building or campus.

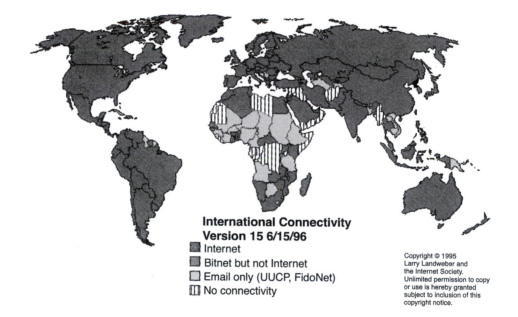

Figure 4.5 A representation of the extent of the Internet as of June 1996[11]

In the construction industry, a range of networking technologies exist that can enable architects, engineers and other designers to work in collaboration with each other, using either special-purpose networks or virtual private networks (VPN).[12]

Private networks are created by connecting a known number of participants in a workgroup (as illustrated in Figure 4.6). This enables specific hardware and software to be used for high-speed and secure methods of data and document transfer. These networks typically make use of technologies such as ISDN and Frame Relay and all of the required equipment is usually owned by the parties establishing the network. Because of the relatively high establishment costs associated with this approach, it is more suited to projects that are located within a local geographical area.

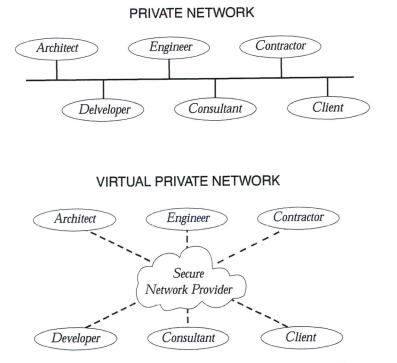

Figure 4.6 A representation of private and virtual private networks[12]

By contrast, VPNs are designed to deliver intercompany networking that is flexible, secure and allows participants to very easily modify networks on a project to project basis. Typically, the use of VPNs is made possible by the use of a public network infrastructure such a public subscriber telephone network or the Internet. Since they make use of these public infrastructures, they make use of very strong cryptographic techniques to encode data being transferred.

The use of VPNs has introduced a new paradigm – that of 'virtual organisations'. A virtual organisation can be considered to be one formed from strategic alliances between individual AEC firms which come together for a particular venture.[10] Given the fragmented nature of the construction industry, and the increasing use of the Internet, this type of network is highly suited as a method of establishing project communication where the participants are distributed over large geographical distances.

Principal Functions of a Network

Networking technology is highly specialised. It often involves levels of communication that use a very wide range of different protocols, software and hardware. Requirements for networking vary from simple file transfer and asynchronous communication (such as email), up to highly complex real-time video streaming. Underlying the various technologies currently in use, there are three major functions networks can perform:

- the sharing and transfer of data;
- the sharing of processing power; and
- the sharing of peripheral devices.

Sharing and Transfer of Data

The most powerful use of networks, and the most relevant to document use, is for the remote access of data. This is commonly achieved by centralising information on any number of servers, and then making this information available to remote computers, for either viewing or processing.

For example, an architect in the head office of a company, could access a project file from a server in another office located many kilometres away, view its contents, make some necessary changes, and then save the file back to the original server. They could then send an office memo via email, stating that these changes have been made and suggesting further possible amendments by the engineers, who might also be connected to the network and can also access the same files. There are also a large number of other potential uses of networks by the construction industry. Some of the major technologies are listed in Table 4.1.

Table 4.1 Potential applications of network technologies in the AEC industry

Network Use	Description
Email	Electronic mail enables messages created on one computer to be sent to another computer via a network.
WWW	The World Wide Web consists of a network of hyperlinked text, graphic and multimedia pages distributed on servers across the Internet.
FTP	The File Transfer Protocol enables the transfer of files from one location to another over the Internet.
EDI	Electronic Data Interchange is a protocol for the secure messaging of business information such as invoices, receipts and quotations.
EDMS	Electronic Document Management Systems enable a group of users on a network to store, distribute and track the use of a range of document types. Many EDMS systems use workflow techniques to automate the routing of documents through a designated series of approval or notification processes.
Video Conferencing	This is a high level collaborative use of networks, whereby live video, audio, virtual whiteboards and application sharing can be used by a number of participants in a design session. Capabilities exist for this technology to be used over high-speed leased-lines or the Internet.
CTI	Computer/Telephone Integration merges the technologies of computers and telephones with the use of specialised networking protocols and inter-application programming standards. Digital computer telephony can be used in conjunction with workflow systems and can also be used for the automated report entry and filing of documents using touch-tone input.
Remote Data Collection	Using a number of infrared, cellular and other communication devices, data can be collected in the field and transmitted to specific areas on a computer network.
OPACs	On-line Public Access Catalogues are used commonly used by libraries, where large databases of books and journals can be remotely queried by users and the results displayed on the local computer. This technique can also be used in the access of on-line building products catalogues.

Figure 4.7 illustrates the appearance of a computer screen during a video conferencing session. In this picture an architect is talking to a consultant and discussing design issues on a project. The CAD drawing is displayed next to a digital photo of a model. Talking and working in real time, the architect and consultant are able to discuss issues across the network and markup the images using a virtual whiteboard that is shared between the two users.

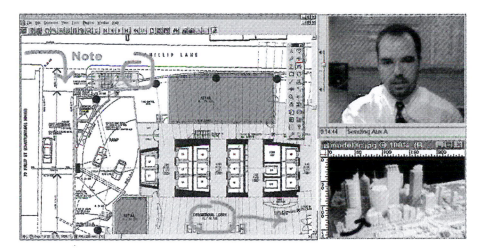

Figure 4.7 Use of video conferencing to discuss a design between remote users

For high-fidelity images and transmission speeds, video conferencing systems usually require the use of high bandwidth leased-lines using ISDN or Frame Relay. There are, however, lower cost and lower quality systems also available for video conferencing over the Internet.

Sharing of Peripherals

The simplest and most common use of networks is for the sharing of resources such as printers, plotters, scanners and other such peripheral devices. For example, by networking computers together the need for individual printing devices for each computer can be significantly reduced. Figure 4.8 illustrates a typical LAN.

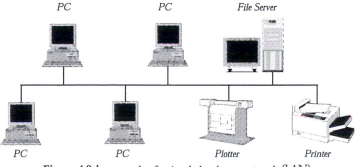

Figure 4.8 An example of a simple local area network (LAN)

Sharing of Processing

The earliest types of WANs used a powerful centralised server to serve a number of dumb terminals. This approach was often necessary because of the enormous cost of computers at the time. By increasing access and centralising processing, these costs could be significantly reduced.

In the early 1980s, this situation changed considerably with the introduction of large numbers of affordable personal computers. Eventually, this enabled a more economical and localised processing of data, but initially resulted in standalone rather than networked configurations. As networking standards were eventually developed for PCs, a model of distributed processing and resource sharing then became possible. Figure 4.9 illustrates these developments.

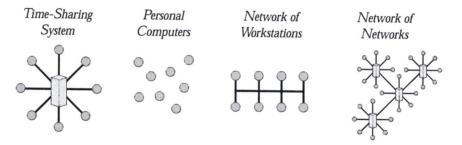

Time-Sharing System   **Personal Computers**   **Network of Workstations**   **Network of Networks**

Figure 4.9 The progress of network communication methods

Today, there are still occasions where remote processing is necessary. For example, scientists often require the use of extremely powerful and expensive mainframes for the processing of weather and astrophysics data. These types of computers tend to be situated in a central location so that they can easily serve a number of different research institutions.

It is also possible to distribute processing on a network of low cost workstations or PCs. This approach can be used to emulate the performance of powerful multi-processor computers. A common example is in the use of network rendering. By using a group of networked computers and a single 3D model, each computer can be assigned unique sequence of frames to render. By distributing the processing, the rendering can be completed in only a fraction of the time it would take using just one computer.

A further development of network computing is the emergence of the so-called NC or 'network computer'. These devices are specifically designed to run as low-cost, low-administration client workstations on an Intranet (a LAN using Internet protocols), using web browser technology and the Java language/runtime environment. An NC computer consists of a processor with RAM as its main memory, and flash RAM to store settings. There is no hard disk on an NC and software is distributed to it automatically, where it is compiled and run on the fly. Booting, administration and data storage of these devices are handled by servers that support a network of these systems. These simplified workstations are not intended to be used for the creation of data or documents but to be used for browsing and accessing information over a network. (A discussion on the Java technology which these computers use is covered later in this chapter.)

Interconnectivity between Networks

One of the greatest realisations to have emerged from the use of networks, is the need for standardisation. On large networks, the potential interaction between different types of computers, operating systems and network protocols is enormous. Added to this, there are an enormous number of different file and document types which have to be transported across them. Without the standardisation of a number of essential protocols, network systems would soon grind to a halt and the benefits of file and document sharing would rapidly diminish.

OSI

One model that has been used to increase the interoperability between various network protocols, is the Open Systems Interconnection Reference Model, or OSIRM as it is more commonly referred to. This model is based on a proposal developed by the International Standards Organisation (ISO) and deals with methods of connecting systems that are open for communication with other systems.

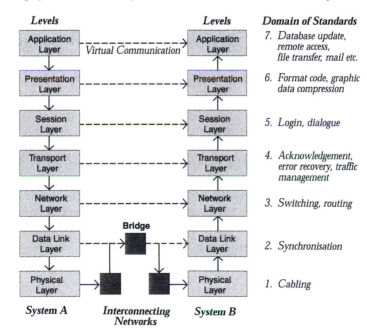

Figure 4.10 The OSI reference model

Open systems integration is quite complex, and involves the use of special network devices called bridges, gateways, and routers to handle data being transmitted by heterogeneous networks – i.e. networks composed of many different types of protocols and hardware (e.g. AppleTalk, and Systems Network Architecture).

In essence, the OSIRM specifies the way that messages can be broken down into simple parts, transmitted and, then, reconstituted at the other end. By complying to this standard, files from almost any type of application (graphic, text, audio or video) can be transparently moved from one end of a network to another, without the user intervening or requiring knowledge of the protocols being used. Figure 4.10 illustrates the seven open systems integration protocol layers and their main functions.

TCP/IP

The most popular implementation of the OSIRM has been the Transmission Control Protocol/Internet Protocol which encompasses a whole family of related protocols that are designed to transfer information easily and seamlessly across a network. TCP/IP enables such functions as sending email, remotely logging on to systems, transferring files, and routing messages.

The TCP/IP protocol is the fundamental enabling technology of the Internet and its use enables different networks to be easily interconnected. Communication over the Internet is typically achieved by using TCP/IP applications and protocols such as:

- Telnet   *for remote login*
- SMTP (Simple Mail Transfer Protocol)   *for email*
- FTP (File Transfer Protocol)   *for file transfer*
- HTTP (Hypertext Transfer Protocol)   *for hypermedia (Web) documents*

Because every computer on the Internet communicates using this protocol, it does not matter what type of computer or operating system is being used by the sender or receiver of information. Web browsers, for example, make use of HTTP to access hypermedia documents and are available for practically every operating system on the market. As a result of the extensive use of the Internet, TCP/IP is now the most widely used networking software protocol in the world.[13]

Internet Technologies on Networks

Following the extraordinary success of the Internet, TCP/IP protocols and associated applications such as web browsers have been applied for use on and between local area networks. The two principal models are referred to as an intranet and an extranet.

The Intranet

An intranet is a private network that is contained within an organisation and makes use of Internet networking technologies. An intranet may consist of many interlinked local area networks and may or may not include connections through a security 'firewall' to the outside Internet. The use of a firewall ensures that messages in both directions are filtered so that company security can be maintained.

Usually, the main purpose of an intranet is to share company information and computing resources among employees. The principle benefit of adopting Internet technologies to achieve this aim is that the software required is relatively low cost, highly standardised and readily available. Once an intranet is established, the same set of communication and information management tools that are used within an office, can also be used to collaborate with project participants using the Internet.

The Extranet

An extranet is a collaborative network that uses Internet technologies to link a business with its suppliers, clients, consultants or other businesses that share common goals. An extranet can be viewed as part of a company's intranet that is made accessible to other companies. In many respects, therefore, an extranet can be considered to be a type of VPN. The information that is shared, might be accessible only to the collaborating parties or might also be made public.

Examples of some extranet applications might include:

- Private newsgroups that special interest groups or strategically aligned companies might use to share valuable experiences and ideas.
- Project management tools that are shared between offices that are part of the same construction project.
- Shared product catalogues that are accessible only to wholesalers or those in the same industry.
- Training programmes or other educational material that companies could develop and share between themselves.

When the same set of network communication tools can be used within an office, as well as with external business contacts, it eventually does not matter whether project participants are located down the corridor or thousands of kilometres away on another network. In the context of the fragmented and temporary nature of most design and construction projects, the use of an office intranet, a collaborative extranet or the Internet, offer highly suitable methods of working in networked environments.

Network Security

An important issue in the use of networks is that of security. By opening up an array of computers to what, in many cases, amounts to open office or public accessibility, there is always a danger of information being unnecessarily modified, corrupted, erased or illegally accessed. To overcome these problems there are a number of inter- and intra-network approaches that can be taken.

While most of the documents in an architectural or engineering office are generally accessible to most employees, certain measures occasionally need to be taken to ensure that unnecessary duplication or prohibited access does not occur. This can be easily achieved by providing some or all of the following methods, including: password access methods, network file permissions, firewall access, file locking or file encryption.

Logins

The first level of security on a network is often provided with the use of logins, such as those that are found in many popular network operating systems. These network systems are usually written to cater for large numbers of simultaneous users, unlike operating systems such as DOS which were designed for standalone computers.

At the entry level to most network systems, security is controlled by the basic requirement that all users have a unique username and password. The username provides an identity for all of the users of the system and is also used for purposes such as the addressing of email. The password, however, is only known to the user and is protected by various forms of encryption. By using a username and password, users are able to register their presence, protect their work and secure the system from unauthorised access by others. This is particularly important when the computer is connected to a large network of many users.

File Permissions

The setting of file permissions is usually provided by operating systems (such as Windows NT and Unix), networking software (such as Novell Netware, Banyan Vines, and Appleshare) and from within certain applications (such as spreadsheets and databases).

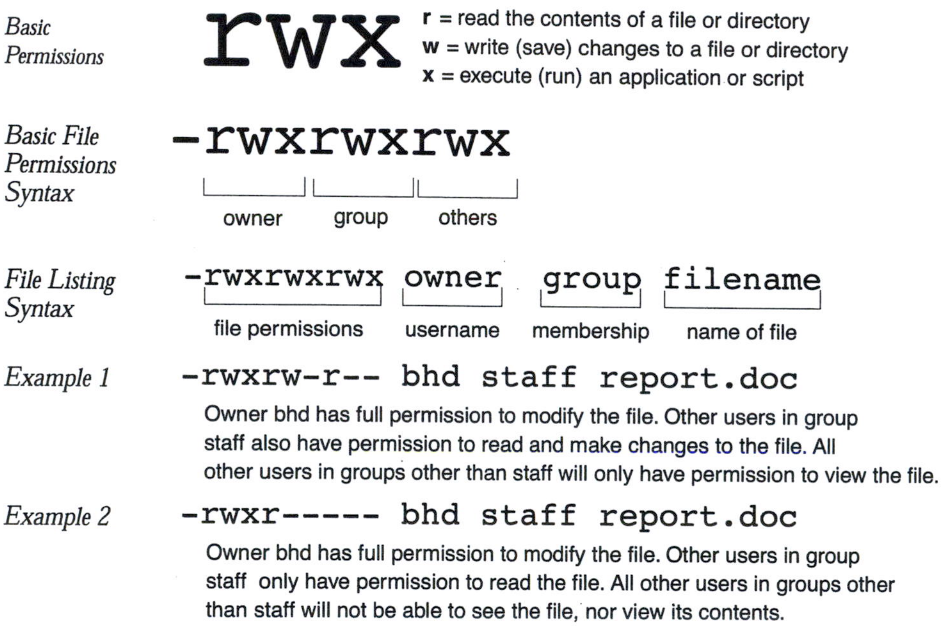

Basic Permissions

rwx
r = read the contents of a file or directory
w = write (save) changes to a file or directory
x = execute (run) an application or script

Basic File Permissions Syntax

-rwxrwxrwx
owner   group   others

File Listing Syntax

-rwxrwxrwx owner   group filename
file permissions   username   membership   name of file

Example 1

-rwxrw-r-- bhd staff report.doc
Owner bhd has full permission to modify the file. Other users in group staff also have permission to read and make changes to the file. All other users in groups other than staff will only have permission to view the file.

Example 2

-rwxr----- bhd staff report.doc
Owner bhd has full permission to modify the file. Other users in group staff only have permission to read the file. All other users in groups other than staff will not be able to see the file, nor view its contents.

Figure 4.11 Basic Unix file permissions

Once registered to a network system, users can be given access to different directories across the network, according to the permission levels that have been assigned to them by a systems administrator. By assigning these access levels, users are restricted to being able to read information from certain directories, save files in certain locations and run particular applications. The essential aim of this method of organisation is to enable large number of users to effectively coexist in the one computing environment.

The primary method of organising users on a network is to assign them to an organisational unit known as a *group*. Then, when a user creates a document the associated file is given an access code according to who owns it, which group the owner is in and what permissions other people outside that group can have to access it. By establishing appropriate permissions, only members of the same group (for example, people working on the same project) will be able to view a particular file, and only the author will have permissions to modify it. Figure 4.11 illustrates a common method of assigning file permissions in Unix.

Firewalls

When a private network can be accessed from a public one, such as an intranet being connected to the Internet, it is essential to use a firewall. A firewall is a combination of special hardware and software that blocks external intruders from accessing the resources of a private network, while still allowing internal users to access external resources on the Internet.

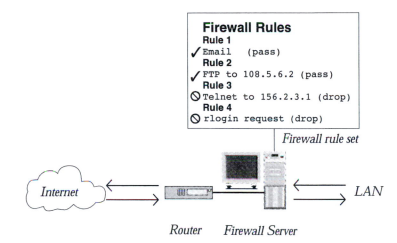

Figure 4.12 A typical firewall set-up

Most firewalls consist of a server, router and software that is configured to filter packets of information that pass between two networks. A filtering router works by testing a set of access rules against inbound and outbound network traffic. Typically, rules are established to only allow certain IP (Internet Protocol) addresses or protocols (such as WWW, FTP or Telnet) to be used. If a prohibited request is made by a user, the request is either dropped or denied by the firewall software. The concept of a firewall is illustrated in Figure 4.12.

File Locking

Another method of protecting documents in a network involves the use of file locking. This method is used to prevent the parallel editing of files by users who have the same permission to modify a file. For example, when a number of engineers are working on a project, they might each need to have access to a common set of CAD drawings. In a networked environment, there is a potential for each of these architects to inadvertently access a drawing while it is still in use. If this were to happen, each persons work could be overwritten by the other whenever the file is saved. To prevent this happening, file locking can be used to protect a file from the moment it is first accessed. Once a document is locked, users are either prevented from accessing the file altogether, or are restricted to simply viewing its contents. The document will then remain locked until the first user has released the file back to the system.

Figure 4.13 illustrates this principle. In this case, user A has opened a document and, in doing so, the editing software has automatically generated a lock file. When user B tries to open the same document, the presence of the lock file indicates to them that it is in use by another user.

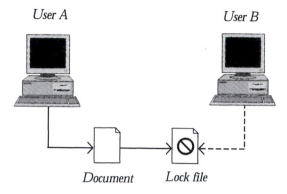

Figure 4.13 File locking of documents to prevent simultaneous editing

File Encryption

In general, the last level of security for a document on a network is the use of encryption mechanisms. Data or document encryption, involves the conversion of information into a code or cipher. Documents protected in this way are unable to be decrypted unless a secret *key* or password is used. Some of these methods are provided as part of the functionality of proprietary applications, while others involve the use of international data encryption standards. Encryption methods can also be used in the creation of digital signatures which can be used to verify the authenticity of documents on a network. These methods will be discussed in more detail in Chapter 7.

The Future of Networking

There are a number of developments in networking technology that are indicating how computers might be used in the future. The introduction of high-speed network protocols like B-ISDN (Broadband Integrated Services Digital Networks), ATM (Asynchronous Transfer Mode) and Frame Relay, are enabling dramatic improvements in networking speed and performance.

In particular, the introduction of fibre optic cables are destined to dramatically affect the quantity and speed at which information that can be transported over networks. A standard copper-based, twisted-pair telephone cable can deliver a theoretical maximum of 6 million bits per second. So far, research indicates that fibre optic alternatives can deliver close to 1 billion bits per second, and there are no signs of any future limitations to this capacity.[14] At that speed, every issue of *the Wall Street Journal* ever produced can be transported down a fibre cable the size of a human hair in less than a second.[15]

The use of high-capacity network technologies will mean that an increasing number of applications will become available for distributed computing, image transfer, and CAD and video conferencing. In addition to becoming real-time conduits for the exchange of data, networks will also support the use of intelligent software agents that can be used to roam a network and seek out information on a user's behalf. These agents will also be able to store, forward and filter messages, prioritise work, and eliminate irrelevant data that is found.[16]

Regardless of the eventual delivery time of these technologies, it is clear that with the use of networks, the computer has begun a transformation from an office automation tool, to that of a global information and communication device.

From the brief analysis of networks, it can be seen that they provide a strong and necessary framework for most modern computational work. The principals involved range from the structures within a computer, to the interconnections which are used between peripheral devices and other computers on large-scale networks. The conclusion to be drawn, is that there is already a well-developed range of technologies to provide a suitable work and communication environment for the use of digital documents. With the use of Internet networking technologies, this environment extends globally.

OPERATING SYSTEMS

Since the very beginnings of microcomputing, users and developers alike, have argued with each other over the relative merits of various operating systems.[17] In the past, the availability of a large number of operating systems were responsible for many incompatibilities that occurred between different applications and the documents created from them. While many of these problems still exist today, there is a common goal to increase the compatibilities of various data types, digital documents, applications and operating systems, in order to deliver a more effective approach to the creation and management of information.

The Basics of an Operating System

An operating system, or OS, is essentially a software program that is used to control the main functions and working environment of a computer. The OS is able to co-ordinate the processor, memory and various input/output devices according the degree of functionality with which it has been provided. In many ways it behaves like a human manager by delegating resources and tasks in a number of different ways.

Initially, simple operating systems like DOS were only capable of controlling single-users. Today however, with the proliferation of networks and windowed environments (where multiple applications can be used simultaneously), there is a tendency for the use of more complex and sophisticated multi-user and multi-tasking systems.

In the last ten years there have been four main operating systems in use by users of personal computers: DOS (disk operating system), MacOS (Macintosh operating system), Windows (such as Windows 95 and Windows NT), and Unix (such as Solaris, HP UX, A/UX, OSF, AIX, Linux, Irix).[18] The main difference between systems like DOS and the MacOS, has been the use of a graphical user interface or GUI. A GUI allows a user to point and interact with objects using a mouse, rather than by typing in arcane commands at an OS command prompt.

When the Windows interface was introduced by Microsoft in the early 1980s, a GUI interface was developed for the DOS operating system. This move eventually prompted many other developers to follow the same approach to OS and application design. Today, almost all applications use a GUI of some sort. Programmers sometimes refer to this approach as using WIMP (Windows/icon/mouse programming) techniques.

New-Generation Operating Systems

Many new-generation operating systems are extending the use of the GUI even further. Most of these systems are highly object-oriented and incorporate many multi-tasking operations to improve operational performance and usability.

In order to obtain these higher levels of performance, and intensive use of graphics, a considerable amount of processing power is required. Currently, the most common type of processor is the CISC (complex instruction set computer) CPU and the most popular example of this type is the Intel brand. Intel have produced a range of microprocessors that have been used in the majority of personal computers since the early 1980s. In successive order, and increasing power, there has been the 8088, 80286, 386 DX, i486, Pentium and Pentium II processors. Due to the vast number of required transistors on CISC processors, there is an increasing degree of complexity associated with further development of this type of design.

Many new-generation operating systemsn therefore, are being developed around the use of the RISC (reduced instruction set computer) CPU. Examples of RISC processors include the Alpha, MIPS, SPARC and PowerPC chips. These processors have been designed to operate from a reduced set of instructions, without any loss in performance or additional power requirements. The performance gains from this type of processor are arguably better suited to delivering the type of processing required for highly object-oriented and multi-tasking operating systems.

While the differences between the internal structures and approaches to the development of operating systems vary considerably, there are three common design themes between them: microkernels, object-orientation and user interface. The last two affect the way in which digital documents can be created and interacted with.

Microkernels

A microkernal is a tiny operating-system core that provides the foundation for modular and portable extensions.[19] Microkernals are now being used as an approach to the design of many new operating systems because they enable the OS to be easily adapted when new and possibly unforeseen technologies emerge. This extensible approach, differs from previous operating systems which were monolithic in nature, and attempted to include every possible function when they were first written.

Object-orientation

One of the approaches to OS design that will have a dramatic affect on the way documents are created and modified, is the use of object-oriented programming (OOP) techniques. An 'object', in programming terms, is considered to be unit of code that has data attributes and an associated set of methods (also called operations or functions) for handling items of that type.[20] By using this object-oriented approach, programmers are able to assemble code in a modularised manner that can be more easily reused and integrated with other systems.

Object oriented programming also enables data to be stored in objects which might exist on a local hard disk as well as remotely on some distant part of a network such as the Internet. These are known as distributed objects and can have a self-contained intelligence that enables them to be called independently of the operating system and location where they reside.

User Interface

The final theme which has emerged from the development of many new-generation operating systems, has been the importance of the user interface. As previously mentioned, most applications today use a GUI. A GUI is usually designed using a set of interface guidelines that are associated with a software application or operating system – such as the MacOS, Windows or Unix computers using Motif.

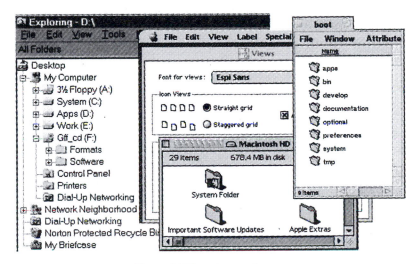

Figure 4.14 Sample user interfaces

By standardising the design of a user interface, users of a particular operating system can begin to expect certain common characteristics in the usability of applications, and of the organisational structure used for filing and managing documents. From a software developer's perspective, standardisation of the interface also enables programming and program maintenance times to be reduced by eliminating costly duplication of programming effort.

A common metaphor used in many GUI OS interfaces, is that of a desktop. By using a series of icons to represent files or applications, objects can be easily moved around the 'desktop' from one logical location to another. This also enables the user to perform certain operations in a visual manner, rather than the abstract verbal manner which was required of many text-based operating systems like DOS.

In terms of application use, a standardised GUI interface usually enables some of the following functionalities:

- placement of open documents in scrolling windows that can be realised or moved on the desktop background;
- standardised placement of file management commands in menus, such as File, Open, Save and Close;
- standardised methods of selecting items from menus; and
- standardised methods of storing files using the metaphor of a hierarchical arrangement of folders.

Using these approaches to application design, ensures that the user of a particular operating system can become easily accustomed to the way in which applications look and feel on that platform. Eventually, many users end up preferring just one particular platform in which to run their applications and are said to prefer the 'personality' of an operating system's functionality.[21] Figure 4.14 illustrates the interface of some common operating systems.

With the prolific use of Web browsers on the Internet, user interfaces are now gravitating towards the use of a browser interface and web navigation methods as a means of gaining access to all the documents, applications and system functions that can be found locally on a computer or on a network.

Personalised Operating System Interfaces

A further development in the use of GUI interfaces, has resulted from the emergence of pen-based computers and PDAs (personal digital assistants). A PDA is defined as a highly portable, easy-to-use computing and communications device aimed at the mass market. Typically, a PDA uses some form of pen-based and/or miniaturised keyboard input and relies on a special operating system, such as Apple's Newton OS or Microsoft's Windows CE. In the case of the Newton OS, the system is able to recognise and interpret the pen gestures that a user makes on the display device.

While this technology has yet to reach its full potential, it has resulted in some new approaches to interface design. A number of PDAs make use of what is known as a STICI (Self-Teaching and Interpretative Communicating Interface). The 'self-teaching' aspect of this interface, means that the STICI is able to customise itself for each person that uses it. 'Interpretative' refers to way that the interface stores and recognises personal information; and 'communicating' refers to its ability to provide seamless management of person-to-person communications.[22]

APPLICATIONS

Applications are one of the primary methods of manipulating and creating data on a computer. In the analysis of different types of applications, it is helpful to categorise them according to their basic functionality and to think of them as tools for the creation and editing of data. Ultimately, every architect and engineer will have a suite of software applications and utilities that can be used to interact with a range of document types. Figure 4.15 illustrates a suggested hierarchical organisation of a designer's software tools.

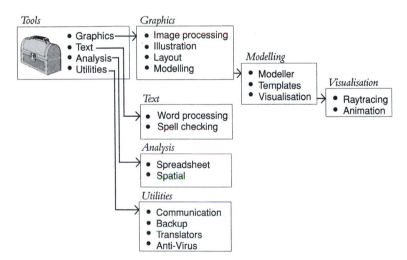

Figure 4.15 A typical suite of software tools used by a designer

Applications for the Construction Industry

An architect or engineer can use an enormous range of different software applications for the creation of practically every document type used in professional practice today. These applications can range from simple text processors through to powerful CAD, rendering and numerical analysis packages.

In Table 4.2 a range of typical software tools are listed. They have been categorised under different classes according to the complexity and specialisation of their functionality.

- **General**: Common software found in a majority of offices of all professions.
- **Intermediate**: Software used at varying levels of sophistication.
- **Specialist**: Software used only by specialists.

Table 4.2 A range of typical software tools

Software Tool	Class	Primary functions
Text/Word-processors	General	Text editing, and word-processing
Spreadsheets	General	Information tables
Databases	General	Data management
Communication	General	Email, messaging
Utilities	General	Archive, backup, conversion, productivity
Reference	Intermediate	Help files, hypermedia, hypertext, viewer documents
Finances/Accounting	Intermediate	Invoicing, book-keeping
Graphics	Intermediate	Vector Illustration and bitmap photo-editing
Multimedia Authoring	Intermediate	Tutorial, instructional, presentation
Structured Authoring Tools	Intermediate	Structural mark-up authoring tools for neutral format documents e.g. SGML and Web documents
Desktop Publishers	Specialist	Document layout
CAD	Specialist	2D documentation, 3D modelling
GIS	Specialist	Geographic Information Systems provide spatial information processing and mapping capabilities
Visualisation	Specialist	Rendering, animation
Time/Project Management	Specialist	Project based scheduling and programming software
Database Publishing	Specialist	Automatic generation of documents from a database
Document Image Processing	Specialist	Creation of digital versions of paper documents via scanning, OCR and image processing
Equation Editors	Specialist	Formatting and typesetting of mathematical expressions
Analysis	Specialist	Financial, statistical, acoustic, thermal, electrical, lighting, structural, hydraulic, mechanical

While many documents can be created using data created from a single application, it is also common that multiple applications can be used. A common scenario is to generate data from specialist software packages and then combine the resulting information into a more generic composition or reporting program. Figure 4.16 illustrates the use of three software packages used to create a single document.

Figure 4.16 Use of multiple applications to create a single document

Applications for Text-Based Document Creation

In the production of documents which are primarily text-based, there are a significant number of applications available. These systems can be categorised under word-processing, desktop publishing, and technical publishing. Each of these classes of applications have different capabilities for the types of documents they can produce. Figure 4.17 illustrates the relationship between these systems.

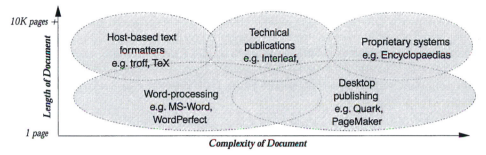

Figure 4.17 The capabilities of various text-based document creation systems[23]

Along the X axis of this illustration is an increasing scale of complexity for the content of various document types. This complexity varies from plain text through to complex, full colour documents. Along the Y axis is an increasing scale for the number of pages contained within a document.

Word-processing applications which are used in the production of relatively simple documents such as business letters and reports, dominate the lower left of the graph. These types of applications run mainly on personal desktop computers. Desktop publishing which is used extensively in the graphics, publishing and advertising industries, occupies the lower right. Host-based text formatters like troff and TeX dominate the upper left. These systems are usually Unix based and are supplied as part of the operating system. Proprietary systems which are used for long and highly complex documents such as encyclopaedias have traditionally dominated the upper right. These systems, however, are being gradually replaced by other types of document creation systems, such as those which occupy the middle of the graph, called technical publication systems. These systems are typically used to create long technical manuals for machinery and equipment.[23]

In this illustration, many of the areas overlap. For example, many word-processors now provide excellent page layout and design capabilities, and are beginning to cross over into a part of the domain of desktop publishing systems. Likewise, many desktop publishing systems are now able to handle longer document types, and are crossing over into the domain of technical publication systems.

Component-Based Applications and Document Centricity

For the users of object-oriented operating systems, the concept of component-based software and document centricity is becoming an increasingly important topic.

The fundamental notion of component software is to build applications from reusable parts that can be plugged into some kind of 'container'. A component is a standalone object that is not bound to a particular program, computer language or implementation.[24]

Components can be specifically written for an application or can be reused from other applications located locally on a computer, or on some other location on a network server. The aim of this approach is to enable software to be developed more quickly, more economically, in compliance with industry standards, and be capable of being easily accessed over a network. This in turn enables different component-based applications to access and modify data objects found in a document, regardless of data content or formatting.[25] As will be discussed in Chapter 6, this is the basis of the compound document type. This approach also leads to the notion of document-centric computing.

The traditional model of computing is based around an *application-centric* approach, whereby all of the functions that are required to perform a task are contained within a single application. Using this approach, the size and complexity of an application increases considerably as new features are continually added, resulting in what are known as 'monolithic' applications.[26]

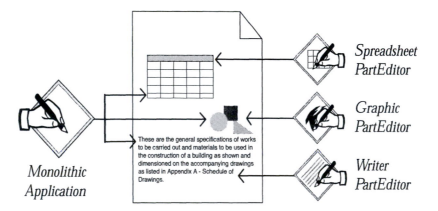

Figure 4.18 The concept of a document-centric approach to editing documents

In many instances the features added to applications are also common to a number of other applications. For example, in many software applications there is often a need for a spelling dictionary, a text editor, basic tables and a simple set of graphics tools. Yet when a new application is developed, unique code to provide these functions is often recreated, resulting in slight variations of functionality and interface from industry standards.

By using a *document-centric* approach to computing, the user does not have to be bound to the features of a single application. Instead, there is an emphasis upon the interoperability and capabilities of the document as a container for various object parts. In this model, applications can be referred to as component editors. Figure 4.18 illustrates the principle of using component editors versus a monolithic application.

Functionally, an application that has been written using components might work in the following manner. Consider a feasibility report that includes some text, a portion of a spreadsheet and part of a CAD drawing. When editing this document, the user only has to select the spreadsheet part and an appropriate component editor is called and the menu will change to give the necessary editing tools. By selecting the graphics object, the menu changes again, but this time providing a set of graphic tools that have been called from a separate component editor. The necessary components required to perform these tasks might be installed on a local computer or be located remotely on another network. This latter approach refers to the use of distributed object computing methods and is being heavily promoted as a method for developing applications for the Internet.[25]

Document-centric computing is still in its infancy, and to date there have only been a limited number of examples that have implemented or demonstrated as component based application technologies, namely: OLE (ActiveX), OpenDoc and Java Beans.

The principle example is Microsoft's OLE (Object Linking and Embedding), which is the object-based foundation of the Windows platform. OLE is also a part of ActiveX which is used for Internet-based applications. As the name implies, OLE enables users to easily link and embed information between documents that has been created from different applications. When objects, such as a graphic, text or table, are linked between their source and the place it was originally created, the object can be edited in either location and the changes be simultaneously updated. Embedded objects actually store a copy of the source data in a document and can be edited by the originating application when the object is clicked on. The underlying communication mechanism between objects using OLE (and ActiveX), is Microsoft's Component Object Model (COM).

A major contender to OLE was the OpenDoc document standard developed by Component Integration Laboratories in 1993 (originally made up of a consortium of companies from Apple, Novell, Sun, Xerox, Oracle and IBM). It was designed around the use of reusable and highly compatible building blocks of code known as 'part editors'. Documents created using this technology were literally regarded as 'containers' of object parts and could be edited using tools from a variety of vendors.[27] The underlying communication mechanism between OpenDoc objects was CORBA (Common Object Request Broker Architecture) that is based on the System Object Model (SOM).

Despite the promise that OpenDoc offered as a platform-neutral application development environment, CI Labs ceased operation in June 1997, with only one major commercial application being developed, Apple's Cyberdog Web browser. A number of the technologies that were developed from this initiative were then refocused upon Java-based application development.

A further, component-based application technology, is called Java Beans. Java Beans is an Application Program Interface (API) that has been designed to provide a reusable software components for the Java Platform.[28] (Java is a programming language expressly designed for use in the distributed environment of the Internet and is described in more detail in the following section). Java Beans components, or Beans, can be combined to create applications and compound documents in a manner similar manner to ActiveX and OpenDoc technologies.

To conclude, there are a number of advantages that can be realised in the use of applications which make use of interoperable components and document-centric computing principles, namely:

- a reduction in application sizes (thereby decreasing disk storage requirements);
- an increased level of integration between applications (thereby allowing users to build up customised sets of application tools that utilise the best features from a number of different applications);
- a substantially increased level of interoperability between documents (thereby reducing the number of incompatible document types);
- a standardisation of application interfaces (thereby decreasing the required learning curve of applications);
- an increased availability of specialised editing tools for documents; and
- an increased capability to distribute application functions across networked environments such as the Internet.

While component-based application development has yet to reach its full potential, there is a significant amount of work being carried out in this area. Most of the progress in this area is now almost exclusively focused upon the development of Internet-based applications.

Internet-Based Applications
The final group of software tools to consider are those which have been specifically developed for use on the Internet. Many of these types of applications are also written as component software.

In the case of Internet-based applications, a web browser can act as a container in which application components can be loaded from a local disk, local area network server, a corporate intranet or a Web server on the Internet. To the end-user, this means that they can download text and graphics data in the normal manner, and can also download code that can be used to interact with that data.

Using this approach, very flexible and powerful applications can be written to interact with exist data sets or applications, and then be widely distributed to users using a common browser interface. At a rudimentary level, interactive or data processing applications can be written for the Web using scripting languages such as CGI (Common Gateway Interface), JavaScript, or Microsoft's Visual Basic Script. More complex and functional components are written using Java applets and Microsoft's ActiveX.

Scripting Applications
CGI programs are server-based applications that can be written in a choice of languages such as: C, C++, PERL, Visual Basic, TCL, or Python. Typically, CGI is

used to interact with existing data sets and can be used for submitting database queries, dynamically generating pages of information based upon those queries, or emailing and processing web-based forms.

JavaScript is a cross-platform, object-based scripting language for developing client- and server-based Internet applications. Client-side JavaScript statements can be embedded into Web pages and, when downloaded into the Web browser, can respond to user interaction using mouse-clicks, form input, and page navigation. When JavaScript is used as a server application, the code is usually far more complex and is therefore compiled and run at the server end similar to CGI programs. Microsoft's Visual Basic Script offers similar functionality at both the client and server end but is limited to use in Microsoft's own Web browser technologies.

Java

Java is a programming language that enables applications to be compiled and run on the Java platform. The Java platform is a software platform for delivering and running highly interactive, dynamic, and secure applets and applications on networked computer systems.[29] A unique aspect of the Java Platform is that it sits on top of other platforms such as Microsoft Windows, Macintosh, OS/2 and Unix, and operates on what is known as a Virtual Machine (VM). In other words, applications written in Java are designed to run on the Java VM, independently of any underlying operating system. This enables developers to write an application once rather than having to write a version for each underlying operating system. This dramatically increases the portability of the application as illustrated in Figure 4.19.

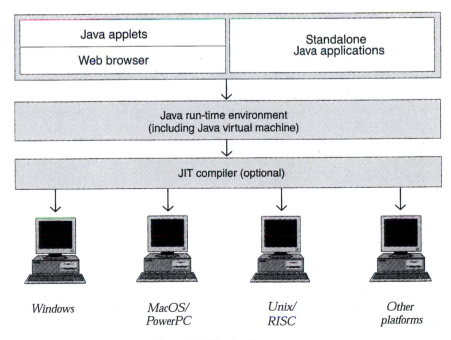

Figure 4.19 The Java Environment

The Java Platform enables two types of programs to be written: applets and applications.

- A *Java applet* requires a Web browser with a Java VM built into it. An applet is then called by the code in a Web page where it is downloaded from a server and executed by the Web browser. Applets tend to be smaller in size and modular in functionality to avoid long download times.
- A *Java application* is a program that does not require a browser to run and does not require to be downloaded. The only requirement is that it must run on a Java VM. When a Java application is called it acts just like any other program such as a word-processor, database interface or spreadsheet.

The capability to write applications once and have them run on top of any operating system is the major drawcard for many developers. However, Java also offers the capability to run applications independently of a host operating system. The JavaOS is a small and efficient operating environment that allows Java applications to run on multiple platform devices such as network computers (NCs), set-top boxes (cable network computing devices), PDAs and, even, electronic devices without any graphical display, such as telephones and smart cards.

Since its official release by Sun Microsystems in 1994, the Java Platform and language has received unprecedented support from software and OS developers, resulting in many new industry alliances and formalised standardisation groups.[30] One significant divergence from this industry model of unified co-operation has been the efforts of Microsoft in the promotion of its own Internet-based technologies.

ActiveX

When Microsoft made a strategic direction in late 1995 to encompass the Internet in all of its software development efforts, it introduced a technology called ActiveX controls.[31] In general, ActiveX makes Microsoft's Object Linking and Embedding (OLE) technology accessible using Internet enabled applications. Like Java applets, ActiveX is also designed to operate in some kind of container such as a Web browser, but can also run in other containers such as native document types. However, unlike Java, ActiveX controls can be written using a range of different languages and are compiled as binaries specifically targeted for use on the Windows platform.

There are a number of pros and cons associated with Microsoft's approach to ActiveX. These issues relate to availability, platform independence, speed and security.

Because ActiveX is based upon the use of OLE technologies, that are already used in the majority of Windows-based applications, there is an obvious advantage in the large availability of controls that can be used. For example, application controls that have already been developed to integrate with Microsoft word-processing, spreadsheet, database and graphics applications, can be immediately ported for use as ActiveX controls. Given the extensive user base of Microsoft products and applications that have been written for the Windows platform, this is a major advantage for developers who want to quickly deliver a product to the market.

What ActiveX gains in availability of existing application controls, it loses in cross-platform capability. ActiveX is specifically designed to work best on the Windows platform and in doing so, sacrifices the platform independence offered by the Java environment.[31] Ultimately this capability depends upon the target environment. If intended users of an application are all using the Windows platform, a developer may choose to make maximum use of ActiveX controls. However, if an application is required to be developed so that it can be used by the largest possible market in a range of computing environments, then the use of Java applets would be the preferred approach.[32]

ActiveX controls are binary in nature and as a result, they offer enhanced performance capabilities because they can run immediately they are downloaded. Java applets, however, need to be interpreted as they are downloaded, and require an intermediate process of compilation before they can be used. In general, interpreted applications tend to run in the order of ten times slower than compiled applications.[32]

One of the most contentious issues concerning the use of ActiveX technologies is that of security. Because Web-based applications that use ActiveX or Java download a program that is run on a computer, there is an element of risk associated with this activity. On an intranet it could be assumed that such applications can be trusted. On the Internet, however, an application could be written by anyone, and it is important to make sure that applications do not contain some type of malicious code such as a virus or data-corrupting program that could affect the operating system.

Because ActiveX controls also offer the capability to talk directly to a host operating system and other applications that reside on a computer, there is an inherent risk with this approach. Java applications, however, are constrained to operate on the Java VM using an approach known as 'sandboxing'. This guarantees security because Java applets are not able to operate outside of this environment. The downside of this approach is that they cannot perform functions that on occasions might be useful, such as being able to write to or save a file on a server.

Both Java and ActiveX offer many new opportunities for the development of applications that can be distributed across a network. The technology and techniques they employ are being subjected to continual and rapid development that is affected by a number of competing market forces. As a result, it is expected that the development and use of applications for the Internet will vary significantly over the next decade and will offer a computing environment for digital documents that might be vastly different from what we know today.

REFERENCES

1.   Sharaz, M. K. (1993), 'Automatic identification in construction', *Construction Computing*, no. 40, Spring, p. 14.

2.   van der Roest, M. (1994), 'EDM: how it makes business more productive', *EDM '94*, Washington, DC.

3.   Radford, A. D. and Stevens, G. (1987), *CADD Made Easy*, New York: McGraw-Hill.

4.   Platt, C. (1997), 'Digital ink', *Wired*, vol. 5, no. 5, p. 162–211.

5.   Negroponte, N. (1997), 'Surfaces and displays', *Wired*, vol. 5, no. 1, p. 212.

6.   Richardson, S., Blackmore, E., Cuffaro, D. and Gavorski, M. (1994), 'Architek Input Device', *I.D. Magazine*, July/August, p. 168.

7.   Sharpe, R. (1995), 'IT in the construction industry – future directions', *Promotional Forum for Electronic Commerce in the Construction and Building Industries*, Melbourne: AUSDEC.

8.   Tapscott, D. and Caston, A. (1993), *Paradigm Shift – the New Promise of Information Technology*, New York: McGraw-Hill.

9.   Tesler, A. (1991), 'Networked computing in the 1990s', *Scientific American*, September, p. 54–61.

10.   Newton, P., Wilson, B., Crawford, J. and Tucker, S. (1993), 'Networking CAD in the AEC sector: an introduction', *Networking CAD*, Melbourne: CSIRO Division of Building, Construction and Engineering.

11.   ISOC (1996), 'Global connectivity table', *http://www.isoc.org/*, Internet Society.

12.   Montgomery, M. (1993), 'Wide area networking within Australia', *Networking CAD*, Melbourne: CSIRO Division of Building, Construction and Engineering.

13.   Pike, M. A. (1995), *Using the Internet*, 2nd edn, Indianapolis: Que.

14.   Voss, D. (1995), 'You say you want more bandwidth? Solitons and the erbium gain factor', *Wired*, vol. 3, no. 7, p. 64.

15.   Negroponte, N. (1995), *Being Digital*, Rydalmere: Hodder and Stoughton.

16.   Reinhardt, A. (1994), 'The network with smarts', *BYTE*, vol. 19, no. 10, p. 51.

17.   Udell, J. (1994), 'The great OS debate', *BYTE*, vol. 19, no. 1, p. 117.

18.   Salus, P. (1994), 'Unix at 25', *BYTE*, vol. 19, no. 10, p. 75.

19.   Varhol, P. D. (1994), 'Small kernels hit it big', *BYTE*, vol. 19, no. 1, p. 119.

20.   Stroustrup, B. (1992), *C++ Programming Language*, Reading: Addison-Wesley.

21.   Hayes, F. (1994), 'Personality plus', *BYTE*, vol. 19, no. 1, p. 155.

22.   MacWorld (1993), 'Off the beam: update on the personal digital assistant scene', *Australian MacWorld*, October, p. 26.

23.   Lewis, C. (1995), 'comp.text FAQ', *news://comp.text*, Usenet newsgroup.

24.   Orfali, R., Harkey, D. and Edwards, J. (1996), *The Essential Distributed Objects Survival Guide*, New York: Wiley.

25. Shah, A. B. (1996), *World Wide Web and object technology*, in '*WWW Beyond the Basics*', Virginia Polytechnic Institute & State University: http://ei.cs.vt.edu/~wwwbtb/book.

26. Williams, G. (1994), 'Why OpenDoc makes sense in more places than you think', *Apple Directions*, December, p. 2.

27. Apple (1994), *OpenDoc for Macintosh: an Overview for Developers*, Cupertino: Apple Computer Inc.

28. JavaSoft (1996), 'Java Beans: a component architecture for Java', *http://splash.javasoft.com/beans/WhitePaper.html*, Sun Microsystems.

29. Kramer, D. (1996), 'The Java Platform', *http://www.javasoft.com*, JavaSoft.

30. Halfhill, T. R. (1997), 'Today the Web, tomorrow the world', *BYTE*, vol. 22, no. 1, pp. 68–80.

31. OMG (1997), 'Comparing ActiveX and CORBA/IIOP', *http://www.omg.org/news/activex.htm*, Object Management Group.

32. Chappell, D. (1996), 'Component software meets the Web: Java applets vs. ActiveX controls', *http://www.chappellassoc.com/JavaActX.htm*, Chappell Associates.

Chapter 5
Digital Data Types

BASIC PRINCIPLES

In some of the earliest uses of computers, the work that was carried out was often referred to as electronic data processing or EDP.[1] Even though the technologies have changed dramatically since then, the principles involved have largely remained the same.

Today, practically all computers are binary based. The information contained within data files they use, are encoded using a series of binary numbers which are made up of a string of 1s or 0s known as *bits* (derived from the term binary digits). A bit can travel at the speed of light and has no colour, size or weight. It represents the smallest element possible in the composition of information. In almost all cases, information that is processed by a computer has to be in this binary format.

Base-ten (Decimal)	Base-two (Binary)
1	1
2	10
3	11
4	100
5	101
6	110
7	111
8	1000
9	1001
10	1010
50	110010
100	1100100

Figure 5.1 A comparison between decimal and binary numbers

Since each bit can store only two possible states, on or off, data such as numbers, text and graphics have to be described using a series of bits. Figure 5.1 illustrates a comparison between common decimal (base-ten) numbers and the binary (base-two) numbers that are used by computers.

At the fundamental level of computing, a software application can be used to create integers, real numbers and alphabetic characters from a series of bits. More complex types of digital data such as audio, graphics, and text can also be formed. Once they have been created, data can then be stored in individual computer files for later retrieval. For example, a data file might contain a sound, a picture or some text output from a numerical analysis application. These data files can then used in the composition of digital documents, which exist at the highest level of this hierarchy, as illustrated in Figure 5.2.

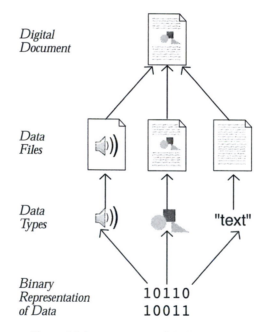

Figure 5.2 A representation of the flow of data

When data is stored in a file, it is usually structured in a manner that is tailored to specific types of information. It is also structured in a manner that allows recovery of the data with a reasonable degree of efficiency. By using these methods, data independency can be achieved, whereby information can be used and reused with a wide range of applications, operating systems, and computer types.

NUMERICAL DATA

In the early use of computers there was an emphasis upon their use as 'number crunchers'. Typically, numerical data was accepted as input, and then processed according to a number of mathematical formulae. In modern computing environments, however, the user is shielded from this level of operation by the operating system and user interface. In most cases the user only needs to be concerned with the representations of numerical data in the form of graphics, texts and sounds as illustrated in Figure 5.3.

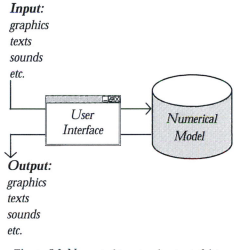

Figure 5.3 Numerical input and output of data

TEXT DATA

In order to maintain effective and consistent results in the exchange of textual data across multiple platforms, an encoding scheme must be used to represent alphanumeric characters as a set of binary digits. As with most computer technologies, there have been a number of competing standards that have been used to achieve this aim.

The four most widely used codes that have been developed for this purpose are:

- ASCII (American Standard Code for Information Interchange);
- BCD (Binary Coded Decimal);
- EBCDIC (Extended Binary Coded Interchange Code); and
- UNICODE (Universal Code)

In each of these schemes, a different number of bits are used to represent a defined set of possible characters. These range from the 7-bit character sets used by BCD through to the 16-bit character sets as used by UNICODE.

Due to the many difficulties which arose from the exchange of information between these different systems, ASCII eventually become the *de facto* standard and is now used in most personal computers. UNICODE, however, is beginning to emerge as a solution for many non-English speaking countries.

ASCII

The ASCII standard describes a coded character set which is primarily intended for the interchange of information. The character set is applicable to all Latin alphabets, and is based upon a 7-bit coded representation of a minimum number of 128 control and graphic characters such as letters, digits and symbols.[2]

In fact, 8 bits (one byte) are commonly used to represent each character in ASCII code. The eighth bit is used as either a control character for parity checking, or to provide the capacity to define an additional 128 characters (for applications which have this requirement). In the early days of computing, parity checking was important since information transmitted by computer was quite often susceptible to corruption. The description and allocation of codes for these additional characters, is usually left open to individual developers and, therefore, only the first 128 characters are ever consistently defined. These additional set of characters are often referred to as extended ASCII codes.

ASCII works by allocating a unique position number on a table for each alphanumeric character. That way, when information is exchanged, equivalent ASCII codes will always represent the same character. Table 5.1 illustrates a series of printable ASCII characters and their corresponding ASCII character number.

Table 5.1 ASCII codes for printable characters

32	sp.	44	,	56	8	68	D	80	P	92	\	104	h	116	t
33	!	45	–	57	9	69	E	81	Q	93	]	105	i	117	u
34	"	46	.	58	:	70	F	82	R	94	^	106	j	118	v
35	#	47	/	59	;	71	G	83	S	95	_	107	k	119	w
36	$	48	0	60	<	72	H	84	T	96	`	108	l	120	x
37	%	49	1	61	=	73	I	85	U	97	a	109	m	121	y
38	&	50	2	62	>	74	J	86	V	98	b	110	n	122	z
39	'	51	3	63	?	75	K	87	W	99	c	111	o	123	{
40	(	52	4	64	@	76	L	88	X	100	d	112	p	124	|
41	)	53	5	65	A	77	M	89	Y	101	e	113	q	125	}
41	*	54	6	66	B	78	N	90	Z	102	f	114	r	126	~
43	+	55	7	67	C	79	O	91	[	103	g	115	s		

The practical application of using the ASCII encoding scheme, is that text files created using this system, can be transferred to almost any other operating system without the need for translation. Its use, therefore, has become synonymous with most methods of platform independent data exchange.

While ASCII has a large number of benefits for cross-platform data exchange, it also has a number of limitations, such as having no immediate method of providing formatting control. This means that it is not possible to vary the typeface, or point size of individual characters (as used in a word-processing applications). ASCII files are also unable to embed other data types such as complex graphics or audio elements. To provide either of these functionalities requires the use of a proprietary document structure, and a resulting loss of data independency.

Table 5.2 Examples of some common uses of ASCII text data

Purpose	Description	Example
Plain text files	These are unformatted text files which are created when the author does not require control of the presentation, but needs to ensure that the reader can display and read the information contained in the file.	Checklists Instructions Software install notes
Application output files	These are application output data files used to store the results of processing. They can also be used as input data for other applications.	Scientific applications Structural analysis GIS applications
Configuration files	Files used to store the data that records certain user customisable features of an application or OS.	autoexec.bat win.ini
Programming source code	Before a software application is compiled into a binary program file, the source code exists as an editable text file.	C LISP
Application interchange files	A method of translating between proprietary file formats is to use an intermediate and editable interchange files.	Microsoft RTF AutoCAD DXF
Metalanguages	Metalanguages can be used to mark-up text files to give them structural meaning.	SGML HTML
Email	All electronic communications via email use 7-bit ASCII to ensure that the message contents are transportable across a variety of different network and operating systems.	SMTP Mail cc:Mail QuickMail
Output / Page Description Languages	Files containing control codes for all of the procedural and printing information required to produce a document on an output device.	PCL HPGL PostScript
Compression files	Certain applications are able to convert binary files into compact ASCII based files so that they can be easily exchanged across unknown networks or operating systems.	BinHex UUencoding Base64 (MIME)

There are, however, a number of ways to extend the capabilities of ASCII files by using delimiters to punctuate the text using an accepted set of encoding rules. Common delimiters include the use of commas (,), dollar signs ($), ampersands (&), less than (<), and greater than (>) characters. Using these, and a number of other methods (which will be discussed later), ASCII files can be used for many different purposes, some of which are shown in Table 5.2. The main benefits of their use in each of these examples, extends from the fact that ASCII text is a neutral data type.

UNICODE

One of the obvious problems for countries which require the use of more than 256 alphanumeric characters, is that ASCII will simply not suffice. To overcome this problem, a standard called UNICODE has been developed by a large consortium of computing companies including: Apple, DEC, HP, IBM, Lotus, Microsoft, NeXT, Novell, Unisys and others. The UNICODE World-wide Character Standard (ISO/IEC 10646) is a character coding scheme designed to support the interchange, processing, and display of the written texts of the diverse languages of the modern world. It also supports classical and historical texts of many other written languages.[3]

The UNICODE (v2.0) encoding scheme, enables the generation of 38,885 distinct coded characters. Using this system, characters and glyphs are derived from 25 primary scripts. An additional number of secondary (or pseudo) scripts are also used to encode a collection of symbols such as: numbers, diacritics (e.g. exposé), punctuation, mathematical symbols, technical symbols, dingbats (e.g. §, ‡, μ,♥), arrows, and geometric shapes. By using scripts, rather than separate character sets, a set of symbols can be generated that may be useful for more than one language. A single script, such as Latin for example, may contribute to the source of hundreds of languages. Other scripts, such as Hangul, may only contribute to just one language.

The characters which can be produced from UNICODE, are able to support the principal written languages of the Americas, Europe, the Middle East, Africa, India, Asia and Pacifica. The UNICODE scripts that have been developed so far are listed in Table 5.3.

Table 5.3 Primary scripts currently supported by UNICODE[3]

Arabic	Devangari	Han	Katakana	Phonetic
Armenian	Georgian	Hangul	Latin	Tamil
Bengali	Greek	Hebrew	Lao	Telugu
Bopomofo	Gujarati	Hiragana	Malayalam	Thai
Cyrillic	Gurmkhi	Kannada	Oriya	Tibetan

The development and adoption of UNICODE provides a mechanism to transcend many of the problems associated with producing text based data in languages other than English.

Fonts

A significant property of a document is the way in which it is formatted for rendering to either a screen or printer. When text is displayed on a screen, or printed on to a page, the characters are given shapes and spacings using a typeface design known as a font.

A font is used to specify the design of individual characters and uses characteristics such as body height, cap height, character width, body width, character origin, stroke, serif, ascender height, descender depth, and so on. The design of fonts is a very exact and esoteric science that is carried out by a profession known as typographers. The techniques they use to design fonts date back to many of the conventions that were developed by scribes in medieval times. For example, the fact that most left- and right-hand edges of text are vertically aligned, relates to the fact that the scribes often wanted to make the facing pages in books perfectly symmetrical.[4] Figure 5.4 illustrates some examples of different fonts and their attributes.

In a document creation or document display system, it is common for a number of different fonts to be supported. Supplied with most operating systems are a basic set of fonts, including such typefaces as 'Roman', 'Courier', and 'Helvetica', but there are literally thousands of different typefaces and incremental variations to choose from. These fonts have usually been created by a number of different creators known as type foundries (a term relating back to the time when metal foundries produced type for use on printing-presses). These foundries also use a number of different ways to construct fonts. Some of the more common font types are listed in Table 5.4.

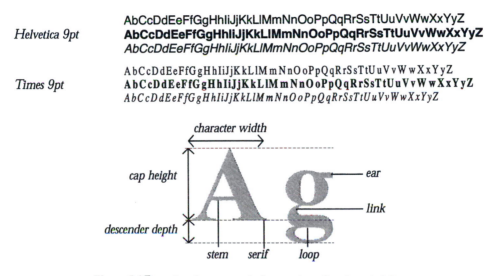

Helvetica 9pt

AbCcDdEeFfGgHhIiJjKkLlMmNnOoPpQqRrSsTtUuVvWwXxYyZ
AbCcDdEeFfGgHhIiJjKkLlMmNnOoPpQqRrSsTtUuVvWwXxYyZ
AbCcDdEeFfGgHhIiJjKkLlMmNnOoPpQqRrSsTtUuVvWwXxYyZ

Times 9pt

AbCcDdEeFfGgHhIiJjKkLlMmNnOoPpQqRrSsTtUuVvWwXxYyZ
AbCcDdEeFfGgHhIiJjKkLlMmNnOoPpQqRrSsTtUuVvWwXxYyZ
AbCcDdEeFfGgHhIiJjKkLlMmNnOoPpQqRrSsTtUuVvWwXxYyZ

Figure 5.4 Examples of some sample fonts and typeface characteristics

A common problem resulting from the exchange of digital documents, is the variety of fonts that can be used. If a document has been formatted using a particular font and the recipient of the document does not have the same font, problems can arise. For example, unless an alternative font is chosen, some or all of the text may be missing from the document, or the layout and pagination can be altered. This can be significant, considering that the layout of documents is often determined by the proportions and spacings of the fonts which have been used.

A number of solutions exist for this problem. A common solution is to restrict the use of complex fonts that fall outside the range of common fonts (such as 'Times' or 'Helvetica'). An alternative solution is to send the document with a copy of the fonts that are used. This method, however, can infringe copyright and may not be a viable solution for cross-platform or cross-application interchange. Some applications also allow a copy of a font to be embedded into the structure of the document itself.

Yet another solution is to use a multiple master font to emulate missing fonts. Multiple master fonts work by substituting an unknown typeface for a generic multiple master typeface that is capable of generating similar characteristics such as weight, width, size and style. This enables the look and feel of a document to be maintained, even though the original font used by the author, may not be present on the recipient's computer.

Table 5.4 Examples of some common font types

Font Type	Description	Creator
Bitmap or Screen	A font description that is made up of a series of dots. Fixed sizes are required for each point size and, therefore these fonts are non-scalable.	Various
Vector	A font description made up of a series of vectors. These fonts are scalable but usually not smooth when enlarged. They are commonly used in CAD systems.	Various
PostScript (Type 1)	A proprietary PDL font that is infinitely scalable. Requires the use of a bitmap screen display font and a PostScript compatible printer.	Adobe Systems
PostScript (Type 3)	Similar to Type 1 fonts but licensed to non-Adobe foundries. (There was no type 2).	Adobe/Various
TrueType	Similar to PostScript fonts but does not require a separate screen font or a PostScript compatible printer.	Apple Computer
QuickDraw GX	A new font technology based on TrueType fonts but enables up to 65,000 character or glyphs per font as well as other features such as: optical alignment, variable style options, and automatic kerning and tracking.	Apple Computer

While fonts are generally considered important to the appearance and usability of a document, it is generally considered that most people want to focus upon the content rather than the details of the formatting.

GRAPHICAL DATA

The process of including graphics data in documents does not seem to be a very complex task. In fact, practically every major software application today is able to create and store some form of graphics data.[5] Even extended ASCII characters can be used in a text file to create rough-looking images. Anecdotal evidence however, seems to suggest that many users often experience difficulties with using graphics files. This could be attributable to a number of factors:

- Graphics data is quite often substantially larger in file size compared to text-based data, and is therefore more difficult to manipulate and store.
- The manipulation of graphics data often requires the use of specialist computing equipment such as scanners, high-resolution graphics cards, high-quality display devices and high-quality printers.
- There is a very large range of graphics file formats to choose from.
- Many graphics file formats often have proprietary and undocumented features that makes them difficult to exchange with other users.

- Many graphics file formats are software and/or platform specific, and are therefore difficult to exchange between different systems.

To be used effectively, therefore, most graphics files will usually require some level of understanding on the author's behalf.

An understanding of computer graphics standards should be considered an essential requirement for most designers. This is because graphic images are often the principle mechanism for the communication of design information. By understanding the underlying principles and features of a variety of graphics data, far more productive, imaginative and effective solutions can be achieved in the use of digital documents.

An Introduction to Computer Graphics

Graphics are required for an enormous number of different purposes, including: user interfaces, graphing, charting, desktop publishing, electronic publishing, CAD, simulation, animation, art, photography, process control and cartography. Almost all of these uses can in some way be associated with architecture or engineering. Currently, almost all interactive application programs use graphics extensively in their user interface, and for the visualisation and manipulation of application specific objects. Therefore, it is perhaps not surprising that an equally diverse range of alternatives have been developed to fulfil these different requirements. As with many other computing technologies, the range of alternatives are related to the development of rapid improvements in technology, the competitiveness of rival marketing forces, and the proliferation of industry standards.

Up until the early 1980s, computer graphics were considered to be a small and specialised field that had a limited choice of software and required the use of very expensive hardware.[6] Early graphics systems were primarily vector based (consisting of individual lines) and required the use of special display monitors. It was not until the introduction of inexpensive personal computers such as the Macintosh and IBM PC in the early 1980s, that a more affordable solution was offered. One of the significant contributions of these systems is that they made use of bitmap graphics (images consisting of a series of individual points), rather than the use of computationally intensive vector graphics.

Basic Graphics Terminology

In order to understand some of the basic characteristics of different graphics file formats (vector, bitmap and others), it is necessary to gain an understanding of some basic graphics terminology.

The subject of computer graphics has become almost too large to grasp in its entirety without some considerable background experience in computing. For the average user of computer graphics, much of the confusion relates to the convolution of lexical terminologies that has occurred over time. In many cases, much of the jargon associated with this field has been evolutional. As a consequence, there are many terms which are no longer relevant to the type of hardware and software that is now in common use, yet their common use still persists.

One typical cause of confusion, appears to be the lack of distinction between what is *displayed* as a graphic, and what is *stored* as a graphic. As previously mentioned, computers use binary numbers to store information. Accordingly, computer graphics are stored as a set of mathematical coordinate points, called *logical* pixels. A computer monitor is made up of a number of *physical* pixels. The distinction is important.

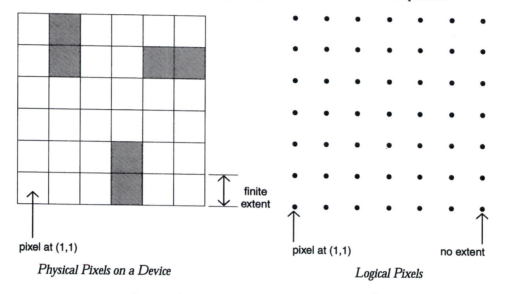

Figure 5.5 A representation of physical vs logical pixels[5]

Physical pixels are the actual dots displayed on an output device, such as those found on the screen surface of a monitor. Because they must cover a fixed area of the display surface, there are physical limitations to how close the dots can be positioned. This size of a physical pixel is often referred to as either the dot size, spot size or dot pitch. In the specification of computer monitors, the smaller this dot pitch, the higher the quality of the resolution. An effect of the limitation of dot pitch is observed when trying to display an image that is too high a resolution for a display, and a blurring or deterioration effect results. Conversely, when a low resolution image is magnified on a large screen, it appears to be made up of large blocks of colour.

Logical pixels are like mathematical points, in that they specify a location, but are assumed to occupy no specific area, as illustrated in Figure 5.5. It is the arrangement and specification of these logical pixels, that are the basis of the contents of a graphical file.

A common term which is often associated with the use of computer graphics is *raster*. As was discussed in the previous chapter, the majority of monitors today are raster monitors – whereby images are formed by rows of physical pixels on a raster line. Over time, the term raster has somewhat confusingly been associated with both the graphics data and the device used to display it with. It is perhaps more appropriate, therefore, to use the term raster in association with display devices, and bitmap in association with graphics files. (In general terms, bitmap and raster files can be regarded as being equivalent to each other).

In Chapter 2 the concept of virtual and actual documents was introduced. These same principles can also be applied to the use of computer graphics. A *graphics file*, therefore, can be defined as the *container* of the specification for an *actual* graphic that is to be displayed or printed. Each specification will consist of a set of data structures, that have been composed according to the rules of a production system (such as a CAD system.)

In addition to existing as individual graphics files, graphics data can also exist as discrete elements as part of a compound document (as shown in Figure 5.2). However, for the purpose of future discussions, it is perhaps easier to think of graphics data in terms of separate files, since the content of these files can almost always be included as part of a compound document. Consequently, it is relevant to discuss *graphics file formats* as being the various methods which are used to store graphics data into files.

From this point on, further discussions could be made on many other terminologies and principles associated with computer graphics, such as colour theory, colour systems, palettes, channels, quantisation, convolution, and so on. Discussions resulting from the description of many of these abstracted concepts, however, are beyond the scope of this book. Fortunately, for most general purposes, the user does need to get involved to this level of understanding. Today, most computer hardware and software that is used for graphics production, is able to shield the user from this requirement. Therefore, only a general understanding of the basic classes of graphics file formats and their capabilities is usually required.

Graphics file formats are traditionally divided into three main classes: bitmap, vector and metafile. In addition to these classes, there are also a number of other file formats used for animation, multimedia and various other hybrid uses. Each of these additional formats still use these three basic classes of graphics in some way.

Contained within every graphics file format will be data containing structural, colour and other descriptive information. This information is included to enable the rendering device (monitor, printer, plotter etc.) to reconstruct and display an image.

Bitmaps

A bitmap is described as a rectangular array of points (pixels) which are used to form an image.[6] In a bitmap, each pixel has a numerical value that specifies the number of colours the pixel can show. This is referred to as the *pixel depth*. For example, a 1-bit pixel can be only one of two colours (usually black or white), a 4-bit pixel can show 16 colours, an 8-bit pixel 256 colours, and so on. The most commonly found pixel depths, are 1, 2, 4, 8, 15, 16, 24 and 32 bits. The number of possible colours from each of these pixel depths is calculated as 2^x where x is the pixel depth. An example of a simple bitmap image is shown in Figure 5.6.

It has been argued that the human eye is only capable of discriminating between 16,777,216 (24-bit) colours simultaneously.[6] Therefore, 24-bit is often used as a practical maximum for the number colours that should be required in any bitmap image. Any device which is capable of matching this level of colours is said to display *truecolour*. Despite this theoretical maximum, there are still a number of bitmap file formats that support image depths higher than 24-bit. Developers of these formats argue that there is a perceptible difference in image quality that can be obtained.

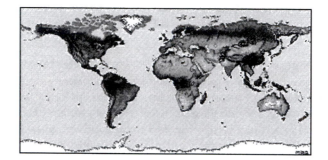

Figure 5.6 A bitmap image

Colour is not always a requirement of a bitmap image. An alternative is to use grey-scale images whereby the value of any of the three primary colours (red, green or blue) making up an image, are of the same value. There are 256 possible grey levels that can be obtained from 8-bit data. This number of greys is usually what is required to obtain a smooth gradation from black to white without seeing tonal jumps or bands. Figure 5.7 illustrates a range of grey-scale tones and a gradation from black to white using all 256 grey tones.

Figure 5.7 A range of grey scale tones

To provide a progressively larger numbers of colours and pixels in a bitmap image, requires a proportionally larger amount of storage space. Therefore, there is usually some form of trade-off that is needed between the number of colours and the number of pixels, if an economical and workable solution is required. As a result of the large size of bitmap files, compression methods are frequently used.

Once a bitmap image has been captured by an input device such as a scanner, digital camera or video frame grabber, it can then be manipulated using different types of software tools. These tools range from simple paint packages that offer a limited range of editing capabilities such as cutting, pasting, painting, spraying, and so on, to sophisticated photo-editing packages that offer a suite of complex editing and special effect tools. Alternatively, these same packages can also be used to create original work. One of the most common sources for many designers, will be from the use of rendering and visualisation applications.

Table 5.5 Examples of some common bitmap file types

File Type	Description
Adobe PSD	A graphics file format used by the popular photo-editing package, Photoshop. Supports multiple colours and RLE compression.
CALS Raster	A monochrome graphics file format used for desktop publishing of CALS-related digital documents. Uses CCITT Gr. 4 compression.
FAX formats	Fax images can be exchanged via computer-based fax-modem cards. There are a number of fax file formats that can be used including PCX and TIFF. All are monochrome. Compression methods vary.
FIF	The Fractal Image Format is used for the storage of high-quality scalable images that are 'resolution independent'. This is achieved through the use of fractal image compression technology. Compression methods are proprietary.
GIF	GIF supports 1-bit to 8-bit colour images and was originally designed to facilitate the transfer and storage of images for CompuServe users. Most commonly used for Web page images. GIF can use LZW compression.
JPEG, JPG, JFIF	JFIF is a common graphics file format used for the compression of high-quality 24-bit colour images. This format is also used for Web page images and uses the JPEG compression method.
Kodak PhotoCD	The Kodak PCD format is designed for the storage of multi-resolution truecolour images on to CD-ROM. PCD uses a proprietary method of compression.
Macintosh Paint	The MacPaint format is a monochrome bitmap format for use in illustration and clip art. It supports RLE compression.
MS Windows Bitmap	The BMP format is designed primarily for the exchange and storage of bitmap images. It supports 1, 4, 8 and 24-bit images and uses RLE compression.
PBM, PGM, PNM PPM	These formats are part of the Unix- and Intel-based Portable Bitmap Utilities. This tool kit was designed to facilitate the conversion of bitmap images to other formats. These graphics file formats use no compression.
PCX	PCX is a popular paintbrush file format as used in Microsoft Windows. It supports mono, 4-bit, 8 bit and 24-bit images and uses RLE compression.
PNG	The Portable Network Graphic format has been developed as an alternative to the use of GIF images as the preferred graphics file format for Internet Web pages. It supports up to 48-bit images and uses the zlib method of compression.
SGI Image File Format	This format is used as a generic image file format on Silicon Graphics computers. It supports black and white, greyscale and colour images up to 24-bit. It supports RLE compression.
Sun Raster	Sun Raster format is the native bitmap format for UNIX-based Sun computers. It has similar characteristics to the SGI image file format.
TGA	The targa image file format is used widely in paint, graphics and imaging applications (such as rendering software) that require storage of image data up to 32-bit. It supports RLE compression.
TIFF	The Tagged Image File Format is used extensively for the storage of bitmap graphics on may different platforms. It is used extensively in desktop publishing and supports up to 24-bit images using a wide variety of compression methods including: RLE, LZW, JPEG and CCITT Gr. 3 and 4.

In Table 5.5 a number of common bitmap file types are listed. Some of the compression methods are described later in the chapter.

There are a number of benefits and drawbacks associated with the use of bitmap files.

Benefits of Bitmap Files

- Bitmap files can be easily created from existing pixel data stored in memory.
- Pixel values in a bitmap image can be individually altered, offering enormous control over the appearance of an image.
- Bitmap files tend to translate well between monitor displays and printers.
- Bitmaps can use free form graphics and are therefore able to emulate many of the characteristics of painting.

Limitations of Bitmap Files

- Bitmap files can be vast, especially if the image contains a large number of colours and pixels.
- Bitmaps do not scale very well. Scaling in either direction usually involves some distortion of the image. Therefore, bitmaps usually need to be displayed or printed at the same resolution at which they were originally created.
- Once primitives in a bitmap image have been drawn, they cannot be treated as separate objects such as lines, circles or polygons. (This requires a process of vectorisation.)
- The inherent nature of the bitmap means that it has a tendency to produce the effect of aliasing (a stair-stepped outline on the edges of rounded objects).

Vectors

In computer graphics, vector data usually refers to a means of representing graphic entities such as lines, polygons or curves, by numerically specifying key points to control their generation.[5] Vector files therefore, are collections of points, which are used by an application (such as a CAD or illustration package) to connect lines (vectors) between points. In order to consistently represent graphic entities, associated attribute information and rendering conventions have to be used to specify colour, line type, line thickness, fill colours and fill patterns. Some typical vector graphics are illustrated in Figure 5.8.

Vector data usually consists of sets of two-dimensional Cartesian coordinates, whereby individual points are specified by a pair of numbers representing a specific X and Y location on a grid. Using this coordinate system, geometric entities can be simply specified as a group of lines consisting of a starting-point, a direction and a length. Other entities such as circles, rectangles, polygons, and splines, can also be created. By using a three-dimensional coordinate system, these entities can also be used in the creation of spheres, cubes and polyhedrons. Characteristically, vector entities can be easily rotated, moved and scaled without loss of resolution. The ability to scale indefinitely, however, will sometimes depend on the allowable precision of the coordinate system used.

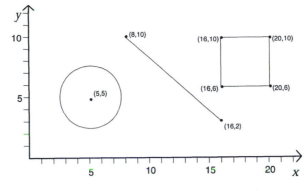

Figure 5.8 Some entities created using vector coordinates

As a result of these attributes, vector files are most commonly used for CAD and drafting purposes. Some common vector file formats are listed in Table 5.6.

Table 5.6 Examples of some common vector file types

File Type	Description
AutoCAD DWG	The proprietary AutoCAD drawing file format. Supports multiple entity types. Uses no compression.
Microstation DGN	The proprietary Microstation drawing file format. Supports multiple entity types. Uses no compression.
AutoCAD DXF	A text-based interchange format, used for the storage and exchange of CAD data from the AutoCAD software package. Uses no compression.
Lotus DIF	The Lotus Data Interchange Format is used for the exchange of numerical data associated with spreadsheets. The format is ASCII based and uses no compression.
Microsoft SYLK	The Microsoft Symbolic Link Format is also used for the interchange of spreadsheet information. Uses no compression.
SGO	The Silicon Graphics Object format is a binary format that is used to store 3D image rendering information as used by the SGI Showcase software. It uses no compression.
Wavefront OBJ	Wavefront OBJ files are used by Wavefront's Advanced Visualiser software. Both an ASCII and binary form of this file type exist. Neither uses compression.

Of the formats listed, many differ in structure and complexity from each other, according to the main function they were written for. As a result, it is quite difficult to generalise about common characteristics of vector file formats, other than those which have been previously mentioned.

Vector files also have a number of associated benefits and limitations which can be summarised as follows.[5]

Benefits of Vector Files
- Vector files are highly suited to storing images composed of line-based two dimensional or three dimensional entities.

- Vector data is easily scaled and manipulated to suit the resolution of a range of output devices.
- Many vector formats are ASCII based and are therefore easily edited and interchanged across a range of different platforms.

Limitations of Vector Files

- Vector images can vary considerably in appearance depending on an applications ability to interpret the data contained within a vector file. For example, not all vector-based applications support complex NURB (Non-Uniform Rational B-Spline) curves.
- Vector images usually require high-resolution monitors for display purposes and are usually not at their highest resolution until output to a hardcopy device such as a printer or plotter.
- Vector files are not suited to storing complex images such as photographs.
- Display of vector data on a monitor is relatively slower, compared to the display of other data formats such as bitmaps. This is because each vector has to be drawn on the screen individually and in the order of creation. Consequently, special video display cards and software drivers are usually required to achieve improved performance.

Metafiles

Metafiles usually contain both bitmap and vector data. This class of file format was initially conceived during the mid-1970s as an attempt to define a device and platform independent graphics file format. Today, however, this aim can be largely met by a number of other formats which are either exclusively bitmap or vector in nature.

Metafiles are widely used to transport bitmap or vector data between hardware platforms. This is often achieved because many of the formats are ASCII based.

Many metafiles work by using the bitmap data for display purposes, and then using the more accurate and scalable vector data for printing purposes. Some typical examples of metafiles are listed in Table 5.7.

Many of the benefits and limitations of metafiles are the same as those for bitmap and vector files. Individual file formats vary according to the proportion of bitmap and vector data contained within them. However, the following generalisations can be made:

- Most ASCII-based metafiles are usually very portable.
- Metafiles containing mixtures of vector and bitmap data can, in some cases, be smaller than fully rendered bitmap versions of the same image.
- Metafiles usually compress quite well.
- Most metafile format specifications are very complex and inflexible.

Table 5.7 Examples of some common metafile file types

File Type	Description
CGM	The Computer Graphics Metafile was developed by ISO and ANSI as a platform independent format for the interchange of bitmap and vector data. CGM files typically contain either bitmap or vector data, but rarely both. It can supported an unlimited number of colours and uses RLE and CCITT Group 3 and 4 compression.
Encapsulated PostScript	Data in an EPS file is encoded as a subset of the PostScript page description language (PDL). It is used extensively in illustration and desktop publishing applications and for bitmap and vector data interchange. EPS files are ASCII based and use various forms of compression.
Macintosh PICT	The Macintosh picture format is a complex and highly platform-specific graphics format that is used for desktop publishing, paint and imaging applications. It supports up to 24-bit colour depth and uses PackBits and JPEG compression.
Microsoft RTF	The Rich Text Format is a metafile standard developed by Microsoft for the interchange of formatted text and graphics data. RTF files are 7-bit ASCII and therefore provides excellent cross-platform exchange. It uses no compression and only supports 256 colours.
Microsoft Windows Metafile	WMF files are used to store both bitmap and vector data for the Windows platform. It is used widely for file interchange and device support. It supports 24-bit depth graphics and does not have a known compression method.
WordPerfect Graphics Metafile	WGM is used for the storage of document and image data for the company's range of software applications. It supports up to 256 colours from a palette of more than one million and uses RLE compression.

Animation Formats

Animation file formats are used for recording a sequence of two dimensional images (usually bitmaps) that are designed to be displayed in a fixed order.

Table 5.8 Examples of some common animation file types

File Type	Description
FLI, FLC	The FLI format was developed by Autodesk to store animation sequences for graphics, CAD and computer games. The FLI format only supports 320 x 200 pixels and 64 colours. The FLC format supports up to 64K x 64K pixel images and 256 colours. It uses Raw, RLE and delta compression. It does not support sound.
M-JPEG	The Motion JPEG format stores each frame using the JPEG compression method and supports 24-bit images.
MPEG	MPEG was created by a working group from ISO known as the Motion Picture Experts Group. This standard was developed for the storage of sound and motion-video data on standard audio CDs and Digital Audio Tape (DAT). A number of different versions exist. MPEG supports a maximum image size of 4095 x 4095 pixels at 30 frames per second at up to 24-bit colour. It uses DCT and other special compression methods.
GIF89a	The GIF89a format supports animations by storing a sequence of GIF images, and can be set up to display the images one after another or in a loop. Supports 256 colours and LZW compression.

Simple animation formats store every individual frame, and hence the size of the files can become very large. More advanced formats use a reduced number of frames and vary the image by loading in a new colour map to simulate movement of the image from frame to frame. Animation files are more likely to exist as individual files than graphic elements of a compound document. Some common animation formats are listed in Table 5.8. While animation formats are still widely used, they are gradually making way to more adaptable digital video and multimedia formats.

Multimedia Formats

Multimedia formats are designed to allow the storage of a number of different data types such as graphics, audio and video in the same file. One of the advantages of multimedia file formats is that they can be easily placed in documents as graphic elements just like any normal graphic. Some examples are listed in Table 5.9.

Table 5.9 Examples of some common multimedia file formats

File Type	Description
Intel DVI	The Intel Digital Video Interactive format is associated with the use of a digital video hardware system of the same name. It is designed for audio/video multimedia applications and supports 16 million colours and uses JPEG and a proprietary method of compression.
Microsoft RIFF, (AVI, WAV, RDI, RMI, BND)	The Resource Interchange File Format is a collection of data type formats used for multimedia applications. The standard covers audio/visual interleaved data (AVI), Waveform data (WAV), Bitmapped data (RDI), and MIDI information (RMI). The standards support 24-bit colour and various compression methods
VRML	The Virtual Reality Modelling Language is file format for describing interactive 3D objects and environments for integrated 3D graphics and multimedia use over the Internet. VRML models an be compressed or uncompressed.
Quicktime Quicktime-VR	Quicktime was designed by Apple for the storage of time-based information under the Macintosh and Windows environments. It is used extensively on those platforms and supports 24-bit colour for images up to 64K x 64K pixels, video, audio, and 3D and uses RLE, JPEG, and other compression methods. Quicktime-VR supports the storage of continuous scenes to rotate objects, zoom in or out of a scene, look around 360 degrees, and navigate from one scene to another.

AUDIO DATA

Digital audio data is an important addition to many multimedia file formats. Its use is also becoming increasing important for inclusion into many different types of digital documents such as CAD drawings, email and, even, standard word-processor documents. Similar to graphics data, audio data has its own special set of requirements for the way in which it can be interpreted and compressed.

Sound is normally transmitted in an analogue manner, existing as a series of undulating air pressure curves over time. When this information has to be represented in a digital form, it is replicated by taking samples of the original analogue sound and converting them to a series of binary numbers. Consequently, the quality of the digitised sound will vary according to:

- The sample resolution (i.e. number of bits per sample), e.g. 8 bits 16 bits.
- The sampling rate (i.e. number of times per second the analogue wave form was read to collect the data), e.g. 11.025 kHz, 22.254 kHz.
- The number of audio channels sampled, e.g. 1 (monaural), 2 (stereo).

As with graphics data, increasing the quality also increases the associated file size. As a means of comparison, a 10-second sound sample recorded at a low quality (one channel, 8-bit sample resolution and 11.025 kHz sampling rate) produces 108K of data. At the highest quality (two channels, 16-bit sample resolution and 44.1 kHz sampling rate) the same 10 seconds of sound occupies 1720K of data. These principles are illustrated in Figure 5.9.

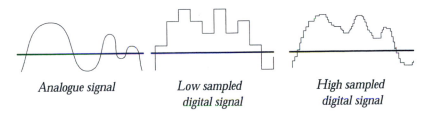

Analogue signal   Low sampled   High sampled
                         digital signal   digital signal

Figure 5.9 An analogue signal replicated digitally with increasing precision levels

Many audio file formats are platform specific, however there are a number of direct conversion utilities and Web browser plug-ins that support a range of formats. Some typical audio file formats are listed in Table 5.10.

Table 5.10 Examples of some typical audio file types

Format or Extension	Platform/Vendor
.AU	Sun Microsystems
.SND	Amiga
uLAW	NeXt
HCOM	Apple Macintosh
.VOC	SoundBlaster
.WAV	Microsoft Waveform
AIFF	Apple/SGI
MP2, MPA	MPEG audio files
8SVX	Apple/SGI

A further common standard for representing sound in a binary format, is the Musical Instrument Digital Interface (MIDI) format. The MIDI standard differs to the previous examples in that it does not actually sample sounds. Instead it stores a description of sounds, using measures for pitch, duration and volume. This encoded data is then interpreted by a MIDI-compatible hardware device.

DIGITAL INK DATA

Many pen-based computers use a data type called digital ink. Digital ink is any type of information that is created when a stylus is used to draw strokes on the screen of a pen computer.[7] Most pen-based computers work by recording strokes on a digitiser surface and then rendering these marks to a screen where they can be subsequently kept as ink data or translated to text or graphics objects. A common example of the use of digital ink data is that used by the Apple Newton as illustrated in Figure 5.10.

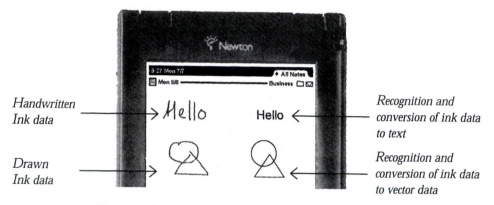

Handwritten Ink data

Drawn Ink data

Recognition and conversion of ink data to text

Recognition and conversion of ink data to vector data

Figure 5.10 Ink data and its conversion on an Apple Newton PDA

While the appearance of ink data may seem to be the bitmapped equivalent of pen marks on a piece of paper, it can actually hold far greater amounts of information than are immediately apparent. For example, ink data is able to record almost every nuance of the way the stylus was used to create the marks.

A standard called Jot has been developed to define ink data.[8] This standard was developed in anticipation of the increasing use of pen-based applications and has been designed to specifically cater for the exchange of ink data in a platform and application independent format.[7] The standard itself is able to record information such as the:

- coordinates of the path of the pen;
- pressure used to create strokes;
- stylus angle;
- type of pen tip;
- height of the stylus above the digitiser;
- use of multiple strokes of ink combined into single objects;
- scale;
- numbered groupings of strokes;
- colour;
- opacity; and
- timing information.

From these properties, it can be seen that ink data is quite similar to MIDI data, in that information is recorded not only about the type of note, but about the pressure and duration that should be used when playing it. By recording all of these pieces of information, ink data can be used for such purposes as handwritten signatures, handwritten email messages, sketches, and the annotation of digital documents.

Ink data should not be confused with another form of temporary data used in pen-based computing, called *gestures*. Whereas ink data is written and *saved* as a data structure, gestures are used as a form of command interface between the user and the application they are using.

Pen-based operating systems, such as the Newton OS, use a series of basic gestures which allow the user to perform functions such as erasing text and graphics, hiding windows, inserting spaces or deleting items. For example, to erase a piece of text or a graphic, the user simply crosses out or scribbles over it. The gestures themselves are usually interpreted in real time, and are done so in context with the position of the stylus in relation to the document being edited. A sample of some typical pen gestures are illustrated in Figure 5.11.

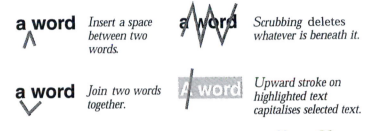

a word   *Insert a space between two words.*

a word   *Scrubbing deletes whatever is beneath it.*

a word   *Join two words together.*

A word   *Upward stroke on highlighted text capitalises selected text.*

Figure 5.11 Some typical pen gestures as used in the Newton OS

COMPRESSION OF DATA

In the specification, transfer and storage of many different types of data, it is often necessary to use some form of compression. By compressing the size of data a number of benefits can be gained including:

- increasing the amount of information that can be placed in a given storage space;
- decreasing the cost of storage for general, backup, and archiving purposes;
- decreasing the amount of time taken to transfer or transmit a given amount of information; and
- reducing the cost of transferring or transmitting information.

There are quite a number of different compression algorithms which can be used to compress data. As was shown in the previous examples, some file formats can use just one or a combination of these different types of compression in their specification. Fortunately, in most cases, the user is also shielded from having to understand the type of compression which a file format uses. An understanding of the basic principles of compression however, will explain which types of data can be more easily compressed and, consequently, why some file formats are more efficient with the amount of space they occupy than others.

Data compression is a method of reducing the physical size of a block of information.[5] In order for the process to be used effectively, a standard encoding scheme must be used to determine how data is to be compressed when it is not in use, and decompressed when it is in use. The difference in the file size between these two states is referred to as the compression ratio or compression per centage. A ratio of 10:1 or 10 per cent for example, would imply that the algorithm used is capable of compressing the raw data to one tenth of its original size.

Compression technology is quite diverse. The algorithms that can be used include: physical, logical, symmetrical, asymmetrical, adaptive, semi-adaptive, non-adaptive, lossy and lossless methods. The most important of these types of compression to understand, is the difference between *lossy* and *lossless* compression.

Most compression schemes use the lossless method of compression, whereby data can be compressed and recompressed without any loss of data. By comparison, lossy compression removes some of the relatively superfluous data in a file, in order to achieve better compression ratios.

Lossy compression systems generally work by using complex heuristic algorithms to rationalise the number of required colours in an image. The process works by replacing adjacent and similarly coloured pixels within a certain range, with another common colour. While this process may seem to reduce the overall quality of an image, most lossy compression algorithms can achieve compression ratios of 20:1 to 25:1 without any perceptible loss of image detail.

Some of the most commonly used compression algorithms for graphics files and digital documents include RLE, LZW, CCITT and JPEG. Other emerging standards include fractal and wavelet compression.

RLE

Run-length encoding is a data compression technique that is used mainly by bitmap file formats such as TIFF, BMP and PCX, but is also used for many other data types. Run length encoding works by reducing long strings of successive pixels (runs) along the raster line, of an image into a coded representation of the same value. For example, an image containing 20 successive characters, normally required 20 bytes.

```
BBBBBBBBBBBBBBBBBBBB
```

By using RLE, this same string could be represented by the code:

```
20B
```

This code only requires two bytes, one for the number and one for the character being repeated. Similarly, the following examples also demonstrate the use of RLE:

```
wwXXXXXXYYYZZZ    -> 2w6X3Y3Z

Specifications    -> 1S1p1e1c1i1f1i1c1a1t1i1o1n1s
```

In the latter example, it can be seen how this method of compression is not always effective on certain types of data, where there is little repetition of values. Consequently, RLE tends to be used more for bitmap data where there are often large areas of contiguous information. Therefore, RLE becomes decreasingly effective as the number of individual colours in an image increases.

LZW

Another common compression algorithm used for many different data types is the Lempel-Ziv-Welch (LZW) method. This is a lossless algorithm that uses a dictionary-based encoding technique. It works by identifying patterns of data and assigning them a unique code from a dictionary of known patterns. Unknown patterns can also be added to the dictionary just like a spelling dictionary in a word-processor. Since its initial development in 1984, LZW has been used extensively in a number of different data file formats such as the graphics file formats GIF and TIFF, and the PC file compression formats LHA, ZOO and PKZIP.

CCITT

One very common use of compression, occurs millions of times per day across the world. Almost all facsimiles machines use a form of lossless compression called CCITT encoding. Named after the French initiated Consultative Committee for International Telephony and Telegraphy, the standard was developed specifically for the transmission of black and white (1-bit) images over telephone lines and data networks.[5] Officially, the protocols used are referred to as CCITT T.4 and T.6, but are more commonly known as Group 3 and Group 4 FAX file formats.

The difference between the two CCITT formats are related to their intended use. Group 3 FAX files are intended for the transmission of data over telephones and uses in-built error detection. Typically, an A4 size document transmitted at 200 dpi will compress to a ratio of 5:1 to 8:1. Group 4 documents however, can compress up to twice that value with ratios of 15:1 or better. However, Group 4 was primarily designed for use on data networks and contains none of the error detection mechanisms that are necessary for image transfer over telephone lines.

CCITT Group 3 and Group 4 are practically identical to the TIFF Type 3 and Type 4 compression algorithms. As a consequence, FAX files are sometimes referred to as TIFF files and vice versa. Apart from its use with FAXs, CCITT encoding has also been adopted for implementation as part of the CALS supported standards.

JPEG

One of the most popular compression technologies to have been developed in recent times is the JPEG standard. The standard was developed by the Joint Photographics Experts Group (as a subset of CCITT) in an effort to develop a standard for the facsimile transmission of colour and greyscale data. While there has been a lack of products on the market for this specific purpose, its most common implementation is for the compression of 24-bit colour images.

True colour (24-bit) images can be encoded using only a limited number of graphics file formats, such as the TGA (Targa Image File) format. The problem with these file formats, is that the compression methods they use are relatively inefficient, and file sizes tend to remain relatively large. The JPEG standard however, offers a far more efficient method of compression. As a result it is being used with increasing regularity where there is a requirement for high-quality 24-bit images but where only a limited amount of storage space or network bandwidth is available.

The JPEG standard works by using a combination of different compression algorithms to provide varying degrees of compactness, according to the intended purpose of the graphic. In most JPEG-supported software, the user is able to specify the amount of compression that is used on an image by changing a quality setting known as a *Q factor*. This Q factor ranges from 1 to 100, where 100 represents the highest quality possible. Being a lossy compression method, JPEG will discard varying degrees of information, related to this Q factor. Typically, compression of 20:1 to 25:1 can be performed without any noticeable loss of image quality.

Fractal

Another compression algorithm, which is receiving increasing amounts of attention, is based upon the use of fractal geometry. A fractal is described as anything which has a substantial measure of exact or statistical self-similarity.[6]

Fractal images can be created by using relatively simple fractal formula to generate one small image, and then repeat it endlessly at smaller and smaller scales in a defined pattern. (A similar effect can be observed when two mirrors are reflected into each other.) By combining various fractal formulae, this technique can also be used to generate images of real-world objects and natural landscapes. By reversing this process, images can also be reduced down to derivative formulae using algorithms based upon Iterated Function Theory using a process known as a Fractal Transform.[9]

The fractal transform model offers a fundamentally different process for the storage and compression of graphic data image file formats. As has been discussed, one of the main disadvantages of bitmaps is that the resolution of a file is limited to the number of pixels that can be used to represent a given area. Fractal compression, however, enables the storage of image data as a record of repeated patterns with no reference to a particular pixel grid. The advantage of this approach is that there are no native scaling properties of the image and it is said to become 'resolution independent'. Fractal image files can therefore be displayed and printed at almost any resolution. For example, the same image can be viewed or printed as a small thumbnail, or as a large A3-size image with no perceptible loss of resolution.

Wavelet

Wavelet compression is a technique used to represent images in terms of special mathematical functions called wavelets. Unlike many other methods of compression which compress data based upon regularly shaped block-like areas, wavelet compression is able to identify flexibly shaped regions of similarly coloured pixels. It does this by using mathematical functions to divide data into different frequency components, and then defining a resolution matched to the images scale.[10] This method holds a number of significant advantages over JPEG and fractal compression, in both the speed of compression and decompression, and the quality of the results.[11] A significant example of the use of wavelet compression, is the system being used by the FBI to store the 30 million sets of fingerprints it has kept on record since 1924. Uncompressed, this amount of data would represent about 200 terabytes (i.e. 200 000 gigabytes) of storage.[10]

Compression File Formats

In addition to compressing data inside a file, it is also necessary, in a number of instances, to compress files or groups of files into a single archive format. This is often required when large documents or groups of logically associated documents (such as a set of CAD files) need to be stored in an efficient manner for archive or transmission purposes.

Table 5.11 Some popular digital archive standards

Format	Description
tar	Unix tape to archive standard
gz	Unix Gunzip standard
z	Unix compression standard
zip	Proprietary DOS PKzip compression standard
lzw	Lempel-Ziv-Welch
zoo	DOS compression standard
sea	Macintosh Self Extracting Archive
cpt	Proprietary Macintosh 'Compact Pro' compression standard

Compression or decompression of files is usually performed using a utility program that supports one or more compression algorithms. These utilities can vary considerably in their functionality and effectiveness from platform to platform. One common capability is to create compression files that are self-extracting. These files require no application to decompress, and the contents can be automatically expanded when they are executed. Some of the more popular file compression formats are listed in table 5.11.

In Chapter 2, it was shown how the archiving of documents is a mandatory requirement in professions in the construction industry. In the archiving of digital documents a number of physical, fiscal and logistical factors have to be considered. To meet these requirements, useful data often has to be backed-up or archived using hardware devices such as additional hard disks, CD-ROMs or archive tapes. To conserve the amount of space taken up on these devices, and to therefore reduce the cost of archiving, file compression techniques are commonly used.

File compression is also commonly used for the storage and transmission of files over networks such as the Internet. By compressing a file or groups of files, significant improvements in download times (and hence cost) can be achieved.

Application of Compression Algorithms

One of the reasons for the diversity of compression algorithms, is that not all data can be compressed in a similar manner. Some data types can be compressed easily, while others can only be compressed with great difficulty. The effectiveness of compression methods upon various types of data are shown in Table 5.12.

Table 5.12 Effectiveness of compression techniques upon data types

Data Type	Methods of Compression
Text	ASCII text files use no form of internal compression. Usually, compression is only used upon text files for archiving or transmission purposes. When text files are compressed the results are usually highly effective.
Bitmap	Almost all bitmap file formats use some form of compression (such as those listed in this chapter). The image data relating to the numbers of pixels and colours can usually be effectively compressed.
Vector	Vector files usually do not incorporate a native form of compression, because the data is already stored using a mathematical description of the image. Therefore, compression results are usually less effective than for text or bitmaps.
Metafile	The effectiveness of the compression of metafiles, usually resembles that of bitmaps. Results depend on the proportions of bitmap and vector data in a file.
Sound	Digitally encoded sound can be compressed using lossy and lossless compression techniques similar to graphics files, but use specific sound compression algorithms. Almost all sound file formats use some form of compression in their specification due to the inherently large size of audio data.
Multimedia	Compression of digital video data is an essential component of most multimedia formats. The majority of formats use a transform coding scheme which reduces the size of the video data by discarding between 10–25% of the file in the form of unused data. Using this method, compression ratios of 20:1 to 40:1 are possible. Using more complex methods such as MPEG compression, can yield results as effective as 200:1.
Animation	Animation formats usually require less complex forms of compression than that of digital video. Most formats use a form of RLE that stores and compresses the difference between two frames rather than compressing each frame individually.

DATA RETRIEVAL

One significant area in the management of data, is the development of indexing and retrieval systems. To date, text-based information is the most easily indexed data type. Most search engines on the Internet for example, only index text-based documents. When text data is in an ASCII form, it is relatively easy to build databases that comprehensively index the content of individual files. These databases can use techniques such as boolean, and relevance-ranked search methods to rapidly and effectively locate information. Searching through other types of data is considerably more difficult.

Typically, most indexing systems that store graphics, audio and video data are file based. In these systems, searches are based upon user defined keywords, and the success of the results is largely dependent on the accuracy of the information that is provided when the files are added to the database. However, there are a number of technologies being developed to enable searches based on the content of complex data types.

Conceptually, the ability to search through the content of audio data is not insurmountable. The main difficulties in this area relate to limitations of PC microprocessor performance, and the limitations of speech and audio recognition algorithms.[12] Advances in both of these areas will eventually enable users to provide a small sample of music, or an audio track, and have a search engine inspect a database for similar sounds.

Because of its inherently complex nature, the most difficult data type to search through is graphics data.[13] These types of searches, require the use of neural network pattern recognition algorithms to identify such characteristics as colour, shape, and texture. Software applications such as IBM's *QBIC* (Query By Image Content) and Excalibur's *Visual RetrievalWare* enables searches through image databases based upon attributes such as colour percentages, colour layout, image texture, or pattern recognition.[14,15] These cataloguing and search engines are accessible from Web servers and the technologies they employ will eventually be combined into the capabilities of standard text based search engines.

Considering that architects, engineers and designers use a very wide range of data types in their work, the use of search engines that are capable of finding the content of text, graphical, audio and multimedia files is an increasingly important capability.

REFERENCES

1. Bindslev, B. and Bindslev, K. (1964), 'The computer and CBC', *Architects' Journal*, 27 May, p. 1193.

2. AS-1776 (1980), *7-bit Coded Character Set for Information Interchange*. North Sydney: Standards Association Australia.

3. Unicode (1997), 'Unicode home page', *http://www.unicode.org*, Unicode Consortium.

4. Campbell, A. (1992), *The Mac Designer's Handbook*, Pymble: Angus & Robertson.

5. Murray, J. D. and vanRyper, W. (1994), *Encyclopedia of Graphics File Formats*, Sebastapol: O'Reilly & Associates.

6. Foley, J. D., van Dam, A., Feiner, S. K. and Hughes, J. F. (1990), *Computer Graphics: Principles and Practice*, 2nd ed, Reading: Addison-Wesley.

7. Bricklin, D. (1993), 'Jot defines electronic ink', *BYTE*, vol. 18, no. 10, p. 110.

8. Apiki, S. (1993), 'A unified ink standard', *BYTE*, vol. 18, no. 10, p. 26.

9. Kominek, J. (1997), 'comp.compression FAQ (Part 2): Introduction to Fractal Compression', *ftp://rtfm.mit.edu/pub/usenet-by-hierarchy/comp/compression/*. Usenet newsgroup.

10. Graps, A. (1995), 'An introduction to wavelets', *IEEE Computational Science and Engineering*, vol. 2, no. 2, p. 50–61.

11. Schroder, P. (1995), 'Wavelet image compression: beating the bandwidth bottleneck', *Wired*, vol. 3, no. 5, p. 78.

12. Lu, C. (1993), 'Publish it electronically', *BYTE*, vol. 18, no. 10, p. 95.

13.   Halfhill, T. R. (1994), 'Image retrieval for compound documents', *BYTE*, vol. 19, no. 8, p. 104.

14.   Excalibur (1997), 'Excalibur Visual RetrievalWare', *http://www.excalib.com/*, Excalibur Technologies.

15.   IBM (1997), 'IBM's Query By Image Content', *http://wwwqbic.almaden.ibm.com/*, The QBIC Project.

Chapter 6
Digital Document Types

AN OVERVIEW OF DIGITAL DOCUMENTS

The Relationship of Software, Data and Documents

Previously, it was established that a document is a container of information used to convey messages between an author and a reader.

In the analysis of this model, so far, the tools for creating documents (the software), and the elements from which they are composed (the data) have been examined.

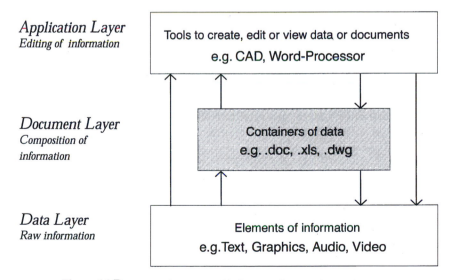

Application Layer
Editing of information

Tools to create, edit or view data or documents
e.g. CAD, Word-Processor

Document Layer
Composition of information

Containers of data
e.g. .doc, .xls, .dwg

Data Layer
Raw information

Elements of information
e.g. Text, Graphics, Audio, Video

Figure 6.1 Documents in context with the general computing environment

It can be seen that a relationship must exist between software and data, in that one is often used to create the other, and vice versa. Sitting somewhere in between are documents, which are created by software applications, and act as containers of data.

To better illustrate this principle, it helps to think of each of them in terms of layers (as shown in Figure 6.1).

While this abstracted view of the relationship between data, documents and software may be oversimplifying some cases, it does help to illustrate one way in which documents can be seen to fit into the overall picture of computing technology.

This particular view also relates back to the concept that was introduced in Chapter 4, regarding document centricity. In a document-centric approach to computing, there is an emphasis placed upon the importance of the *structure* of documents, rather than the particular applications (software tools) used to create them. By using appropriate document structures, the information content can become far more usable and accessible.

The Need for Appropriately Structured Documents

The need for easily accessible and reusable information is extremely important. Architects and engineers in particular, deal with large volumes of information from a range of different sources. Documents such as drawings, schedules, and specifications are constantly in demand during a project, and they need to be accessible to a large number of different participants. It is also often necessary to refer back to previous projects, where valuable construction details or specifications (which might be related to the current project) can be found and reused.

Important reusable data is referred to as legacy data, and there has been a realisation in many industries of the enormous value of information contained in documents of this nature. By using appropriate standards to structure information, a powerful and highly valuable information repository can soon be created. The content of individual documents can then be regarded as a subset of a much larger information or knowledge base.

One of the main objectives of the computing industry, is to develop standards that will allow information and documents to be easily managed, distributed, accessed and processed by dissimilar applications running in multi-platform computing environments. A significant contributor to this aim has been the emergence of the World Wide Web.

Traditional Methods of Structuring Documents

Despite the considerable progress that has been made in computing, the exchange of documents in heterogeneous computing environments still remains relatively difficult to achieve. The principle reason for this difficulty is due to the enormous number of proprietary document structures that are in use. Historically, as each new type of application came on to the market, developers have used their own proprietary method of document mark-up to encode text, graphics and other forms of data. The end result is large-scale incompatibilities that exist between most document types.

Most of the difficulties encountered in the exchange of data and documents, result from a general lack of knowledge about data and document standards, and a lack of suitable software tools to deal with them. For example, it is quite common for architects, engineers and their consultants to encounter enormous difficulties when exchanging computer-based documents for the first time.[1,2] These difficulties usually result from incompatibilities between the different types of software or computing systems being used, and are interfaced at the level of the document.

The Rationale of Proprietary Formats

When software is first written, there are often fairly valid reasons for developers needing or wanting to structure their document format differently to their competitors. These relate to:

- the nature of the data contained in the document;
- developer control of the format; and
- brand loyalty.

The main reason for the use of proprietary formats relates to the nature of the data contained in a document structure. Depending on the type of authoring application, a document might contain any mixture of bitmap, vector or text data. For example, in the case of applications which are mainly graphical in nature, a document structure might have been developed to suit a required bit-depth, or to create a compact file size. Similarly, a text-based application might use a document structure that relates to the way in which font information, or graphic objects need to be stored. Document formats therefore, are usually developed to reflect the features and usability of an application.

A further reason for a proprietary approach, relates to the flexibility afforded to developers when they are the sole owner of a document format. When an application is initially developed, the first generation of the document structure is often fairly immature. Then, as the application is further developed and features are added to its functionality, the associated document structure also tends to change. This is often evidenced by the fact that many document formats are closely associated with the particular version of the software used to create them (e.g. the MS-Word 7.0 DOC format or the AutoCAD R.14 DWG format).

Since the development of a software application is often ongoing, it is usually in the developers best interest to keep their document format proprietary. This enables modifications and features to be easily made to a document format without having to worry about achieving consensus with other industry developers. The downside of this approach, is that there may be fewer applications to exchange documents with.[3]

A by-product of the use of proprietary document formats, is that it helps to establish brand loyalty. Anecdotal evidence suggests that one of the reasons that many users tend to use a particular brand or version of software, is the compatibility it offers them when documents need to be exchanged with other users. As a result, many offices tend to standardise on one particular application brand.

If an office standardises on the use of one brand of word-processor, for example, document exchange, document reuse, and document searches, become far easier. If a range of different word-processor software are used, many incompatibility problems can arise. Therefore, whether intentional or not, the use of proprietary document formats by software developers, also tends to promote a continued support of a software product within an organisation.

CLASSIFICATION OF DIGITAL DOCUMENTS

Due to the enormous diversity of data types, software applications, and communication protocols, it is almost impossible to clearly categorise a range of digital document types according to one set of criteria. Digital document technologies are evolving rapidly, and new features and capabilities are being constantly added.

To provide distinct classifications can sometimes be misleading. This is because new features of some document types can often blur the distinguishing features of previously defined classes. There are, however, a number of document classes that can be identified according to a set of common characteristics and similar functionality. These classifications range from traditional application-based and output-specific structures, through to more open, standardised and generic structures. The following document classes have been devised by the author to explain some of the common approaches to the way in which data can been structured in digital documents.

Application-Based Standards

Application-based standards are those document structures which are associated with proprietary and application-centric methods of document production. They can be classified into proprietary application-based documents and output documents.

Proprietary Application-Based Documents
Proprietary application-based documents are those documents which are associated with a specific software application.

Output Documents
Output documents are those documents which are used in the process of rendering a source document to an output device, such as a printer or a plotter.

Open Standards

With the increasing demand for interoperable computing environments, there have been a number of open standards developed for the exchange of both simple and complex document types. In most instances, these document classes tend to have been developed with the intent to provide industry wide compatibility. Consequently, many of these standards are controlled and supported by independent bodies such as ISO or ANSI, or have been made publicly available by individual or collaborative groups of software developers. The classes of open standard documents, can be grouped under the headings of interchange, messaging, compound, reference, viewer and multimedia.

Interchange Documents

Interchange documents are those documents which are used for translating between proprietary document types.

Messaging Documents

Messaging documents are those documents which are used to exchange messages between users on a network.

Dynamic Compound Documents

Dynamic compound documents are those documents which are designed to act as containers of data objects that are dynamically linked to their sources.

Processable Compound Documents

Processable compound documents are those documents which are specifically designed to provide a universal neutral document-encoding model.

Electronic Reference and Hypermedia Documents

Electronic reference documents (ERDs) and hypermedia documents, are those documents which are specifically designed for the rapid delivery of information located within, or between, large collections of digital documents.

Viewer Documents

Viewer documents are those documents which provide a platform, and application independent, read-only structure for the distribution of formatted copies of original documents.

Multimedia Documents

Multimedia documents are those documents which contain a rich mixture of data sources, and are specifically structured for learning or the provision of entertainment.

PROPRIETARY APPLICATION-BASED DOCUMENTS

A more traditional, application-centric view of computing, regards most digital documents as being the specific output of a software application (as shown in Figure 6.2). Although a lot of progress has been made on the development of platform and application independent document structures, proprietary document formats are still highly popular. Document structures which are proprietary to a particular developer and/or software application are also referred to as being native or private in nature. For example, the AutoCAD DWG drawing file format has remained proprietary to its developer, Autodesk, since they first started in 1982.

Characteristically, native document formats use application-specific semantics and are often binary in nature. This means that the developer uses a proprietary system of structural and procedural mark-up to organise the data within their particular document type. Characteristically, most native document types are difficult to exchange between other applications or operating systems, where those forms of mark-up are not recognised.

As mentioned previously, there are a number of contributing factors as to why these proprietary document formats remain popular. However, it is clear that some form of industry standardisation will be required if the unrestricted and accurate exchange of information in digital environments is to occur on a large scale.

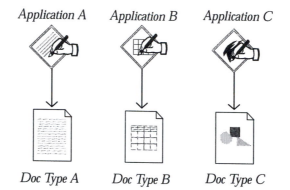

Figure 6.2 The concept of application-specific document formats

Universal standardisation of software applications to overcome document incompatibilities is highly unlikely. Given the speed at which many computing technologies are developing, and the resulting obsolescence of the technologies which precede them, it is unlikely that there will ever be any universal standardisation of software applications to just one vendor. Legislation even exists in many countries to prevent such monopolistic behaviour.

It is also unlikely that there will be any large-scale standardisation of application use among the construction industry sector of the market. This is due to the large number of participants and the diversity of disciplines involved in the industry. Consequently, if large-scale interoperability and productivity gains are to be made in the use of digital documents, industry-standardised neutral formats will have to be adopted.

An alternate approach to this problem that has been adopted among many hardware and software developers, is to develop a diverse range of document interchange, translation and file viewing methods. Some of these methods will be examined later.

There are simply too many different applications and native document formats to enumerate here. Not only are there an enormous range of application-specific formats, but there are also variations among individual standards, according to the version of the software that is used to create them. For example, successive versions of most software, use document formats that are backward incompatible. This means that the most recent version of a software application can read documents created by a previous version, but not vice versa. Some typical examples of native document formats are listed in Table 6.1.

Table 6.1 Examples of some common native document formats

Application	Purpose	Extension	Developer
Microsoft Word	Word-processing	DOC	Microsoft
Microsoft Excel	Spreadsheet	XLS	Microsoft
Microsoft PowerPoint	Presentation	PPT	Microsoft
AutoCAD	CAD drawing	DWG	Autodesk
Microstation	CAD drawing	DGN	Bentley
Lotus 1-2-3	Spreadsheet	WKS	Lotus
FileMaker Pro	Database	FP3	Claris
PageMaker	Desktop publishing	PM5	Adobe

OUTPUT DOCUMENTS

In order to render the contents of a document to a printing device, such as a printer or plotter, an output format has to be used. While these formats are not usually used as editable documents by software applications, they do fit the definition of a document as a container of information.

When a digital document is sent to a printing device, it needs to be intercepted by a part of the printer called a controller. The controller uses a program to interpret the encoded document sent to it, which it then describes to the printer engine in a language that it can use to recreate the document on paper.[4] This language includes information about the way that the document formatting should be translated into instructions for depositing microscopic dots of black or coloured ink on to a page. This translation is usually very complex, and must take into account a number of very subtle typographic issues. For this purpose, there are two main output document types, called output device languages (ODL) and page description languages (PDL).

Output Description Languages
An output device language is defined as a set of commands created by a vendor to communicate with a particular type of output device and may or may not be easily human-readable.[5] A common example is Hewlett-Packard's page control language (PCL), which is used to communicate to HP and HP compatible printers.

Page Description Languages
A page description language is created by a vendor to communicate with a range of output devices. A PDL may be a fully functional language, and is always human-readable. It is also generally more sophisticated than an ODL, and is not tailored to any particular output device. The most popular PDL in use today, is PostScript.

Page description languages have been specifically developed to insulate the application writer from the machine-dependent details of printers.[6] In the past, software developers had to write or provide printer drivers for almost every brand of printer on the market. This meant that in order to print, a user had to configure their software according to the brand of printer connected to their system.

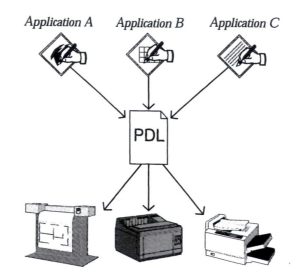

PDL supported output devices

Figure 6.3 A page description language used to support multiple devices

Today, however, most printing devices use ODLs or PDLs in order to communicate with software applications. For example, it is common to see in the specification of many output devices, that they are either PCL or PostScript compatible. This standardisation of output formats has meant that software applications now only have to support a limited number of ODLs or PDLs as illustrated in Figure 6.3. Some typical examples of ODLs and PDLs are listed in Table 6.2.

Table 6.2 Examples of some output and page description languages

Language	Purpose	Developer
PostScript	PDL	Adobe
Interpress	PDL	Xerox
Reprint	PDL	Interleaf
DDL	ODL	Imagen
HPGL	ODL	Hewlett-Packard
PCL	ODL	Hewlett-Packard

The most important aspect of PDLs is that they are a language. This means that when information is being sent to a printer, only short programs, instead of huge volumes of pixel data are sent. An example of a simple PostScript program and its output is illustrated in Figure 6.4. This significantly improves the speed of printing. In addition, it also means that the language can be accurately translated or interpreted by other applications.

```
/Helvetica findfont     # Find font object
                        #  "Helvetica"
188 scalefont           # Make it 188 times
                        # larger than default
setfont                 # Make font current
100 20 moveto           # Move to point on page
45 rotate               # Rotate co-ords 45 deg.
(DRAFT)                 # Place word "DRAFT"
                        # and render it on the
                        # page
```

Figure 6.4 A PostScript program and printed output

PostScript is also commonly used as a method of distributing formatted documents in a relatively neutral manner. By distributing a PostScript version of a document, a user can send it directly to any PostScript compatible printer, view it using a special PostScript viewer (such as GhostView), or import it into applications which support PostScript input.

Despite these conveniences, one of the disadvantages of PostScript, is the relatively large size of the files which are created, compared to the native document format from which they were produced.

INTERCHANGE DOCUMENTS

Digital documents can be exchanged at almost any level in the computing environment. At the simplest level, files can be exchanged using floppy disks and transferred from one computer to another. With the use of networks, file transfer is greatly simplified and a far larger number of computers and information sources can be accessed. However, this also results in many users being exposed to a greater variety of file and document types.

Despite the widespread use of proprietary document formats, there are a number of approaches which can be used to overcome incompatibilities between them. Many of these methods have resulted from interoperability requirements demanded by industry. The basic requirements for the successful exchange of documents are:

- Neutral interchange that is independent of hardware.
- Neutral interchange that is independent of proprietary software.
- The complete exchange of data content.
- The complete exchange of formatting information.

The success of solutions that meet these criteria varies considerably, and is often dependent on the complexity of the information being exchanged.

As illustrated in Figure 6.5, there are basically two separate approaches to the exchange of different native document formats:

- specific system to system translators; and
- neutral interchange formats.

Direct translators are often built into software applications so that other non-native data or document files can be imported or exported. While highly convenient to the user, this method relies heavily on one developer's accuracy in interpreting another developer's proprietary format.

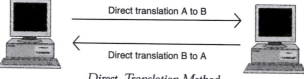

Direct Translation Method

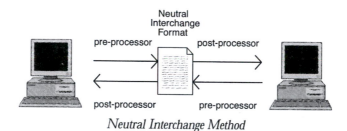

Neutral Interchange Method

Figure 6.5 Methods of exchanging native document formats

The most accurate translators are usually built with the use of programming APIs that have been supplied by the originator of a proprietary document format. However, some translation methods can be highly inaccurate and have been developed from the reverse engineering of a file format. For example, an inaccurate translation process might result in stray vectors, incorrect bit-depths, font changes, missing graphics or altered formatting. Because translation filters are built around proprietary document formats, developers are forced to continually update translation filters as new releases of document formats arrive on the market.

The fundamental problem with direct translation is the huge number of translators that are required. For example, if there are n different formats to be translated, there will be n^2 different translation paths to consider.

To overcome this problem, an alternate approach is to use a neutral interchange format. These interchange formats provide developers with an intermediate document structure that is usually well supported in the industry because it is in the public domain.

By adopting the use of a common interchange format, both users and developers have a more reliable and accurate method of interchanging documents. These interchange formats are usually ASCII based, and are therefore highly portable across a number of different platforms and network protocols. By using an interchange format the number of translators between formats can be reduced from n^2 to $2n$, as illustrated.

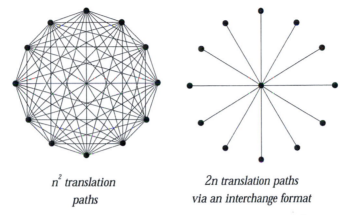

n^2 *translation*
paths

2n translation paths
via an interchange format

Figure 6.6 The effect of using a document interchange file[7]

Text-Based Interchange

One of the simplest methods of exchanging documents is to use an ASCII text interchange method. ASCII is particularly reliable when exchanging documents between different platforms or when there is no other form of direct translator available. The problem with ASCII, however, is that any formatting commands that might be contained in the original document, such as font or layout information, is stripped away. What usually remains is the raw text-based content.

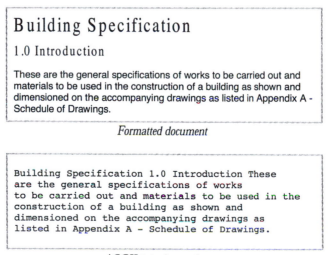

Formatted document

ASCII interchange document

Figure 6.7 The effect of ASCII text interchange from a formatted source

Figure 6.7 illustrates a sample of a document that has been formatted in a word-processor. In order to transfer this document to another system which does not have a direct translator for that document format, the document would have to be saved in an ASCII format. As can be seen in the illustration, all of the font, layout and graphics have been removed. When preservation of these features is required, alternative approaches need to be taken. These will be considered later.

Database and Spreadsheet Interchange

When database or spreadsheet documents have to be exchanged, another form of ASCII transfer can be used. This approach uses ASCII interchange files containing delimiters to separate the information contained in the cells or fields of a database or spreadsheet. The most common delimiters are the comma or tab ASCII characters. An example of a small spreadsheet exported to an ASCII, comma-separated values (CSV) format, is illustrated in Figure 6.8. Notice that all formatting information for fonts, bolding, shading, text colour and borders are lost.

Window Schedule		
No.	Width	Height
1	800	600
2	800	600
3	1200	2400
4	900	300

```
Window Schedule

No.,Width,Height

1,800,600

2,800,600

3,1200,2400

4,900,300
```

Figure 6.8 The effect of delimited ASCII interchange

Retaining Formatting Information in Interchange Files

In the previous examples, it can be seen how the content of a document can be easily exchanged, but that the formatting information is left behind. Sometimes this formatting information can be extremely important to the way a document is interpreted. To enable the formatting of more complex document types to be retained, a neutral form of mark-up is required. These methods can also be ASCII based.

The use of mark-up tags in an interchange format, enables additional information about a document's structure and layout to be conveyed in the exchange process. A number of software developers have produced well-documented and publicly accessible interchange formats such as those listed in Table 6.2.

Table 6.3 Examples of some common document interchange standards

Standard	Purpose	Developer/Maintainer
DXF	CAD	Autodesk
SIF	CAD	Intergraph
IGES	CAD	NIST, ISO
STEP	CAD	ISO
SYLK	Spreadsheet	Microsoft
RTF	Word-Processing	Microsoft

Word-Processing Document Interchange

A well recognised interchange format used for word-processing and desktop publishing is Microsoft RTF (Rich Text Format). This interchange format uses a series of structural and procedural mark-up tags to describe both the content and formatting of a document. An example of a document converted to RTF is shown in Figure 6.9.

Building Specification

1.0 Introduction

These are the general specifications of works to be carried out and materials to be used in the construction of a building as shown and dimensioned on the accompanying drawings as listed in Appendix A - Schedule of Drawings.

Formatted Document (MS-Word)

```
{\rtf1\mac\deff2}
{{\f20\froman Times;}{\f21\fswiss Helvetica;}}
{\stylesheet{\f20 \sbasedon222\snext0 Normal;}}
{\info
{\title Spec1}
{\author Bruce Duyshart}
}

\paperw11880\paperh16800\margl1701\margr1701\margt1417
\margb1417\deftab709\widowctrl\ftnbj\sectd\sbknone
\linemod0\linex0\headery737\footery737\cols1\colsx737
\endnhere \pard\plain \f20

{\fs36 Building Specification}\par
\par
{\b 1.0 Introduction}\par
\par
{\f21\fs20 These are the general specifications of works
to be carried out and materials to be used in the
construction of a building as shown and dimensioned on
the accompanying drawings as listed in Appendix A -
Schedule of Drawings.}\par
}
```

Interchange Format (RTF)

Figure 6.9 An example of the RTF interchange format

While interchange formats appear to solve immediate incompatibility problems, there are still enough alternatives in this class of document to confuse many users. The main reason for this problem is that the majority of interchange formats are still controlled by individual software developers, and most interchange formats change as frequently as the versions of software they are associated with.

CAD Document and Product Data Interchange

One of the most common types of documents exchanged by architects and engineers are CAD documents. As a result, there has been a considerable amount of attention given to the problems associated with this activity. In general, the difficulties encountered are not so different to those that have been mentioned previously. In particular, problems in the exchange of CAD documents result from:

- The large number of CAD systems on the market.
- The large number of CAD file formats and associated software versions.
- The different types of entities used in the creation of a CAD document.
- The different methods used to organise entities within a CAD document.
- The exchange of CAD data across different operating systems.

CAD documents can also be interchanged using the previously mentioned approaches – either by direct translation or by using a neutral interchange format.

One of the biggest problems associated with CAD document exchange, is related to the way that they are structured internally. Despite the fact that CAD systems have been around since the 1960s, there is still a reasonable amount of conjecture about the way a CAD document should be organised. Drawings from two different CAD systems, for example, may provide identical output on paper, but the organisational structure of the CAD documents may be entirely different. This can cause many problems when these documents are exchanged.

There are a number of key organisational methods used in a CAD system. Each of these methods are usually implemented inconsistently between different systems, including some of the following conventions:

- **Layers**: A drawing can be organised by placing drawn entities into common associated groupings such as walls, doors, floor, etc. These layers (or levels as they are also called) can use a variety of naming or numbering conventions. These conventions are rarely well documented or universally accepted.
- **Text/Fonts**: Text can be defined using many different types of fonts. These fonts aren't always available on each system that a drawing is transferred to.
- **Symbols**: A library of pre-drawn objects can be used as part of a CAD system. The naming convention of these symbols (also called blocks or cells) and their organisational structure can vary considerably between systems.

- **Linetypes**: A variety of standard and customised linetypes can be used by some CAD systems. There are no universal standards for the way these linetypes are defined or translated.
- **Plotting**: Drawings can be organised in different ways to provide the scales and layout necessary to produce hard-copy output.
- **Colours**: On some CAD systems colour is used to indicate line widths, and on others is used only for organisational and identity purposes. The range of colours used, and the line widths they represent usually vary between systems.
- **References**: Many CAD drawings, especially those used on large projects, are made up of a number of individual CAD reference files. The organisational method of these files usually varies between CAD systems and can result in numerous complications when translated.

Not only do these organisational methods vary between CAD systems, but they also vary between different architectural and engineering practices, and even within individual offices themselves.

In the development of CAD interchange methods, there have been a number of standards developed, representing varying levels of sophistication. These standards are DXF, SIF, IGES, STEP and IAI/IFC.

At the lowest level of sophistication are the entity-based interchange formats DXF, SIF and IGES. DXF and SIF are the CAD drawing interchange standard used by AutoCAD and Intergraph respectively. Since AutoCAD holds approximately 70 per cent of the CAD market, it has been their DXF format which has come to prominence as the *de facto* standard for CAD document interchange.

DXF

Drawing Interchange format is an ASCII based standard which defines a database of entities found in an AutoCAD drawing file. One of the limitations of this standard is that there are specific versions of DXF for each version of AutoCAD. The standard also only describes entity types which are native to the AutoCAD system, which can potentially cause problems with other CAD systems. A portion of a DXF file is illustrated in Figure 6.10. In a DXF file, codes are used to identify entity types, vector points and data values.

IGES

The Initial Graphics Exchange Specification (IGES), is a standard that was developed in 1980 by Boeing Aircraft, General Electric and the US National Bureau of Standards, to provide a neutral data format for the digital exchange of information among CAD systems.[8] The specification itself is quite complex. Version 5.1 for example, is described in a 600-page manual. As a result of this complexity, its poor implementation and the popularity of CAD systems such as AutoCAD (that offered simpler alternatives such as DXF), IGES has not been widely adopted in the design and construction industry.[9]

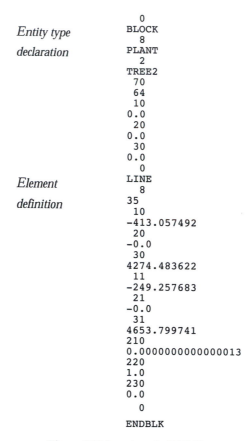

Entity type

declaration

Element

definition

```
           0
         BLOCK
           8
         PLANT
           2
         TREE2
          70
          64
          10
         0.0
          20
         0.0
          30
         0.0
           0
         LINE
           8
          35
          10
         -413.057492
          20
         -0.0
          30
         4274.483622
          11
         -249.257683
          21
         -0.0
          31
         4653.799741
         210
         0.0000000000000013
         220
         1.0
         230
         0.0
           0
         ENDBLK
```

Figure 6.10 A section of a DXF file

STEP

By the early 1980s it was realised that many of the vector-based standards, such as
IGES, were in need of replacement by a new standard that was more comprehensive
and internationally focused.[10] In 1984 the Standard for the Exchange of Product data
(STEP) was initiated by the International Standards Organisation (ISO), for the
computer-interpretable representation and exchange of product data. The objective of
this standard is to provide a mechanism for describing product data throughout its
lifecycle, independent from any particular hardware or software system. STEP can be
used for neutral file exchange as well as for implementing and sharing product
databases and archival information.[11]

Formally known as ISO Standard 10303, STEP is being developed with contributions
from at least 28 countries and representations from practically every major industry in
the world.[12]

This standard is far more complex than any of the previous standards used, because it
is designed to be more than one type of document. The Standard for the Exchange of
Product Data is a set of resources, data exchange methodologies, interfacing

methodologies, and conformance testing procedures. These approaches are combined to prepare a set of application protocols (APs) in which whole industries can base their particular exchange requirements.[13] The APs are based upon a common underlying methodology that uses a common file format and a data definition language called EXPRESS.

An important effect of STEP is that it will enable a wide variety of industries to use concurrent engineering methods to dramatically improve the quality and speed at which products can be developed. Major international companies such as Du Pont and Shell for example, are expecting to make savings of $200 million and $1 billion dollars respectively per annum, when STEP initiatives are fully implemented throughout their organisations.[10]

IAI/IFC

The Industry Alliance for Interoperability (IAI) was established in 1996 as a parallel industry standard to STEP, but is specifically focused upon defining a universal language for collaborative work in the building industry.[14] Similar to STEP, the IAI is also made up of a range of international representatives from many industries including: architecture, engineering, construction, and facilities management.

The IAI is developing Industry Foundation Classes (IFC) as a universal language to improve communication, productivity, delivery time, cost, and quality, using CAD-based tools. Similar to STEP, the focus is upon the use of the information throughout the life cycle of a building during the design, construction, operation and maintenance phases.[15]

Using interoperable software tools based upon object-oriented and component technologies, IFC provides a development environment for creating customisable tools for capturing information about building elements. IFC also enables the relationship between building elements to be defined, so that tasks can be automated for creating wall layouts, door placements, window placements, stair designs, and bubble diagramming for space layouts.

The application of both STEP and IAI will require a paradigm shift in the culture of participants in the design and construction industry if it is to succeed. Because of the fundamental differences in approach that are used over traditional methods of document exchange and information management, companies that wish to make use of this approach will also need to adopt many new methods of practice.

MESSAGING DOCUMENTS

With the escalating use of networked environments in which to share and exchange data, messaging systems are becoming an increasingly important part of normal business practice. Messaging formats associated with these systems, are specifically designed to enable the seamless exchange of text-based (ASCII) information between remotely located parties. Messaging formats use ASCII because of its reliability in being able to pass through different types of networks with varying levels of security, priority and formatting requirements.

Messaging standards fall into three main categories: email (electronic mail), EDI (electronic data interchange), and facsimile. A further technology that is closely associated with these methods is known as electronic forms.

The idea for both electronic mail and facsimile goes back over 100 years. The first fax was sent in 1842 by a Scotsman called Alexander Bain, thirty-three years before Graham Bell patented the telephone.[16] In 1863, Jules Verne wrote the following scenario in a manuscript entitled *Paris in the 20th Century*: 'Photo-telegraphy allowed any writing, signature or illustration to be sent far away, and any contract to be signed at a distance of (20,000 km). Every house was wired.'[17]

Electronic Mail

Electronic mail, or email, is a facility that enables a user on a network to send messages to other computer users connected to the same network. These messages can be regarded as documents (according to the definition of a document being a container of information).

Email can be used to send notes, memos, letters, and many other types of business and personal communication documents. Because email is so easy to use, it has been predicted that it is only a matter of time before email is as pervasive and easy to use as the telephone.[18] Negroponte even goes as far as predicting that 'email will be the predominant interpersonal telecommunications medium, approaching if not overshadowing voice within the next fifteen years'.[17]

There are essentially two parts to an email document – a header and the message itself (as illustrated in Figure 6.11). The header contains all of the details necessary to send the message from one location to another, including information about the sender, details of the addressee, a subject line, and the time and date the message was sent. Additional information about the route the message took in being delivered, is also added to the header. Some mail systems also enable a priority level such as 'important' or 'urgent' to be added to the header, but this is usually only acknowledged by systems supporting this same feature.

An optional signature section can also be appended to email messages. The signature (or 'sig' as it is sometimes referred to) is voluntarily added to a message to indicate more information about the sender, as illustrated in Figure 6.11. (In this example, notice that the header information contains all of the information about the route the message took, and the times, dates, authorship, subject, addressee, referral, content type, length and status of the message.)

Electronic mail can be used to send messages over varying distances. At a simple level, email can be used in a local office environment using a LAN. At the most powerful level, messages can be sent to users anywhere in the world using the Internet. Depending on the load on the network, email can usually be delivered within minutes of it being sent.

One of the greatest benefits of email, is that allows users to exchange information in an asynchronous manner. When email is sent, it does not require the intended recipient to be at the other end waiting to receive the document. Instead, email is stored in an electronic mailbox of an email subsystem (a software application). This enables people to be separated by considerable differences in time and distance, yet still communicate effectively. With the use of mobile computers, it also enables communication to be enabled from practically any location in the world.

```
Header

From mtc@vitruvius.arbld.unimelb.edu.au Mon Jun 26 10:42:31 1995
Received: from ledoux.arbld.unimelb.EDU.AU (ledoux.arbld.unimelb.EDU.AU
[128.250.136.2]) by vitruvius.arbld.unimelb.EDU.AU (8.6.12/8.6.12) with ESMTP
id KAA02694 for <bhd@vitruvius.arbld.unimelb.edu.au>; Mon, 26 Jun 1995
10:42:29 +1000
Received: (from mtc@localhost) by ledoux.arbld.unimelb.EDU.AU (8.6.12/8.6.12)
id KAA03341 for bhd@vitruvius.arbld.unimelb.edu.au; Mon, 26 Jun 1995 10:42:28
+1000
From: Mike Cutter <mtc@vitruvius.arbld.unimelb.edu>
Message-Id: <199506260042.KAA03341@ledoux.arbld.unimelb.EDU.AU>
Subject: Re: Elm & remote access
To: bhd@vitruvius.arbld.unimelb.edu.au (Bruce DUYSHART)
Date: Mon, 26 Jun 1995 10:42:28 +1000 (EST)
In-Reply-To: <199506251258.WAA00630@ledoux.arbld.unimelb.EDU.AU> from "Bruce
DUYSHART" at Jun 25, 95 10:58:07 pm
X-Mailer: ELM [version 2.4 PL24]
Content-Type: text
Content-Length: 324
Status: O
--

Body

Hi Bruce,

Here is a sample e-mail message illustrating a header, body and signature
Mike

--

Signature

name:    Michael Trevor Cutter   email: mtc@arbld.unimelb.edu.au
job:     Mac SysAdmin & Devel   Architecture, Building & Planning,
         University of Melbourne, Parkville, VIC, 3052, AUSTRALIA
```

Figure 6.11 A typical email header, message body and signature

One of the major problems with using email, is the multitude of messaging standards and email systems that are used. Some of the most common standards include: CMC, MAPI, MHS, OCE, VIM, VINES, X.400, and SMTP. These standards have all been developed around different computer platforms, operating systems and vendors. Of these standards, the Simple Mail Transfer Protocol (SMTP) and X.400 MHS (message handling service) are the most popular.

The SMTP protocol is most commonly used on the Internet, and is based on a client/server model in which a mail client is used to create and read mail, and servers do the processing and delivery of it. After a message is sent to an SMTP mail server, it is examined by a program called a mail transfer agent (MTA). The MTA looks at the address of the intended recipient and then sends it to another program called a mail delivery agent (MDA), which sends mail to the appropriate in-box of the user on the server. This process is illustrated in Figure 6.12.

In the exchange of email, a message might pass through a number of different networks and, in doing so, passes through what are known as gateways. In addition to converting data between different network typologies, a gateway performs the task of automatically converting different email formats. For example, the SMTP protocol only supports ASCII text, and any binary files that are attached to a message need be converted to ASCII before they can be passed on. To achieve this conversion, one of three main encoding mechanisms can be used: UUencoding, Base64, or BinHex (MacOS only). At the receiving end, the mail reader automatically decodes the attachment and reassembles the original binary file.

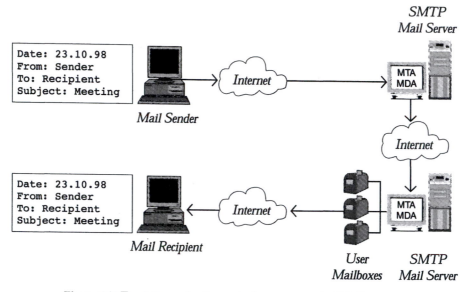

Figure 6.12 The delivery of mail over the Internet using the SMTP protocol

In theory, the process of encoding and decoding attachments is meant to work seamlessly. However, when different systems are in use, and the recipient does not have an email reader that supports the specific form of encoding that was used, the message can arrive as a jumbled mess of code. In order for the recipient to read the attachment they will then have to manually use a decoding utility.

A final consideration is the size of files that can be attached. Although there is usually no theoretical limit to the size of an email message that can be sent, there are practical considerations that should be made. If an email message has a large file attached to itself, such as a CAD file, it can sometimes take a considerable amount of time to pass through the email gateways on a network.

If very large files are encountered, it can sometimes crash the gateway or mail system. As a result, gateways are often configured to reject such files, and the message is simply returned to the sender, or split up and delivered as a set of smaller contiguous files. A practical limit for email messages being sent over the Internet is about 1Mb or less. Larger files should be transferred using network protocols such as FTP (File Transfer Protocol).

MIME

To overcome some of the problems associated with binary file attachments to email messages, a specification called MIME (Multipurpose Internet Mail Extension) has been developed. This is the mechanism for specifying and describing the format of Internet messaging bodies using the SMTP protocol.[19]

The approach MIME takes, is to label the contents of an email message with a plain-text header, which describes the segments contained in the body of the message. This header is then read by MIME-compliant mail readers, which interpret the various types of content and then opens up appropriate tools to act upon the data. For example, if an email message included a graphic GIF image, it would be labelled 'Content-Type:image/GIF' and a GIF graphics viewer could then be automatically used to open the image. (Any binary files that are attached to a MIME message use Base64 encoding.)

The Multipurpose Internet Mail Extension originally defined seven basic types of data: text, images, audio, video, binary enclosures, multipart messages, and enclosed applications. It is also fully extensible to cater for future data types. The benefit for the end-user, is that they are able to send complex document types across multiple platforms, without having to know the end-user's mail system. For international users of email, it also offers the possibility of being able to use foreign character sets. Without MIME, the usual solution is to use the lowest common denominator, plain ASCII text.

Security

The remaining issue to consider with the use of email, is that of security. As with many other forms of digital documents, the ease of duplication and forgery can be high, unless they are managed with appropriate software tools. Since email is used for messaging, it is usually important that the user maintains the confidentiality of the message being sent and provides a level of authentication to prove who the author was.

Confidentiality is often achieved by using a layer of security on top of an email system. This is important for highly confidential email documents. For example, although it is against the ethics of a systems administrator, it is reasonably easy on some systems for an administrator to open a user's account and read the contents of their mail. To prevent this occurrence email encryption should be used.

A wide variety of methods for sending and storing secure and authenticated email are available, including: PGP, S/MIME, PEM and MOSS.[20,21] A number of these systems provide privacy by encrypting entire messages, and adding authentication through the use of digital signatures. (Each of these methods are covered in more detail in Chapter 7.)

EDI

Electronic data interchange is defined as the application-to-application transfer of business data between or within companies (including their agents or intermediaries).[22,23] Such transactions can include the exchange of quotations, purchase orders, invoices, and any other type of business data that are included on any type of business form. The use of EDI is now commonly associated with electronic commerce infrastructures which include the use of email, electronic funds transfer (EFT) and other forms of electronic business transactions.

Electronic Data Interchange is designed to eliminate expensive and time-consuming document handling and data entry and re-entry tasks. With the improvements in performance that are gained, businesses are able to operate more efficiently. The improvements in performance at BHP, for example, have enabled them to reduce lead times for tenders and orders from more than four weeks, down to 24 hours.[24] RJR Nabisco estimates that its traditional processing of paper purchase orders costs the company about $70 per order, but by processing an EDI purchase order, this cost can be reduced to 93 cents.[23] An international study by a Fortune 500 company in the US, also showed that they could save between $US500 to $US700 million by using a corporate-wide EDI system.[25] These savings can be attributable to the fact that:[26]

- the majority of one computer's input is another computer's output;
- the majority of a transaction's cost is data entry and re-entry; and
- many business documents have data entry errors that effect the underlying business transaction.

In simple terms, EDI messages are very similar to email messages. The major difference is that EDI messages are sent in a pre-set format that enables inventory and accounting software to easily process the data. In order to do this, the messages must be sent using an appropriate standard such as ANSI X.12 or the United Nations EDIFACT (EDI For Administration, Commerce and Transport).

Electronic Data Interchange messages which are created according to an EDI standard, must begin with a code that specifies the nature of the particular transaction. For example, under the X.12 standard, all purchase orders begin with the *805* code, and all invoices with the *810* code. Then, for each type of document, there are a number of specified fields including: the address, transaction information, and the total moneys due. An example of an EDIFACT EDI document and its paper equivalent are shown in Figure 6.13.

Electronic data interchange transactions can occur over a range of network types including the public telephone network, the Internet, and special third party organisations known as value added networks (VANs). Value added network providers are responsible for administering and providing a secure infrastructure to transmit sensitive commerce information, and to provide secure electronic mailbox facilities. VANs have been the traditional carriers of EDI data for electronic commerce, but many transactions are now being carried out using TCP/IP-based networks such as the Internet.

While many of the key features of EDI are analogous to paper trading documents, there are some distinct differences. These include the use of digital signatures that can be instantly verified by without the need for identification, digital cash that can be moved anonymously without forgery, and digital time-stamps that can provide incontrovertible proof of a document's existence and content at a particular time.

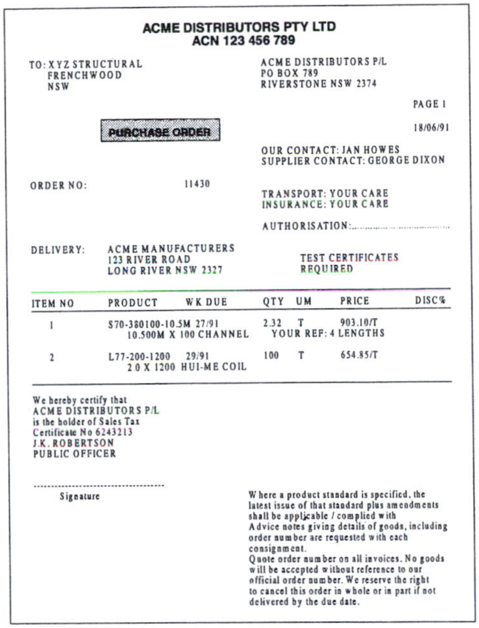

ACME DISTRIBUTORS PTY LTD
ACN 123 456 789

TO: XYZ STRUCTURAL
FRENCHWOOD
NSW

ACME DISTRIBUTORS P/L
PO BOX 789
RIVERSTONE NSW 2374

PAGE 1

PURCHASE ORDER

18/06/91

OUR CONTACT: JAN HOWES
SUPPLIER CONTACT: GEORGE DIXON

ORDER NO: 11430

TRANSPORT: YOUR CARE
INSURANCE: YOUR CARE

AUTHORISATION:..............................

DELIVERY: ACME MANUFACTURERS
123 RIVER ROAD
LONG RIVER NSW 2327

TEST CERTIFICATES
REQUIRED

ITEM NO	PRODUCT	WK DUE	QTY	UM	PRICE	DISC%
1	S70-380100-10.5M 10.500M X 100 CHANNEL	27/91	2.32	T	903.10/T YOUR REF: 4 LENGTHS	
2	L77-200-1200 2.0 X 1200 HUI-ME COIL	29/91	100	T	654.85/T	

We hereby certify that
ACME DISTRIBUTORS P/L
is the holder of Sales Tax
Certificate No 6243213
J.K. ROBERTSON
PUBLIC OFFICER

....
Signature

Where a product standard is specified, the latest issue of that standard plus amendments shall be applicable / complied with
Advice notes giving details of goods, including order number are requested with each consignment.
Quote order number on all invoices. No goods will be accepted without reference to our official order number. We reserve the right to cancel this order in whole or in part if not delivered by the due date.

Printed Purchase Order


```
UNH+002386+ORDERS:1:911:UN'
BGM+220+11430+9
DTM+97:910618'
RFF+XA:123 456 789'
NAD+BY+M8926::91++ACME DISTRIBUTORS+PO BOX
789+RIVERSTONE+NSW+2734'
DOC+4++EI'
CTA+OC+:JAN HOWES;
NAD+VN+XYZ::92++XYZ STRUCTURAL++FRENCHWOOD+NSW'
CTA+OC+:GEORGE DIXON'
NAD+ST+++ACME MANUFACTURERS+123 RIVER ROAD+LONG
RIVER+NSW+2327'
TAX+7+++++6243213'
UNS+D'
LIN+1++S70-380-100-10.5M:BP'
IMD+F++::10.500M 380 X 100 CHANNEL'
QTY+21:2:32:TNE'
DTM+2:9127:615'
MOA+203:2095.192'
PRI+NTP:903.10::::TNE'
LIN+2++1.77-2001200:BP'
IMD+F++;;2.0 X 1200 HUI-ME COIL'
DTY+21:100:TNE'
DTM+2:9129:615'
MOA+203:65485'
PRI+NTP:654.85::::TNE'
UNS+S'
MOA+128:67580.192'
CNT+2:2'
UNT+27+002836'
```


The Equivalent EDIFACT Purchase Order

Figure 6.13 A paper-based purchase order and its EDIFACT EDI equivalent [26]

In the construction industry, EDI is being looked at for additional functions such as:

- project management;
- drawing information;
- tender preparation;
- specifications;
- bill of quantities; and
- contractual documentation.

Electronic data interchange is also being developed as a carrier for CALS based documents, including STEP product data exchange files.[27] With the widespread adoption of EDI through its association with electronic commerce, EDI is predicted to have a significant impact on the business community of many countries.

Facsimile

The inclusion of facsimile as a digital document type could be regarded as somewhat dubious, since it is essentially a graphics file format transmitted via a telephone service. However, since its use is so extensive in business practice, it is worthy of discussion in order to outline its place among other types of documents.

When email started during the 1960s, very few people were computer literate, email tools were quite primitive, and network connectivity between computer users was very scarce. Consequently, email never really became established as an easy to use, and effective means of communication. By the 1980s the facsimile began to quickly established itself as a simple, non-computer-based and verifiable method of communication. It was not long after it was initially introduced that the fax quickly overcame the use of email and other forms of electronic communication.[17]

Negroponte, however, describes the development of the fax as 'a serious blemish on the information landscape, a step backward, whose ramifications will be felt for a long time.'[17] He also states that despite the fact that the fax seems to have revolutionised the way that business is conducted, its use in a digital environment 'is about as sensible as sending each other tea leaves'.

To understand the problems associated with the use of the facsimile, it is important to realise why it was commercially developed. Up until the mass production of the facsimile, most business in Japan was conducted person to person or written by hand. The only alternative if printed documents were to be used, was to use complex typesetting machines capable of producing the 60,000 characters in the Kanji alphabet. With such hindrances to the exchange of documents, the fax was quickly adopted in Japan as an alternate method of communication.[28]

In a computer-based office environment, the use of faxes promotes a very unintelligent medium. While it enables the easy transfer of document *images*, it does nothing to improve the usability of the information being transferred. To illustrate this point, consider the approach that is normally taken to create a fax.

Most documents which are faxed, have been originally created on a computer in a digital format and then printed out (thus losing its digital structure). When a document is faxed, it is scanned as a bitmap image and then transmitted electronically. At the recipient's end, the document is printed out and returned back to a paper document again (usually at a far less resolution than the original). This leaves the recipient with a document that is less intelligent than the original, and absent of any form of processable data that could be stored, retrieved or manipulated.

Faxes can also be sent directly from a computer with a modem, to a fax machine or another modem with the same fax capability. This process, however, is far from economical. As a graphics file, a fax is substantially larger in size than an equivalent text file. On average, an email message contains less than one-tenth of the bits necessary to convey the same message when using a fax machine that transmits at a speed of 9600 baud.[17] This translates to a significant degree of cost savings, especially when higher transmission speeds such as 33,600 baud can be achieved using a computer. By comparison, an email message can cost only 2 per cent of the total cost of a fax equivalent when sent internationally.

Although a number of OCR and OPR technologies have been developed for the conversion of faxed documents, they represent the use of a retrograde technology to solve a problem which would otherwise be a purely straightforward digital transfer of information. One of the few remaining valid uses of the facsimile, in the absence of other alternatives, is for the communication of design sketches which are created by hand. In the digital work environment this requirement is likely to be reduced.

Electronic Forms

A further type of digital document that is closely associated with messaging systems, are electronic forms. These type of documents have a number of alternate methods of implementation, many of which transcend some of the boundaries that have already been established in this book.

In their most simple form, an electronic form is the digital equivalent of pre-printed paper-based form. Forms can be typically used for: applications, pro formas, questionnaires, tax declarations, reports, and so on. Electronic forms can be implemented using two basic approaches:

- using a specialised forms-based application; or
- using a forms-based interface, within an application.

Specialised Forms-Based Applications

Forms-based software usually comes in two parts – a designer application which is used to design the form layout, and a filler application which is used to fill the form out. To create a form using this method, an author must use both parts. A recipient of the form only needs to use the filler application.

Forms designer software allows an author lay out a page similar to a desktop publishing package, and then place items such as:

- empty fields
- pop-down lists
- lookup tables
- command buttons
- check-boxes
- radio buttons
- spreadsheet tables
- graphics
- text.

Once a design is complete, it can look identical to a printed version, although it has far greater functionality. For example, the information in individual fields can be directly linked to the corresponding fields of an external database, or other external applications. The form itself, or the information content, can then be emailed to other users using a number of different techniques.

When an electronic form is sent to a user, it can be automatically routed as part of a workflow or document management system. This means that once a form has been initiated it can then be automatically transmitted, via a network, to a known number of recipients for actioning. If a form interacts with a database and that database is not accessible to the recipient, it is also possible in some systems to embed the appropriate portion of the database into the form. The database information can then be downloaded to the central database at a later time.

In general, forms created from specialised forms software applications cannot be interchanged between different systems. However, a number of them support common email messaging protocols, such as MAPI, VIM and SMTP, to allow data be easily transported across networks. It is also possible to only use the form as an interface, and to transmit the information contained within the fields as a separate delimited ASCII file.

Forms-Based Interfaces

In addition to using specialist electronic forms applications, a number of different software applications also support the use of forms. Two common examples include databases and hypermedia documents.

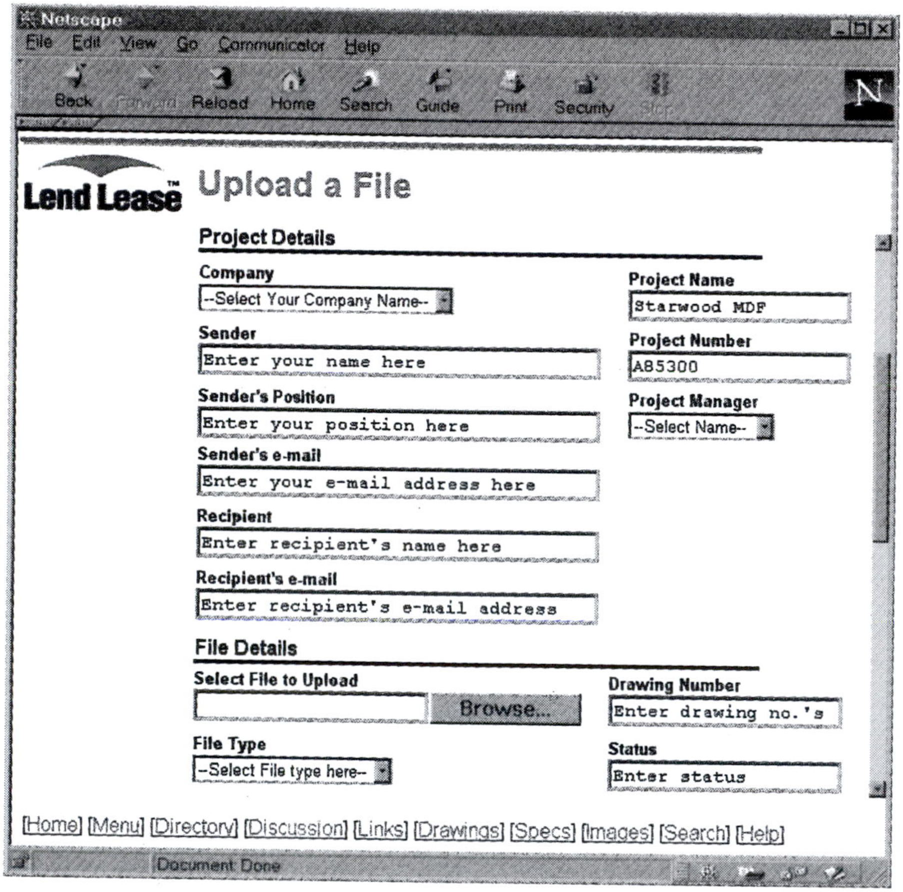

Figure 6.14 A Web form used to upload a file and notify other users

Databases commonly use forms-based interfaces as a method of entering data. Many form elements, such as data entry fields, buttons, check-boxes, and so on, are available to create a user interfaces similar to normal applications. The principle difference is that the form is tightly integrated with the database. The main disadvantage of this approach, is that the form does not become a separate document in its own right, and must be associated with the main database at all times.

Documents created for the World Wide Web, use a hypermedia document structure called HTML (hypertext markup language). The HTML language can also be used to create forms using pop-up lists, text fields, radio buttons and check-boxes. These forms are commonly used to search databases, send mail or interact with information systems. Because HTML is platform independent, it means that the client (using the form) and the server (maintaining the database) can be on completely different platforms. The process of interaction then becomes relatively transparent to the end-user. A Web-based form for a document transmittal is illustrated in Figure 6.14.

DYNAMIC COMPOUND DOCUMENTS

Most documents contain a mix of different data types and are therefore called compound documents. Originally, software applications such as word-processors and graphics packages, used to operate independently of each other. At best they were able to import selected file types into the application for processing. However, with the advent of GUI-based operating systems such as Microsoft Windows and the MacOS, a number of different inter-application communication (IAC) methods have been developed. Inter-application communication enables programs to easily copy, merge or link information from the content of one document to another.

In their most simple form, compound documents can be any mix of text, numerical data, tabular listings, charts, illustrations or bitmapped images. When objects are pasted or merged into a single document, the process is analogous to a paper-based model, whereby cuttings from a number of different sources can be literally laid out and pasted on to a page. This particular approach however, is being gradually outmoded by the development of object-oriented programming and component-based software applications (as discussed in Chapter 4). The aim of document creation applications that have been written in this way, is to enable data objects to be easily exchanged and reused.

Normally, when data from a source is pasted into a document, the link between the source and the document is broken. This means that if the source data changes, the document is not automatically updated. This often leads to the need for multiple revisions of a document which in turn, can lead to errors in the production and management of documentation.[29] By linking a document to its source data however, it can be assured of always containing the latest information.

The approach used in the creation of dynamic documents, enables workgroups to retool and rethink ways of generating and updating documents. For example, it is possible for the data attributes within a document to be encoded with information that prescribes conditional rules about how data content can be shared or updated between other documents. In this manner, a master building specification for example, could be dynamically linked to CAD details or manufacturer's specifications, and be automatically updated at defined intervals.

Table 6.4 Examples of some IAC and dynamic compound document standards

Standard	Purpose	Developer
Cut and Paste	Copy or move data within or between documents (non-dynamic process).	Various
Print merge	Merge data (usually from a database) into empty fields in a document template (non-dynamic process).	Various
Publish and Subscribe	Proprietary method of dynamically sharing data between documents.	Apple
OLE/COM (ActiveX)	Object Linking and Embedding is a standard for the interactive exchange of data objects using the Common Object Model (COM). This enables applications to share data between different compound document structures. ActiveX focuses upon the use of OLE in Web-based environments.	Microsoft
CORBA	Common Object Request Broker Architecture. A specification for distributed computing with portable objects. This technology is being used for the development of Web-based applications and documents.	Object Management Group
Java Beans	Java Beans is an API (application program interface) that enables developers to write software components for the Java platform (as used in Web-based applications).	IBM
PDO	Portable Distribution Object. A specification for compound documents similar to OLE and CORBA.	NeXT

There are a range of dynamic compound document structures that exist at different levels of sophistication. Many of the technologies exist as object-oriented programming tools that are used to write applications, and are therefore not apparent to the end-user of an application or document. The more advanced of these methods are used for Web application development, and are designed to enable data to be shared between documents that exist in a distributed network environment such as the Internet. A number of IAC methods, dynamic document structures and associated programming standards are listed in Table 6.4. (Further details on Internet based applications that make use of some of these technologies are found in Chapter 4).

PROCESSABLE COMPOUND DOCUMENTS

Traditionally ASCII has always been looked upon as the universal method of neutrally exchanging data content. The problem with ASCII, however, is that it expresses meaning in only one direction, that of content. It is limited in its ability to also convey semantic encoding (i.e. the set of rules used to encode a document).

Compound documents usually have information which has been carefully formatted, so it is often necessary to express meaning in three (or more) dimensions using: content, structure, and presentation style.[3] The aim of a neutral document-encoding model is to encode the mixed-data content, layout and presentation information of a document, so that it can be used across multiple types of applications and further edited, processed, stored, printed or retransmitted at a later date.

The International Standards Organisation has so far published two standards for the open interchange of revisable documents, fitting these previous aims. The first standard in this category is SGML, the Standard Generalised Markup Language (ISO 8879) published in 1986. The second is ODA, the Open Document Architecture (ISO 8613) published in 1987. A further, vendor-based model called CDA was formalised in 1989 and is based upon the ODA standard.[30] Other private formats used by proprietary software applications, have also been developed.

Table 6.5 Examples of some common compound document processing models

Standard	Purpose	Maintainer/Developer
SGML (ISO 8879:1986)	General document mark-up	International Standards Organisation (ISO)
ODA (ISO 8613:1989)	Compound document encoding	International Standards Organisation (ISO)
CDA	Compound document encoding	Digital Equipment Corporation

Each of the standards listed in Table 6.5 takes a slightly different approach. Standard Generalised Markup Language is known as a tagging language and uses structural mark-up of ASCII-based documents. ODA and CDA are both compound formats designed to provide a set of standards for the exchange of structurally and procedurally formatted documents across multiple computer platforms and applications. The most widely implemented of these standards is SGML, which is closely associated with the HTML standard used to create Web documents.

While SGML, ODA and CDA all share common principles, it is very difficult to directly compare them using a feature-based comparison method.[31] The broadest distinction that can be made is that SGML is a language used to mark up text based documents, and that ODA and CDA are binary structures. Each has their own particular purpose and method of implementation.

SGML

SGML is formally referred to as the *Information Processing – Text and Office Systems – Standard Generalised Markup Language.* The Standard Generalised Markup Language offers a neutral method of organising a document using structural mark-up. This means that a document can be organised according to organisational elements such as headings, paragraphs, tables, lists and so on. It does *not* use any form of procedural mark-up to describe document formatting such as layouts, fonts, leading, or margins. In other words, the *content* is treated completely separate to the *formatting* of the document. This is analogous to the use of musical scores in which notes rather than sounds are described. Because only the content is described in a score, the information can be read by any musician and played on almost any type of instrument.

The biggest advantage of using structural mark-up like SGML, is that the highly valuable content of a document can be kept separate from processor-dependent formatting technologies. Since there is a propensity for most computing technologies to change over time, the use of SGML can be dramatically increase the long-term usefulness of the information contained within documents .

There are also a number of other advantages that the use of SGML offers including:

- Maximising the benefits of an investment in data entry and authoring.
- Facilitating data exchange across enterprises involving many different customers and business partners.
- Maintaining common data from central sources.
- Accessing data in many different and diverse ways.
- Standardising the way information is conveyed.
- Controlling data quality.
- Reusing documents using multiple forms of presentation.
- Increasing the longevity and usefulness of a document against proprietary and obsolescent technologies.

The Standard Generalised Markup Language is also described as a meta-language. That means that it is not just one language, but a language that describes other languages within its framework.[32] This concept is explained further in the description of an SGML document.

An SGML document is composed of essentially three parts:

- **An SGML declaration**. This declares that the document is an SGML document and specifies the character set to be used.
- **A Document Type Definition (DTD)**. This declares the definition of the tags that are to be used in the mark-up of the document.
- **The document instance**. This is the actual document that has been marked up in accordance to the DTD.

The key to the structure of an SGML document is contained in the elements that are defined in the DTD. A DTD usually defines a tree-like structure in which the elements of a document are hierarchically specified. For example, a set of elements for a book might include a chapter, chapter title, chapter number, appendix and an index. In the DTD, the relationship between these elements are declared. In some SGML editors the organisation of the elements in the DTD can be graphically illustrated to assist the author in the mark-up of an SGML document, as shown in Figure 6.14. In this figure, the words in brackets indicate how many times the elements can be used, or whether they have to be used at all.

Elements in the SGML instance of a document are indicated with the use of angled brackets to form a tag e.g. `<para>`. In general, the basic syntax is that for each starting tag, there must be a corresponding end tag to indicate that a section of document is identified. For example, Figure 6.15 shows the SGML mark-up of a simple catalogue in which a number of different tags are used to identify specific parts of the document.

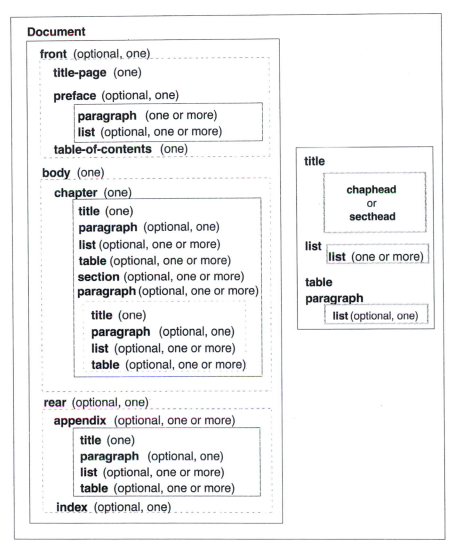

Figure 6.15 A representation of the structure of an SGML DTD

The structural arrangement of the DTD has a large number of benefits for both the author and end-user of a resulting SGML document. For the author, it means that a document can be clearly and consistently marked up using an agreed set of rules. Unlike the use of styles in a word-processor, most elements in an SGML document must be marked up in a correct order. (SGML mark-up software often ensures that only certain mark-up tags can be used, according to the context in which the text is placed.) This improves not only the readability and consistency of a document, but also the quality of its structure.

```
<catalogue>
  <intro>
    <title> Parts Catalogue </title>
    <para>
    This catalogue describes parts
    available for Type A windows.
    A listing of each part,its
    description,and price follows.
    </para>
  </intro>
  <list>
    <item>
        <partno> 00A1 </partno>
        <description>
        Brass window opener.
        </description>
        <price>$25.00 </price>
    </item>
  </list>
</catalogue>
```

Figure 6.16 A typical SGML document instance

To assist authors in ensuring the quality and conformance of their document to the DTD, it can be passed through a piece of software called a parser. A parser is designed to validate the level of conformance of a document to the rules set out in a DTD. If any errors in the document are detected, they will be reported back to the author. Otherwise the document can be considered to be validated. Figure 6.16 illustrates the process used in an SGML authoring system.

Once a document is successfully marked up, it can be presented and used in a number of different ways. For example, documents can be organised according to different levels of complexity – offering simple, standard and advanced levels of access to information. Some items can also be tagged with different security levels, so that only authorised personnel can access appropriate parts of a document when it is displayed on-line. Standard Generalised Markup Language documents, also lend themselves particularly well for inclusion into databases. For example, once an SGML document is in a database, users could search for all instances of a tag such as <warning> that appear in a set of procedures manuals. These documents are also extremely well suited for input into electronic publishing systems.

Creating a DTD to describe a document, can be a very complex procedure. This is because every scenario for the use of a document has to be considered when it is written. It is quite common, therefore, that the approach taken in writing a DTD for a particular purpose, will vary from author to author. Accordingly, a good DTD will often have to be the result of a consensus between a number of different people.

Despite many benefits, SGML is also acknowledged to have some weaknesses. An obvious weakness is that SGML actually defines DTDs and not the documents themselves. This means that if different users do not have the same DTD, then the document is not very usable. Another problem is that because SGML is text based, it cannot store non-text objects. It addresses this problem by providing external pointers to objects (such as a graphic or sound file) to indicate where they are positioned in a document.

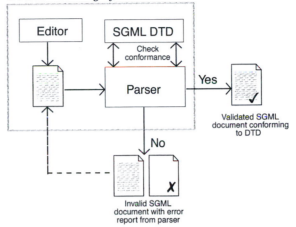

Figure 6.17 An SGML authoring and parsing process

An associated standard called HyTime has been developed to address a number of these issues. HyTime (derived from Hypermedia/Time) is an SGML-based, neutral mark-up language for representing the logical structure of hypertext, multimedia, hypermedia, and time and space-based documents.

Despite many of the advantages of separating document structure from document format, there are some occasions when procedural formatting information of SGML documents also has to be specified. This is particularly important if the intent is to distribute the information in a form suitable for rendering to a screen or printing device. One of the principle standards developed for this purpose is the Document Style Semantics Specification Language (DSSSL).

Application of SGML

The phenomenal success of the World Wide Web has been closely associated with the use of SGML. That is because the mark-up language used to create Web documents (called HTML - Hypertext Markup Language) is actually an example of an SGML DTD. As described in more detail in the following section, HTML defines a generic set of mark-up tags to structure documents. Standard Generalised Markup Language however, is fully extensible and can therefore be customised for very large range of different uses, other than just for the Internet. It can also be used to describe highly complex documents, that would be otherwise impossible to do in HTML alone. Some diverse examples for the applications of SGML include:[33]

- The CAD product data exchange standard STEP is advocating the use of SGML-based documents as a method of supplying product documentation.
- Defence departments in many countries around the world, have endorsed the complete adoption of SGML as a method of creating, exchanging and delivering technical support documents as part of its CALS standards.
- The news industry, in the form of the IPTC (International Press Telecommunications Council) and the NAA (Newspaper Association of America), is developing an SGML-based Universal Text Format, for on-line, broadcast, print and archival news.
- In Europe, ICADD (the International Committee for Accessible Document Design) has developed a project called TIDE (Technology Initiative for the Disabled and Elderly) for delivering electronic newspapers to blind people, based on SGML structured documents.
- In the airline industry, Boeing, Airbus, Pratt and Whitney, General Electric, Rolls Royce, Deutsche Lufthansa, and United Airlines are developing systems for the delivery of technical maintenance manuals using SGML.
- In academic research, the Text Encoding Initiative (TEI) has been developed to produce a formal DTD for the textual features most important to the use of electronic texts in academia.

ODA and CDA

Two alternate standards to SGML that have been developed, are the ISO Open Document Architecture (ODA), and the Compound Document Architecture (CDA) by Digital Equipment Corporation. Both are aimed at neutral document interchange, however, they are designed to encode both content *and* formatting within their structure.

Open Document Architecture and CDA both use a document encoding scheme known as aggregates. Aggregates are lists of programming entities that can represent text, graphics, audio, video and document format.[34]

Compound Document Architecture uses a platform independent set of encoding rules called the Digital Document Interchange Format (DDIF).[35] These rules are used to encode all of a document's structural parts and stylistic presentation information. Implementation of the standard is designed to be transparent to the user, and CDA-compliant applications can revise each other's documents, even if the documents are written in different languages, run under different operating systems, or are located in different parts of a network.

Open Document Architecture, upon which CDA is based, also uses its own encoding scheme called the Open Document Interchange Format (ODIF). Similar to DDIF, the ODIF encoding scheme is able to preserve structural and procedural mark-up. It offers features such as authentication, digital signatures, alternate representations for display and printing, and hyperlinks.[36]

Both ODA and CDA were developed to describe standard office documents, however, the development of these standards are considered to have failed in their aims. One of the principle reasons was that their designs were not robust enough to handle vendor-independent document interchange.[37] There were also too many document types that do not fit into the confines of the generic models that they specified, and consequently, the standards were not widely adopted.

ELECTRONIC REFERENCE AND HYPERMEDIA DOCUMENTS

Electronic reference documents (ERDs) serve the same purpose as hard-copy reference documents. Electronic reference documents are also known by a number of other names such as soft-copy, enhanced documents, hypertext and hypermedia. By structuring digital documents using electronic reference methods, information can be rapidly located within or between large collections of information in a manner which is far superior to that of paper. The concept of linking documents together is illustrated in Figure 6.18.

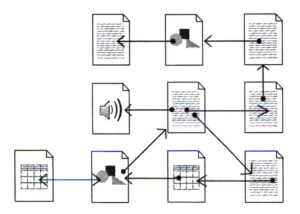

Figure 6.18 A series of hyperlinked documents

The idea for a system used to navigate through large volumes of information was first suggested in 1945, by Dr Vannevar Bush, a science adviser to President Roosevelt during World War II.[38] Bush proposed the use of an electromechanical device called the Memex, which was designed to search through large amounts of text and visual information stored on microfilm. One of the problems with this system, is that it was based around a page-sequential design of a book where information could only be presented in a two-dimensional linear manner.

In a paper-based document such as a book, sentences, paragraphs, pages and chapters follow one another in an order not only determined by the author, but also by the physical and sequential construct of the book itself.[17] In a hypermedia document, however, there is usually a system of links that allows the reader to explore a number of different and non-linear paths through a body of information.

The terms 'hypertext' and 'hypermedia' were first coined by Theodore 'Ted' Nelson in 1965. Nelson described hypertext (non-linear text) as being 'a body of written or pictorial material interconnected in a complex way that it could not be conveniently represented on paper'.[40] Nelson's vision was further developed in a project known as *Xanadu*, which aimed to create a global, unified literary environment which could act as a repository for everything that anybody has ever written. Nelson described Xanadu as being a completely interactive 'docuverse'.[41]

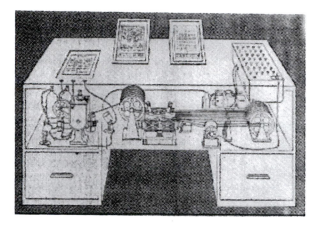

Figure 6.19 Artist's impression of The Memex (1945)[39]

In a hypermedia system, a combination of hypertext and multimedia technologies can be used to create, annotate, link and share information using a variety of media such as text, graphics, audio, video, animation and programs. As a result of these capabilities, hypermedia is emerging as a new class of complex information management system.

Common to all hypermedia systems are the concepts of linking, browsing and navigating.

- **Navigation** refers to the ability to travel between documents using any number of alternate paths to find information on a topic of interest.
- **Browsing** refers to the ability to search and display information on a semi-random basis.
- **Linking** enables two distinct pieces of information to be connected together.

When these techniques are combined, information can be navigated in a non-linear manner, and presented as one-dimensional text, two-dimensional images and drawings, three-dimensional geometric models and, even, four-dimensional kinematic models.[7]

The connections between an information source and a pointer to that location are referred to as nodes and buttons, respectively.[42] The connection itself, is referred to as a hyperlink. For example, in a hypertext system, a button link may be connected to a footnote reference. By clicking on to the hyperlinked footnote number, it would navigate the user to another piece of associated text. That text might also contain links to other related information, and so on. The links are usually created by the author of the document. These principles are illustrated in Figure 6.20.

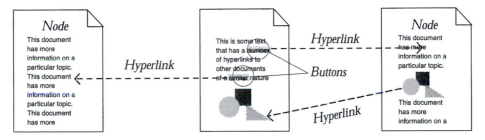

Figure 6.20 The hyperlinking of documents

Hypermedia is an extension of hypertext but can combine the use of text, graphics, sound, animation and video. In a hypermedia system, a user might click on to a part of a drawing and be navigated to an accompanying explanatory text, another more detailed drawing or, even, an audio note from an author.

An important aspect of hypermedia documents is that they abandon the page based model. Despite their familiarity to many users, physical pages can sometimes impede access to information. For example, illustrations in text can sometimes be far removed from their reference, and pages can inconveniently break the flow of information that is being presented. Pages are also usually fixed in size and cannot be re-scaled or re-oriented. By contrast, most hypermedia documents treat the document as a stream of information, through which the user can navigate by scrolling, linking or zooming.

Finding information

In addition to incorporating a number of enhanced navigation tools, hypermedia and ERDs can often incorporate a number of different methods for finding information. When using paper-based documents, the user must resort to using an index or table of contents that may or may not list the information being searched. Alternatively, the reader will have to skim read the contents of a document itself. Hypermedia documents, however, can be searched in number of different ways such as those listed in Table 6.6.

Since architects and engineers have frequently to navigate through large volumes of reference material, the use of hypermedia and other forms of electronic reference documents are highly suited to this purpose. Documents such as building codes, product catalogues, and specifications can all be enhanced with the use of hypermedia and distributed electronically using networks or fixed media technology such as CD-ROMs.

Table 6.6 Methods of searching reference documents

Feature	What it enables
Full-text searching	Using full-text search methods, a user can scan the entire length of a document for every instance of a word or phrase.
Graphical browsing	Some hypertext applications and graphical browsing tools can display the logical connections between units of information by using connecting lines or other visual cues to turn relationships of meaning into easy to understand graphics.
Hypertext links	Hypertext links that are embedded into text, can give the reader live cross-references from a word or phrase to other closely related information within the same or different documents.
Keyword searching	When an author creates a document, it can be stored with a number of keywords to describe its content. These keywords can then be searched to help the reader to locate ideas and data that might be missed by a full-text search.
Live table of contents	A live table of contents can help a user move quickly from general topics to details and back again. It is often coupled with a document outliner expansion capability. A typical example is the Microsoft Windows Help system.

HTML and the World Wide Web

The most pervasive hypermedia system in use today, is the World Wide Web (also known as WWW, W3 or simply 'The Web'). As a computing technology, the Web has been phenomenally successful in all areas of commercial, scientific, academic and private use.

The Web is officially described as a 'wide-area hypermedia information retrieval initiative aiming to give universal access to a large universe of documents'.[43] The Web consists of specialised browser software, and a set of protocols and conventions that enables people to roam, browse and contribute to vast amounts of information that are on the Internet.

The development of the Web began in 1989, at the European Laboratory for Particle Physics in Switzerland called CERN. The Web was conceived as a method of enabling researchers to share documents and images over large geographical distances. Although this aim was quite simple, the existence of a diverse range of communication protocols and document standards hindered an immediate solution.

By the end of 1990, the researchers at CERN had developed a simple text-mode browser, and a graphical browser for the NeXT computer. During 1991, a Web browser was released for general use at CERN and was combined with additional network tools such as WAIS, FTP, Telnet and Gopher under the one user interface.

By 1992, the Web was being heavily promoted with the distribution of a free browser called NCSA Mosaic. Between February and December 1993, the use of this browser grew at an astonishing rate of 11 per cent per week.[17] By the middle of 1994, the Web had become one of the most popular ways to access Internet resources. Since then the Internet has grown exponentially is size, a rise that can almost be entirely attributed to the popularity of the Web.[44,45]

The Web makes use of a number of specific communication, document and software standards. Communication is handled by using the networking protocol TCP/IP (Transfer Connection Protocol / Internet Protocol). Web documents are usually hypertext or hypermedia based, and are structured using a language called the Hypertext Markup Language (HTML).

Figure 6.21 The Netscape browser displaying information from a Web site

The Hypertext Markup Language is in fact, an SGML Document Type Definition (DTD). The HTML specification defines a set of predetermined elements (descriptors), which can be used to mark-up a document for distribution over the Web. A Web browser has the HTML DTD built into it, and is able to interpret and display HTML and other ASCII-based documents. Some common examples of Web browsers, are *Netscape Navigator* by Netscape Communications, and Microsoft's *Internet Explorer*. The Netscape browser and a typical HTML document is illustrated in Figure 6.21.

The HTML specification defines a series of elements that enables an author to define the way a document is structured.[46] Using these elements, the author can use some of the following functions to create a document:

- Specify structure with section headings, paragraphs and line breaks.
- Specify basic text formatting with size and emphasis.

- Integrate in-line pictures (usually GIF or JPEG files).
- Integrate audio, animation and video files.
- Integrate applets and applications.
- Create:
    - hyperlinks
    - interactive forms
    - tables
    - equations
    - lists
    - horizontal rules

A sample HTML document using some of these features is illustrated in Figure 6.22.

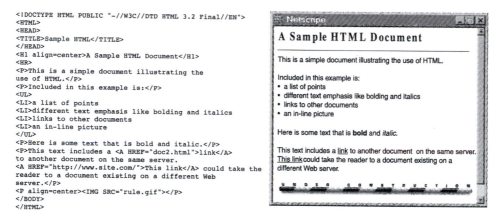

Figure 6.22 HTML source code and its appearance in a WWW browser

In the previous illustration, a number of links have been created. These links are a very powerful feature of HTML documents because they enables a user to transparently link to other documents or application protocols such as FTP, Gopher, Telnet and News by simply picking a highlighted piece of text or outlined graphic. This feature is so powerful and effective, that when a user is browsing the Web, they are often oblivious to the fact that the information they have accessed has been delivered over a range of different network media, traversed a number of different operating systems and travelled thousands of kilometres, in only a few seconds.

As a resource for the design and construction industry, the World Wide Web represents an enormous number of benefits including:

- Access to a global repository of information on practically any topic.
- Local, national and international links to other architectural and engineering practices, industry consultants, building contractors, CAD systems information, building product information, software, job listings, new projects, conference information, conference proceedings, competitions, academic institutions, professional institutions, news groups, discussion groups, mailing lists and electronic magazines.

- An inexpensive method of publishing to the industry, other professional bodies and the public, at both a local and international scale.
- A method of promoting professional services to potential clients.
- A method of interacting with other design professionals to exchange information and project files.

The number of uses of the Web have become so extensive, that most of the computing industry is now focused on providing solutions to extend these capabilities. For example, many software applications are now being developed to provide Internet and Web-based functionality including CAD systems, word-processors, spreadsheets, databases and document management systems.

Browser Plug-ins

The Hypertext Markup Language was originally developed as a very simple mark-up language that offered a generic set of capabilities. By default, if a binary data file (such as an audio or video file) is referenced from a Web page, it requires an additional application to open the file. Because of the binary nature of these files, they are not able to be displayed in the container provided by the browser. In order to handle non-HTML data within a Web browser window, a 'plug-in' or 'control' is required.

A plug-in, or control, is designed to act as an add-on module that extends the basic functionality of a web browser, to handle additional interactive and multimedia capabilities. Plug-ins are available for browsers that enable video and audio streaming, display of native compound documents (such as word-processing files and spreadsheets), display of multimedia applications and the display of CAD files and other graphics file formats.

When a web browser comes across a page that references a non-HTML object, it examines the MIME type of that object to see if an appropriate plug-in has been installed. If installed, the data object is displayed in the browser window as though it was a part of the normal HTML document. The advantage of this approach is that it allows more interactive and content-rich Web pages to be created. The disadvantage of this approach is that plug-ins are often platform specific and, therefore, not always available. There is also an additional cost, download time and installation time associated with acquiring these plug-ins. This procedure is not always practical for the casual visitor to a Web site.

XML

In the use of more complex Web documents, there are a number of limitations to HTML that do not provide the extensibility, structure, and data checking required for large-scale commercial publishing and distributed document processing.[47] To address this need, the World Wide Web Consortium (W3C), has developed the Extensible Markup Language (XML) for document types that require additional functionality beyond HTML. In essence, XML is designed to enable SGML documents to be used on the World Wide Web.

As previously described, the HTML language is an SGML DTD (document type definition) that describes a generic set of tags that can be used to structurally mark up a document. One of the benefits of using SGML over HTML, is that DTDs can be written to suit specific document types using a custom set of tags that suit the way a document needs to be organised, displayed or processed.

Some of the features of XML include:

- richer control over text formatting including font, size, weight, colour, indents, spacing, auto-numbering and invisibility of text;
- the ability to search for content based on structural elements, such as searching for text within a heading, title or table;
- improved linking capabilities including two-way linking and one-to-many linking (where a single hyperlink can open two referred documents); and
- graphic-to-graphic hotspot linking (where an area on a graphic can be hyperlinked to an area on another graphic).

Style Sheets

As a mark-up language, HTML was only originally designed to describe the structural mark-up of a document. This meant that no procedural mark-up could be directly used to specify characteristics such as font, point size, kerning, leading, margins etc. Unless techniques such as the heavy use of graphics and complex table formatting are used, some HTML documents are subject to variations in interpretation, when they are rendered to a different browsers.

To address this issue, a style sheet can be used as a set of guidelines to indicate how the various elements of a document should be presented in a browser window. The use of styles is analogous to those used in a word-processor, where a specific font, point size, colour and emphasis can be specified for a particular section of a document, such as the body text, headings, lists or tables.

There are essentially two style sheet proposals in use, namely Cascading Style Sheets (CSS) from the World Wide Web Consortium (W3C), and the Document Style Semantics and Specifications Language (DSSSL) by ISO. CSS is the style sheet language used for HTML documents and DSSSL is for SGML and XML documents.

A style sheet can be used at three basic levels: local, global and linked. At a local level a style sheet can be used to specify the appearance of a particular section of a document such as a heading or a paragraph. At a global level, a style sheet can be used to describe the formatting of all elements in a document. In its most powerful form, a style sheet can be linked to an entire set of documents. For example, a single style sheet could be used to specify the appearance of an entire set of office procedures, guidelines and standards. All of these documents could then be instantly updated in appearance, by simply modifying the style sheet.

The use of style sheets ensures that the appearance of a document to a reader, is the same as that intended by the author. This technique also allows the author to control a range of typographic attributes, while maintaining platform independence.

Case Study: BCAider

A good example of an ERD product designed for the construction industry, is *BCAider*. BCAider is a hypermedia tool developed by the CSIRO, to deliver the Building Code of Australia (BCA) using an expert-system feature. The BCA is used to regulate standards of structural sufficiency, fire safety, health and amenity, and is used on approximately $30 billion worth of construction per year.[48]

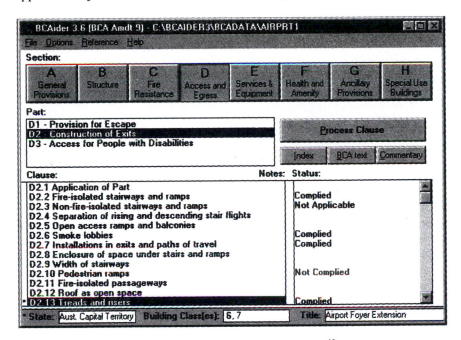

Figure 6.23 The BCAider software interface[49]

When using BCAider, as illustrated in Figure 6.23, a user works though the various clauses of the BCA to see whether a building complies with the regulations. The clauses of the BCA are processed by answering a series of 'Yes/No' or 'Yes/No/Don't Know' questions. Throughout the product, hypertext is used to link users to explanations of terms and regulations, using either text or diagrams. An additional assisting commentary, also helps the user to decide the compliance level of the building they are assessing.

BCAider is able to link into the text of over 400 related Australian Standards which are available in a digital format on CD-ROM. At the end of a session, a report can be generated which states whether the building complies or not, and is accompanied with a list of explanations. A copy of the dialogue (that was used in the checking process) can also be generated.

Using this system has a large number of benefits over the paper-based BCA. The major benefits of BCAider include:

- easier checking of building designs to ensure compliance with relevant clauses of the BCA;
- on-line help and commentary to assist users, and to provide background explanations and examples;
- presentation of the BCA to users in a hypermedia format that includes the use of menus, buttons, hot spots, hypertext, graphics and keyword searches;
- an ability for designers to explore a wider range of design options, by quickly testing out variations (such as changing dimensions, exit locations, or fire protection methods);
- automatic generation of compliance report files for use by authorities;
- automatic generation of job files which may be stored and later recovered for modification or perusal; and
- assistance in the education of building designers and checking officials.

Case Study: IETMS

Electronic Reference Documents are also being used for the delivery of documents on work sites. For example, the US Department of Defence has developed an Interactive Electronic Technical Manual (IETM) to help technicians maintain complex aircraft, weapons systems, ships and submarines. The IETM system is based upon the use of SGML documents. When using these systems, studies have shown that it takes technicians less time to diagnose and repair complex equipment than when using traditional paper documents.[34]

Using a paper-based procedures manual, normally involves the user having to search through a huge number of pages to find a particular reference. These references can also be located in a large number of different manuals and represented in a number of different formats such as books, manuals and large-format shop drawings. By using an ERD system, a user is able to search and collect the information using a single interface. Augmented-reality systems have also been developed to allow documents to be superimposed on a transparent visor worn by a person building or repairing equipment.

The manuals are written using the SGML Hypermedia/Time-Based Structuring Language (ISO/IEC 10744) to provide a method of neutrally representing hypermedia data.[34] This enables complex hypermedia documents to be easily interchanged between equipment manufacturers, suppliers and end-users.

The principles of IETM could also be applied for use in the construction industry, where complex documents are commonly used on building sites. In particular, it would be highly useful for the referral and cross-referencing of specifications to working drawings.

VIEWER DOCUMENTS

It has been estimated that somewhere between 50 to 80 per cent of most end-user's needs can be met by viewing a document on a screen.[50] This fact has led to the development of a number of digital document types, which are specifically aimed at providing a view-only, uneditable version of a document. A number of common document viewer formats are listed in Table 6.7.

Table 6.7 Examples of some common viewer document formats

Format	Purpose	OS	Developer
Acrobat Portable Document Format (PDF)	Document viewer format	MacOS, DOS, Windows, SunOS, Solaris	Adobe Systems
Common Ground Digital Paper	Document viewer format	Mac, Windows, Java	Hummingbird Communications
WorldView	Document viewer format	MacOS, Windows, Unix (various), VMS	Interleaf
Portable Digital Document (PDD)	Document viewer format for computers using QuickDraw GX	MacOS	Apple Computer
FrameViewer	Document viewer format	MacOS, windows, X/motif Unix (various)	Adobe Systems
Envoy	Document viewer format	MacOS, Windows	Corell
GhostView	PostScript file viewer	MacOS, OS/2, Windows, Unix, VMS	GNU public license

While there are a number of different viewer formats that have been designed to read the documents of a single application or platform, the most usable are those which have been specifically designed with cross-platform compatibility in mind.

The aim of a viewer document is to provide a fully formatted document structure, that is capable of being distributed from one computer to another regardless of the hardware platform, operating system or application software used to create the original. When a viewer document is received, the user is able to perform functions such as viewing, navigating, searching, annotating, printing or storing the document on their own system.

Most viewer document formats use a specific software creator and viewer. The document creator usually exists in the form of a printer driver or file format converter. If a printer driver method is used, a viewer document can be created via the standard print function from any software application. Instead of printing to paper, a file can be converted and saved to a viewer document format.

Once a document has been converted to a viewer format, it can then be distributed to users on a range of different platforms and viewed independently of the application that was originally used to create it. To each recipient, the viewer document will maintain the visual fidelity of the author's original document in both formatting and appearance. For example, a complex report including graphic, spreadsheet, text and CAD data could be created using a desktop publishing system on a Macintosh. By converting it to a viewer format, it could then be distributed to other users, irrespective of whether those recipients have the same authoring software or whether they use a Macintosh-,Windows- or Unix-based computer. All the recipient requires is an appropriate document viewer. These principles are illustrated in Figure 6.24.

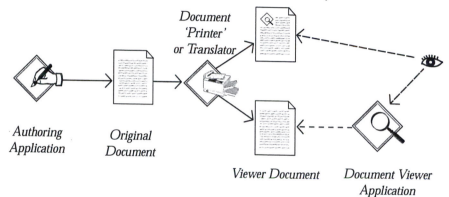

Figure 6.24 The creation and distribution of a viewer document

Document viewers can exist as separate applications, web browser plug-ins, or Java applications. Some software products also embed a simple viewer into the content of the document itself. While this approach helps recipients who do not have the fully featured viewer application, it reduces the cross-platform capability of the document.

The development of viewer document formats represents a new model for document creation and distribution. Of the formats listed in Table 6.6, one of the earliest and most widely adopted is Adobe System's *Acrobat PDF* (Portable Document Format). Because Acrobat (and products like it) represent a whole new type of document, it is well worth examining in detail. Since these document types are read-only and are used mainly for distribution purposes, it is the functionality and usability of this document type more than its specific structure which is of most interest.

Adobe Acrobat PDF

Adobe System's *Acrobat* was released in June 1993 with the aim to provide a document format primarily for the purpose of electronic document delivery.[51]

The PDF Format

Adobe Acrobat software writes and reads (views) a file format called the Portable Document Format or PDF, which is closely based upon PostScript. The files are encoded as 7-bit ASCII, which means that they are extremely portable between diverse hardware and operating system environments and can be easily included as attachments to email. Because PDF documents can contain various types of data, it uses a number of different compression algorithms such as LZW, RLE, CCITT Group 3 and 4, and JPEG to reduce the size of the file.

One of the great problems in the exchange of digital documents is the use of fonts. For example, if a font used in the creation of a document is unavailable on the recipient's computer, then the document can become illegible or, at worst, unreadable. Common solutions around this problem usually involve sending accompanying fonts with the document, restricting the font types used, or sending paper proofs.

The PDF format overcomes this problem with the use of multiple master fonts. A multiple master font is one which is capable of emulating the basic typographical characteristics of another font such as its height, width, spacing, kerning, bolding, italicising and so on. By using this technology, PDF documents are able to consistently maintain the look and feel of the original, even if the fonts originally used by the author to create the document are not available on the computer of the reader.

There are essentially five basic pieces of software that compose the Adobe Acrobat product suite: the PDF writer, Acrobat Distiller, Acrobat Exchange, Acrobat Capture and the Acrobat Reader.

The PDF Writer

The Acrobat PDF writer, is a print driver that is installed on the operating system of a computer, and is available for specific operating systems such as MacOS, DOS, Windows and various Unix platforms. The PDF writer is used to create a PDF file via the standard 'Print' function of an application. However, instead of printing to paper, the document is saved as a PDF file, leaving the original document intact on the author's system.

Acrobat Distiller

The Acrobat Distiller program creates PDF files from PostScript language files. This tool is not essential for the creation of PDF documents, but is intended for more complex compound documents that include a range of illustrations, images and other graphics. Acrobat Distiller takes PostScript documents as input and then converts them to PDF. Much higher compression ratios can be achieved using this software.

Acrobat Exchange

Acrobat Exchange, is a platform-specific application that has a number of tools for viewing, annotating, copying, printing, securing and navigating PDF documents. Some of the basic features of the software interface are illustrated in Figure 6.25.

Navigation of a PDF document can be performed by zooming in or out on pages, or by using a series of buttons similar to a tape recorder, to go to back and forward to the first page, previous page, next page and last page. In addition to linear navigation, hypertext links can be established between any part of a page, to any other part of the same document, different documents connected to the same system, or to a Web site address on the Internet.

An alternate method of navigation, is to use a series of thumbnail views of each page. These thumbnails can be used for previewing the appearance of pages, selecting areas to enlarge, and for rearranging the sequence of pages if necessary. In Figure 6.25, notice how pages can be mixed between portrait and landscape modes. When documents are distributed using a document viewer, the author is not necessarily restricted to one continuous set of formatting rules.

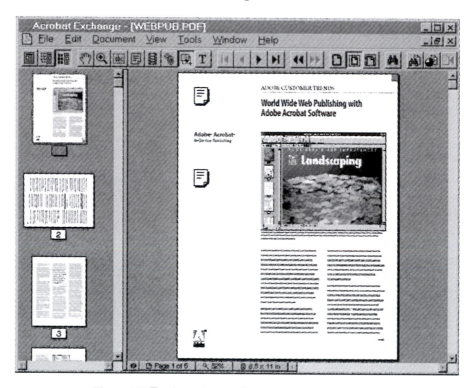

Figure 6.25 The Adobe Acrobat Exchange application interface

Another navigation feature is the use of bookmarks. Bookmarks enable a small table of contents to be established for a document. These bookmarks also provide a means of linking pages together at different magnifications. For example, this mechanism can be used to link a reader from a table of contents, to a particular page *and* a specific magnified location on that page.

Annotations to a PDF document can be made using a digital 'sticky note'. These notes can contain any amount of text information and can be searched as part of the main document. The notes can be iconised, coloured, and freely moved around the page and the notes can be automatically dated, summarised and recorded in a new PDF document.

Acrobat Capture
Acrobat Capture is used for converting scanned images of documents into the PDF format. This software offers optical page recognition (OPR) capabilities, and results in

documents that provide the full visual fidelity of the original document with absolute positioning of both text and graphics. The system operates by importing a scanned image of a document (usually as a TIFF file) and then processing it using optical character recognition (OCR), to convert the bitmap text to text that can be corrected, indexed, searched or copied to other files. Graphic images are left in the same position they were in the original document. Any text which is not recognised in the OCR process, can be left as a bitmap image over the top of the underlying text, thus maintaining the appearance of the original document.

This method is particularly suited to the conversion of large volumes of legacy documents that need to be converted to a digital format. In 1995, the US Department of Defence (DoD) committed to using this technology for the conversion of over 20 million documents. Although the DoD is committed to the use of CALS standards for the creation of new documents the use of Adobe Capture and PDF for converting legacy documents, represented a savings in labour of $5 a page over traditional tagging methods (such as SGML and HTML).[52]

Acrobat Reader

The Acrobat reader is the view and print only product in the Acrobat software suite. This document viewer is available as a standalone application and a browser plug-in. The reader is free to use, and is widely distributed on the Internet. The viewer has less features than the Exchange application and doesn't allow for authoring techniques such as the annotating, saving and linking of PDF documents.

When viewing a document, the user can use exactly the same navigation tools as the Exchange program. There is also a full-text search engine built into the viewer which enables comprehensive searching capabilities. Text and graphics can also be copied from the PDF document and pasted into other documents.

Case Study: the Use of Adobe Acrobat

In 1994, KPMG Peat Marwick made an extensive study which evaluated the benefits of using the Adobe Acrobat product.[53] The study was made by interviewing and analysing the work of forty-one employees throughout Adobe System's World Wide operation. (At the end of 1993 Adobe had approximately 1000 employees and an annual revenue of $US331 million.) Virtually all employees used computers, but in a heterogeneous environment in which DOS, Windows, Macintosh and UNIX were used.

The benefits that were noted from the use of Acrobat, were grouped into five major areas: cost savings, increased document availability, higher quality information, improved organisational performance and enhanced customer service.

Cost Savings

Based on KPMG's analysis of the use of Acrobat, it was conservatively estimated to have saved the company $US950,000 per year. Table 6.8 outlines what those savings were attributable.

Table 6.8 Cost savings from the use of PDF documents[53]

Business Activity	Estimated Annual Savings
Production and distribution of documentation for developers	$462 000
On-line documentation development	$200 000
User training materials production	$94 000
Distribution of manufacturing reports	$50 000
Copier and paper usage	$49 000
Production and order processing	$47 000
Printer OEM documentation production and distribution	$29 000
Outgoing Federal Express documents	$10 000
QA Software documentation for engineering staff	$9 000
Total Annual Cost Savings	**$US950 000**

Increased Document Availability

A key element of success in using the Acrobat software, was the increased accessibility employees had to documents existing on central servers. Of particular importance, was the fact that employees could use any type of computer to view the documents.

Higher Quality Information

Since PDF documents can be created from almost any type of application, the quality of the appearance of documents was also increased. The use of richly formatted documents using colour graphics and text often helped in the interpretation and readability of documents. The addition of navigation features also helped users to quickly search for relevant information. If needed, a section of a document, rather than the entire document, could be printed out by the user.

Improved Organisational Performance

With the use of PDF, Adobe Systems were able to significantly improve their internal organisational performance. These improvements were reflected in savings in time, and improved integration with other sections of the organisation, through the use of a common document exchange method.

In one case, the distribution of a comprehensive 600–700 page finance report was able to be reduced from an average of five working days to one hour. Using PDF, the finance department was able to create the report and store it on a secure central server. The department then broadcast all of the managers by email telling them that the report was available, and notifying them of the network location they could access it from. A comparison between this method and the previous method is illustrated in Figure 6.26 Similar savings in the production and distribution of documents in other areas of the company, ranged from two days for presentations, to three to six months for producing on-line documentation. These savings in time were directly attributable to savings in cost.

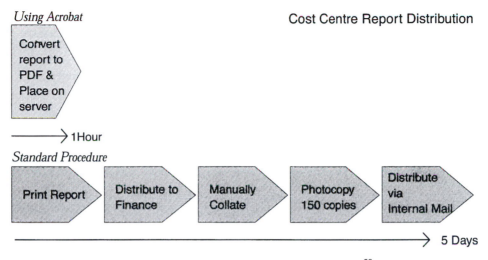

Figure 6.26 Comparative distribution times for a report[53]

Enhanced Customer Service

With the use of PDF documents, it was observed that customer service was significantly enhanced. One of the key improvements was the ability to be able to locate and access documents such as marketing plans, specifications and schedules more quickly. Human Resources were also able to create lists of phone numbers and contact information linked to plans of the office. Portable Document Format documents were also used for all company quality assurance documentation.

Summary

While Adobe Acrobat represents just one of many viewer document formats which are available on the market, it has a majority of the user interface and functionality features which are typical of this document type. As a document distribution method, viewer documents offer a significant cost-saving measure for many companies, considering that the distribution and warehousing of paper can account for at least 60 per cent of the total cost of producing most traditional documents.[51] Other key advantages of viewer documents include:

- Fast creation. Viewer documents can be created very quickly without the need to be structurally marked-up.
- Exact reproduction as intended by the author of the document.
- High portability across different operating systems and networks.
- Varied linear and non-linear presentation capabilities, that allow a document to be used more interactively.
- Capability for use as a presentation method.
- Support for multiple application authoring.
- Different formatting methods, page orientation and page sizes can be used in a single document.

Although the PDF format offers a significant number of benefits, it offers quick solutions for the creation and distribution of documents, that may not be suitable in all circumstances:

- Developer dependent. Although the PDF format is publicly available it is a native file format of one company and not an independent standard.[54]
- Contains no structural mark-up that can be used for processing of the document by other systems.
- Requires a special reader that needs to be downloaded and installed.
- Requires special search engines to search contents.

MULTIMEDIA DOCUMENTS

Similar to hypermedia and electronic reference documents, multimedia documents are capable of using hyperlinks and search engines to enable users to navigate through information. A multimedia document, however, is specifically designed to use large numbers of content rich sources such as graphics, sound and video, to assist with learning and mastery, or to provide entertainment. As illustrated in Figure 6.27, multimedia documents are able to deliver a far greater variety of data types than traditional printed documents.

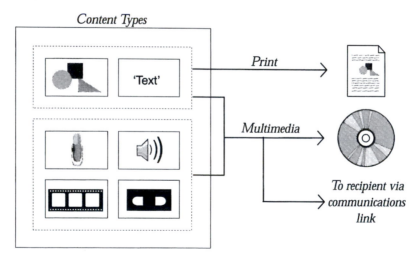

Figure 6.27 Media types used in multimedia and print documents.

Interaction is implicit in all multimedia, and most multimedia titles have been designed to actively engage the user of the document. For example, it is common for a number of different data types to be presented to the user simultaneously, including graphic images, animation, hypertext, voice narration and a background soundtrack. Some common uses for multimedia include: illustrated encyclopaedias, dictionaries, business guides, training guides, teaching aides, art collections and, of course, games.

Due to the diversity of standards which can be used for each type of data incorporated into a multimedia document, there are no industry-wide standards for the formatting, interchange and storage of multimedia documents. The Interactive Multimedia Association, however, is promoting the establishment of multimedia software standards that relate to cross-platform compatibility, intellectual property and technology convergence.[55] One such standard, is the Open Media Framework interchange standard being developed for the digital post-production industry for the exchange of animation, audio, editing, graphics, effects, and video files.[56] Another standard is Java, which can be used to write platform-independent multimedia applets or entire multimedia applications for delivery over the Internet or an intranet.

Table 6.9 Examples of some multimedia document products

Standard/Product	Purpose	Maintainer/Developer
MacroMedia Director	Cross-platform multimedia authoring application for CD-ROM or Internet delivery	Macromedia Inc.
MacroMedia AuthorWare	Cross-platform multimedia authoring application for interactive learning via CD-ROM or Internet delivery	Macromedia Inc.
Macromedia Shockwave/Flash	Browser plug-in to display Director and AuthorWare applications over the Web	Macromedia Inc.
IconAuthor	Cross-platform multimedia authoring software for interactive learning	AimTech
Hypercard	Hypermedia/multimedia authoring application	Apple Computers
MetaCard	Cross-platform multimedia authoring software for interactive learning on Unix/X11 and Windows computers	MetaCard Corporation
SuperCard	Multimedia, Internet, and Application Development	Allegiant Technologies
Open Media Framework (OMF)	Multimedia interchange and storage format used in digital post-production environments	Avid Technologies
Java	Application development language that can also be used to create multimedia applets and documents	Sun Microsystems

Listed in Table 6.9 are some widely used multimedia authoring and development applications. All of these applications produce proprietary document types.

Due to the very large size and/or number of files used in complex multimedia titles such as interactive encyclopaedias, the usual delivery method is via a fixed media such as CD-ROM. Even when complex compression techniques are used, it can be difficult to compress graphic, video and audio data without compromising its quality, thus the need for high-capacity storage media.

With the use of Web browser plug-ins and controls, it is also possible to embed multimedia objects into a Web page. Despite the increased download times and need for proprietary viewers, the use of multimedia to enrich Web pages can be a highly effective means of delivering interactive-documents, to a large or widely distributed audience in a networked environment. Typical uses of multimedia in Web pages include animated graphics, audio and video streaming, navigation, user feedback, education and training.

3D Virtual Reality Environments

Three-dimensional multimedia and virtual reality environments offer a number of different methods of spatially representing information. Systems such as MEME, Quicktime VR, DIVE, Milena, Viscape, and VRML, all use file formats that support a range of techniques for simulating 3D environments. Of these standards, VRML is the most widely used.

Figure 6.28 A VRML world with navigation controls

The Virtual Reality Modelling Language (VRML, often pronounced 'vermal') is an open industry standard that defines a file format for Three-dimensional multimedia and shared virtual worlds on the Internet.[57] This language is used to create a VRML 'world' or 'scene' in which a user can navigate a space in real-time, by moving, tilting, rotating and zooming. In a VRML world, the user can click on to objects that are linked to other documents, HTML Web pages, sounds, video or other VRML worlds. Typically, VRML worlds are embedded into HTML documents and viewed in a Web browser using a plug-in or control, although they can also be viewed outside this environment.

Virtual Reality Modelling Language files exist as either plain text or compressed text files that can be created using specialist VRML authoring software, or using export filters from 3D CAD and animation systems. In a VRML world, geometry is defined by XYZ coordinates, and surfaces have specific 'material' properties to describe how various forms of light reflect off the surface of an object. Similar to a rendering system, various levels of shading, colour and texture can also be assigned to surfaces. A typical VRML world is illustrated in Figure 6.28.

Since VRML is very closely associated with the use of Internet protocols and Web browser technologies, it has often been suggested that VRML could be used as an advanced method of navigating the World Wide Web.[58]

Applications for Multimedia in the Construction Industry

The use of multimedia in the construction industry, falls into three main categories: design, product information, and education/reference.

Design

In the design process a number of multimedia tools can be used for purposes such as: collaborative design, design analysis, design presentation and marketing. Each of these approaches can incorporate the use of CAD, text, graphics, video, sound, animation and database sources. Figure 6.29 illustrates the types of sources that can be used in the creation of a multimedia document for design purposes.

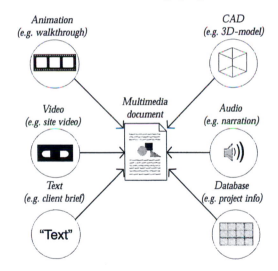

Figure 6.29 Design sources for a multimedia document

Product Information

A number of manufacturers use multimedia to create a highly interactive product catalogues.[61,62] These catalogues enable users to browse and select products using a range of data types. For example, a multimedia catalogue could be used to help select a type of brick or tile. Rather than seeing one picture of the brick and a brief description, a multimedia document can use graphic overlays to allow a user to interactively select a building design upon which to test the contextual appearance of the brick. Audio descriptions of the product, as well as digital video clips of completed projects using the product, could also be included.

Typically, in a multimedia catalogue, product information can be searched or sorted by industry classification codes, manufacturers names, trade names or keywords. Extensive hyperlinking can also be used to cross-reference products and link to relevant supporting files such as CAD documents containing construction details. Figure 6.30 illustrates a CD-ROM based multimedia catalogue.

Although CD-ROM is used extensively for this purpose, the use of on-line catalogues via a Web site is also popular. While a product catalogue on a Web site is likely to use less interactivity due to restrictions of bandwidth, its major advantage is that it offers a direct connection to the manufacturer. This enables more current information to be published, and larger and more powerful server-based databases to be used.

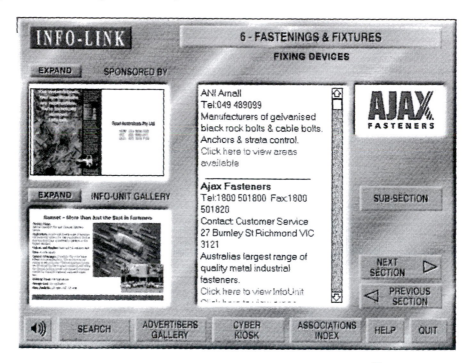

Figure 6.30 A CD-ROM based multimedia product catalogue[62]

Education and Reference

Multimedia documents are widely available for education and reference purposes. Typical applications include encyclopaedias, teaching aids for techniques in building construction, and demonstration of principles of building science.

Some good examples of interactive multimedia encyclopaedias include the *Great Buildings Collection* and the *Frank Lloyd Wright Companion*.[63,64]

In the *Great Building Collection* a range of information is available on a building's name, architect, location, date, building type, construction type, climate and context. These are all combined with interactive three-dimensional models, Quicktime movies, drawings, sketches, images, narrative commentary, maps, and a history timeline. The *Frank Lloyd Wright Companion* includes a multimedia encyclopaedia of the complete works of the architect Frank Lloyd Wright from 1888 to 1959, a screen shot of which is illustrated in Figure 6.31.

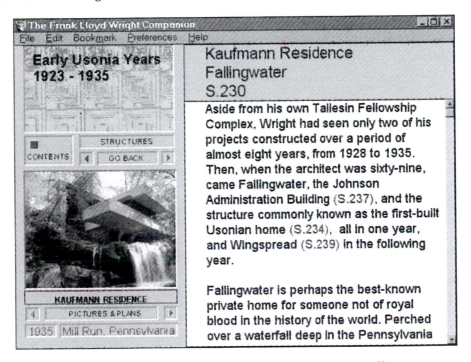

Figure 6.31 An example of a multimedia reference encyclopaedia[63]

A COMPARISON OF DIGITAL DOCUMENTS

In the previous sections, an extensive range of digital document types have been examined and a summary of their main features are listed in Table 6.10.

As was stated at the beginning of this chapter, it is very difficult to find a common set of criteria by which to directly compare all types of digital documents. Making comprehensive, feature-for-feature comparisons is not only very difficult, it is possibly misleading due to ongoing developments that are occurring with many standards. Most digital document types have been developed with a number of different design criteria in mind.

While many digital documents support common features, such as hyperlinks or neutral encoding, this does not mean that the document types that share these features can be considered equivalents. For example, both PDF and HTML support hyperlinks, yet they are most commonly used for quite different purposes. In this case, hyperlinks are just a mechanism that can be used to enable a reader to move quickly from one part of a document to another.

Table 6.10 A summary of the main digital document groups

Document Type	Definition	Principle Use	Major Standards
Proprietary	An application-specific document structure	Storage of application specific data	various
Output	A standardised formatting structure used to communicate with output devices	Printing and distribution of formatted documents	PostScript PCL
Interchange	A standardised translation structure used between proprietary document types	Document exchange between specialist applications	DXF RTF
Messaging	A standardised messaging structure for asynchronous communication	Communication of information between remotely located individuals	Email EDI Facsimile
Dynamic Compound	A semi-intelligent, editable document structure that is dynamically linked to its data sources	Documents that reference editable data sources	OLE (ActiveX)
Processable Compound	A neutral, editable, cross-platform document structure	Highly structured, platform-independent documents that can be reused and formatted to suit different purposes	SGML
Viewer	A semi-neutral, cross-platform, read-only document structure	Distribution of documents	PDF
Hypermedia/ Reference	A referable, hyperlinked, cross-platform, document structure	Reference documents, electronic publishing	HTML
Multimedia	A highly structured, content-rich document structure	Education, learning or entertainment	various

One general observation of digital documents, is that many navigation and portability features are becoming increasingly similar between different document types. What remains, is the principle function that the document type was intended for – such as printing, distribution or interchange.

Listed in Table 6.11 are some of the common features of a range of different digital document types. Some of these features are related to the structure of documents, others are related to the features of the software tools used to create them.

Table 6.11 Some common features of digital documents

Feature	Description	Examples
Hyperlinks	The ability to navigate from one section of a document to another, using a series of buttons and nodes. Hyperlinks can exist either within a single document or between a group of documents located on a local or remote computer system.	HTML SGML PDF
Reference links	The ability of a document to create active links to its data sources. This enables automatic updates to the master document.	OLE (ActiveX)
Navigable interface	The ability to move to specifically defined portions of a document, such as its start, end, next or previous page.	various
Neutral structure	The ability for a document's structure to be portable across different operating systems, networks and software applications. A neutral structure may or may not also include the formatting information used to render the document to a display or printing device.	SMGL HTML Email EDI
Searchable content	The ability for a document structure to facilitate searches through its content.	SGML HTML PDF
Extensible structure	The ability for a document to be easily modified or added to using a variety of editing tools.	various
Compact nature	The ability for a document to be stored in a minimal amount of storage space Some document structures also incorporate compression methods to further improve storage and transfer capabilities.	General PDF
Reusable nature	The ability for a document's content to be easily reused, duplicated, referenced, rescaled, or presented in a number of different ways.	general
Securable content	The ability for a document's contents to be protected with the use of encryption and secure methods of transfer.	various

SUMMARY

In this chapter, a comprehensive range of digital documents have been identified, categorised, described by their principle functions, briefly examined in their structural approach and evidenced in their use. It is clear that a comprehensive range of digital document types are commonly available, and they can be applied for an extensive number of different purposes.

The principle function of all digital documents is to provide a structural mechanism for containing data. The method of structuring, however, will vary considerably according to the function or functions that a document has to perform. These functions include:

- storage of data;
- printing;
- interchange;
- messaging;

- publishing;
- distribution;
- reference;
- learning; and
- intelligent document assembly.

In general, there are four other major observations that can be made about digital documents. They are becoming:

- more open in nature;
- more easily distributed;
- increasingly multi-functional; and
- smarter.

Digital documents are becoming more open, in the sense that their underlying structure is becoming less proprietary, and more compatible with a wider variety of computing systems and work environments. Digital documents used to be regarded as output files from an application. Currently, there is a focus upon the interoperability of documents, and a realisation that once data has been structured and formatted it should be possible to easily reuse and distribute the information content, regardless of its location or the hardware or software that is being used.

This observation is most clearly evidenced by the rapid adoption of the World Wide Web. One of the principle reasons for its success, is that it uses a neutral and vendor-independent method of structuring and distributing documents. This enables documents to be distributed and displayed on almost any type of computer, on any location on the Internet, in almost any location in the world.

Documents used to be identifiable by a principle function such as data storage, printing or distribution. Developments in both software applications and document structures however, have begun to blur the boundaries between many principle functions. For example:

- Viewer documents such as PDF can also be used for authoring, printing, distribution, viewing, storage, forms interface and multimedia.
- HTML is being further developed to allow the use of style sheets so that authors can also include advanced formatting features the same as those found in desktop publishing software such as multiple fonts, drop capitals, text colour and multiple columns.
- Many software developers are now distributing free browsers for their proprietary document formats.
- Many software developers are also supporting generation, of SGML, HTML and viewer documents from their proprietary document-authoring software.

All of these developments point to a higher level of integration and compatibility, in the exchange of information between different computer systems. It also means that a number of different document models and platforms will be available for performing similar document functions. Over the next decade, the document classifications which have been used here will be expected to erode considerably.

The final observation to be made is that digital documents are changing from being fairly static file structures, to structures that are more dynamic and smarter in nature. In the past, documents tended to be dumb and knew little about themselves.[65] Now, many digital document types can carry information with them, about their origin and identity, as well as executable code that knows how to manipulate and render themselves according to certain conditions.

REFERENCES

1. ACADS (1993), *CADD Data Exchange: an Australian Perspective*, U293 Rev. 2, Association of Computer Aided Design.

2. AIA (1993), *CAD–the Medium of Exchange*, The American Institute of Architects.

3. Williams, L. (1993), 'Compound documents: what could be better than ASCII?', *Dr. Dobb's Journal*, March, p. 32–39.

4. Campbell, A. (1992), *The Mac Designer's Handbook*, Pymble: Angus and Robertson.

5. Murray, J. D. and vanRyper, W. (1994), *Encyclopedia of Graphics File Formats*, Sebastapol: O'Reilly and Associates.

6. Foley, J. D., van Dam, A., Feiner, S. K. and Hughes, J. F. (1990), *Computer Graphics: Principles and Practice*, 2nd ed, Reading: Addison-Wesley.

7. Mitchell, W. J. and McCullough, M. (1995), *Digital Design Media*, New York: Van Nostrand Reinhold.

8. Haase, B. (1990), 'By Definition . . . IGES is not for everyone', *Cadence*, vol. 5, no. 11, p. 57.

9. Douglas, B. (1992), 'Data exchange standards', *Technical Computing*, no. 71, pp. 12–14.

10. Jones, M. (1996), 'STEP - Standard for the Exchange of Product data ISO TC184/SC4', *STEP Search Conference*, Melbourne: DIST.

11. ISO (1997), 'ISO 10303 - Industrial automation systems and integration – product data representation and exchange', *http://www.nist.gov/sc4/*, ISO TC184/SC4.

12. NIST (1997), 'What is STEP?', *http://cic.nist.gov/plantstep/stepinfo/step_def.htm*, PlantSTEP.

13. Mitchell, J. (1994), 'STEP - an international report: sharing information in the AEC sector', *CADEX '95*, Melbourne.

14. IAI (1997), 'International Alliance of Interoperability', *http://www.interoperability.com*, IAI Home Page.

15. Howell, I. (1996), 'The need for interoperability in the construction industry', *InCIT '96*, Sydney: IEAust.

16. New Scientist (1992), 'The world's first fax machine', *New Scientist*, 13 June, no. 1825, p. 11.

17. Negroponte, N. (1995), *Being Digital*, Rydalmere: Hodder and Stoughton.

18. Reinhardt, A. (1993), 'Smarter e-mail is coming', *BYTE*, vol. 18, no. 3, p. 90.

19. RFC1341 (1993), *MIME: Mechanisms for Specifying and Describing the Format of Internet Message Bodies*. Network Working Group.

20. PGP (1997), 'Pretty Good Privacy Inc. home page', *http://www.pgp.com/*, PGP Inc.

21. RSA (1997), 'S/MIME resources', *http://www.rsa.com/rsa/S-MIME/*, RSA Laboratories.

22. DAS (1992), *EDI – A Better Way: Streamlining Purchasing*, Canberra: Standards Australia.

23. Premnos (1997), 'Getting started with EDI', *http://www.premenos.com/edi/edi.html*, Premnos Technology Corporation.

24. Corporate Review (1993), 'EDI paperless purchasing', *Corporate Review*, vol. 4, no. 3, p. 125.

25. Wayner, P. (1994), 'EDI Moves the Data', *BYTE*, vol. 19, no. 10, p. 121.

26. EDICA (1993), *The Essential EDI*, Strathfield: Standards Australia.

27. CALS (1997), 'Commerce at light speed', *http://www.cals.com/*, CALS Home Page.

28. Hunkin, T. (1993), 'Just give me the fax', *New Scientist*, 13 February, no. 1860, pp. 33–37.

29. NPWC (1993), *Integration of Documents: Quality Management of Documentation for Construction*, Procurement Management Series, Canberra: National Public Works Council.

30. Travis Jr., R. L. (1990), 'CDA overview', *Digital Technical Journal*, vol. 2, no. 1, p. 8.

31. Bramhall, M. and Stewart, J. A. (1992), 'Comparing compound document processing models', *Connexions: the Interoperability Report*, vol. 6, no. 8, p. 2.

32. Naggum, E. (1992), 'SGML FAQ', *ftp://ftp.ifi.uio.no/pub/SGML/FAQ/FAQ.0.0*, SGML Repository.

33. Cover, R. (1997), 'The SGML Web page', *http://www.sil.org/sgml/sgml.html*, Summer Institute of Linguistics.

34. Wood, J. M. (1995), *Desktop Magic: Electronic Publishing, Document Management, and Workgroups*, New York: Van Nostrand Reinhold.

35. Laurune, W. R. and Travis Jr, R. L. (1990), 'The Digital Document Interchange Format', *Digital Technical Journal*, vol. 2, no. 1, p. 16.

36.   PODA-SAX (1992), *The ODA Brochure*, Project 5320, ESPRIT project 5320.

37.   Walter, M. (1996), 'HTML's success doesn't spell SGML's doom', *Seybold Bulletin on Computer Publishing*, vol. 1, no. 15.

38.   Bush, V. (1945), 'As we may think', *The Atlantic Monthly*, pp. 104–107, http://www.theAtlantic.com/atlantic/atlweb/flashbks/computer/bushf.htm.

39.   Life (1945), 'Memex', *Life Magazine*, September 8, p. 122.

40.   Nelson, T. (1965), 'A file structure for the complex, the changing and the intermediate', *ACM 20th National Conference*.

41.   Xanadu (1994), 'Xanadu: theinformation future', *http://www.xanadu.com.au/xanadu/future.html*, Xanadu Australia.

42.   Rao, U. and Turoff, M. (1990), 'Hypertext functionality: a theoretical framework', *International Journal of Human-Computer Interaction*.

43.   Berners-Lee, T. (1993), 'World Wide Web: an illustrated seminar', *http://www.w3.org/hypertext/WWW/Talks/General.html*, CERN.

44.   NW (1997), 'Internet domain survey', *http://www.nw.com/zone/WWW/top.html*, Network Wizards.

45.   Gray, M. (1997), 'Internet growth summary', *http://www.mit.edu/people/mkgray/net/internet-growth-summary.html*, Internet Statistics Growth and Usage of the Web and the Internet.

46.   W3C (1997), 'Hypertext Markup Language (HTML)', *http://www.w3.org/MarkUp/*, World Wide Web Consortium.

47.   Bosak, J. (1997), 'XML, Java, and the future of the Web', *http://sunsite.unc.edu/pub/sun-info/standards/xml/why/xmlapps.html*, Sun SITE.

48.   Haseldon, P. and Sharpe, R. (1994), 'Interface between BCAider and AutoCAD', *CADEX '94*, Melbourne: CADEX.

49.   CSIRO (1994), *BCAider: Building Code of Australia Expert Assistant, User Guide*, Highett: Building Construction & Engineering Division.

50.   van der Roest, M. (1994), 'EDM: how it makes business more productive', *EDM '94*, Washington, DC.

51.   Seybold (1993), 'Adobe Systems' Acrobat', *The Seybold Report on Desktop Publishing*, vol. 8, no. 1, p. 6.

52.   Adobe (1995), *Adobe Customer Trends: Adobe Acrobat Capture*. Mountain View: Adobe Systems Incorporated.

53.   KPMG (1994), *Adobe Acrobat Product Benefits Study*, KPMG Peat Marwick LLP.

54.   Bienz, T. and Cohn, R. (1993), *Portable Document Format Reference Manual*, Reading: Addison Wesley.

55.   IMA (1997), 'Interactive Multimedia Association home page', *http://www.ima.org/*, Interactive Multimedia Association.

56. OMF (1997), 'Open Media Framework', *http://www.omfi.org/*, Open Media Framework Interchange Home Page.

57. VRML (1997), 'The VRML Consortium Home Page', *http://www.vrml.org/*, The VRML Consortium.

58. Pesce, M. D., Kennard, P. and Parisi, A. S. (1994), 'Cyberspace', *http://hyperreal.com/~mpesce/www.html*.

59. Maher, M. L., Cicognani, A. and Simoff, S. (1996), 'An experimental study of computer mediated collaborative design', *http://www.arch.su.edu.au/kcdc/cmcd/paper/index.html*, Key Centre of Design Computing, University of Sydney.

60. Schiffer, M. J. (1994), 'A geographically-based multimedia approach to city planning', in *Human Factors in Computing Systems*, C. Plaisant (ed.), New York: Association for Computing Machinery, pp. 265–266.

61. Sweets (1997), *SweetSource*, CD-ROM: McGraw-Hill.

62. Info-Link (1997), *The Book 97: Building Products and Suppliers*, CD-ROM: Reed Business Publishing.

63. Storrer, W. A. (1995), *The Frank Lloyd Wright Companion*, CD-ROM: Prarie Multimedia Inc.

64. Matthews, K. (1994), *The Great Buildings Collection*, CD-ROM: Van Nostrand Reinhold.

65. Reinhardt, A. (1994), 'Managing the new document', *BYTE*, vol. 19, no. 8, p. 90.

Chapter 7
Applying Digital Documents

SELECTING DIGITAL DOCUMENT TECHNOLOGIES

To determine the most suitable type of digital document or document system to use in any situation, a combination of factors should be considered. Most of these factors are dependent upon the circumstances, capabilities, budget and performance requirements of a particular project, or office environment in which solutions need to be implemented. Considerations that need to be made include the size of a practice, the platform(s) used, required compatibility levels, ease of implementation, cost of implementation and the time to implement a solution.

Size of the Practice

The construction industry is well known for its diversity. Architectural, engineering and design practices vary considerably in size and offices can range in size from sole practitioners, through to large firms of 100 people or more. The size and capability of a practice can often influence the size of projects that are taken on which in turn, influences:

- the number of documents that are used;
- the complexity of a system needed to manage those documents; and
- the amount of capital available to implement a solution.

Main Platform Used

One of the perennial problems in computing, is the incompatibility that exists between different operating systems. Currently, the most common operating systems include Windows, DOS, MacOS and various versions of Unix. By standardising on a particular operating system, the range of digital document solutions are restricted to those available for that platform. However, in a mixed platform environment, networking and file compatibility can also be a problem. Therefore, the most future-proof solutions will be those which are specifically designed to be cross-platform compatible.

While Web technologies address many of the issues concerning the cross-platform distribution of documents, many of these solutions require the use of platform-specific 'plug-ins' to read and view document types that are not pure HTML. The majority of digital document authoring systems also tend to be platform specific.

Required Level of Compatibility

Compatibility should be considered not only on a local level, but on a national and international scale as well. For example, if an architectural practice has a number of interstate offices, system and document type compatibility should be considered between those offices. With the increasing use of large networks such as the Internet, international collaborative projects are becoming increasingly common. The effect of such collaborations should also be an influencing factor in selecting appropriate digital document technologies. Ideally, any solution should be adaptable and extensible enough to cater for current and future scenarios.

Ease of Implementation

The ease at which a solution can be implemented, is often a contributing factor to its success. For example, some systems offer such an extensive number of features that they end up being quite complex, time-consuming and expensive to implement. It should also be assessed whether the expertise to implement a solution exists in-house.

Cost of Implementation

Depending on the answers to the previous questions, implementation costs can vary from very low to very high. To properly analyse the cost of implementing an extensive company-wide digital document solution, a return on investment (ROI) should be considered. Some suggested criteria for this ROI would be:

Paper-based costs
- Cost of labour for performing certain tasks such as creation, distribution, storage and retrieval of paper.
- Cost of paper stock for printing, photocopy, dye-lines etc.
- Cost of consumable supplies such as staples, binders, folders etc.
- Cost of paper document storage including filing cabinets, drawing cabinets and office floor space.

Other costs
- Cost of hardware and software
- Cost of computer file storage
- Cost of labour for performing tasks in the creation, distribution, storage, and retrieval of digital documents.
- Training time required to use the system.
- Productivity loss during training.
- Productivity gains after training.
- Additional costs for consultants, maintenance, upgrades etc.
- Additional savings in time, and quality improvement.

Even though there are extensive calculations that can be performed to calculate ROI, and other measures such as IRR (Initial Rate of Return), these techniques have been demonstrated to be incapable of capturing the entire benefit of investing in IT solutions.[1,2] The reason for the failure of traditional economic measurement techniques is that they do not take into account the so-called 'intangible' or 'soft' factors such as accuracy, quality, convenience, variety, timeliness, flexibility, functionality, reliability, usability, user satisfaction and relevance.[3] Therefore, these additional intangible benefits should be taken into consideration when performing an economic analysis of solutions.

Time to Implement

Due to the tight time constraints imposed on many projects, it is often difficult to implement new technologies. Unfortunately this often results in expedient decisions being made about the appropriateness of certain technologies. It does not necessarily follow that a technology that is very easy to implement will be best for the company in the longer term. Quite often a more holistic view is required that will take into consideration solutions that will meet the requirements of a range of current and potential projects.

The prospect of large-scale and time-consuming solutions, also tend to delay their implementation. What is clear, however, is that the longer an organisation waits to begin a transition to a new and appropriate technology, the more they will eventually have to spend in time and money, even in the short term.[4]

DISTRIBUTION METHODS

In the analysis of various digital document solutions, there are number of important considerations that should be made. These include the way that digital documents can be distributed, managed, secured and stored.

In the previous chapters, a number of different methods of delivering digital documents were alluded to. These included the use of networks, management systems and fixed media such as CD-ROM. There are, however, a number of criteria which should be considered when selecting a document distribution method.

Criteria for Selecting a Distribution Method

There are two main reasons why workgroups use electronically distributed documents. The first reason is speed of access, and the second reason is the ability to easily and quickly update information. Speed of access can be critical in the timely delivery of documents and can lead to improvements in operational performance.

The choice of distribution method will depend on a number of factors including the:

- size of the document;
- relative complexity of the document type;
- distance the document has to be delivered;
- timeliness of the delivery;
- number of recipients to whom it has to be delivered; and
- compatibility of the media used to transfer the document.

Size

The size of the document is usually a reflection of the type and volume of data contained within in it. Documents which contain a lot of graphics or are entirely graphic based, such as CAD drawings, tend to be significantly larger than text-based documents. Figure 7.1 illustrates some of the relative sizes of certain document types.

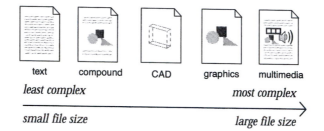

Figure 7.1 The relative complexity and file size of various document types

The size of a document affects the storage space that is required, the media which can be used to store it, and the speed at which it can be transferred. Large documents, such as complex renderings, or large CAD drawings are difficult to compress and, therefore, only certain high-capacity media such as CD-ROM, cartridge or tape can be used.

Networks can also be used to directly transfer information. However, there may not always be a network connection available, and transmission speeds will vary according to the bandwidth of the connection and the size of the data being transferred.

Complexity

The complexity of a document is usually a reflection of the number of different types of data contained within it and the number of referenced links that are used to its data sources. When dynamic compound documents are used, the links to the source data are very important. For example, if the links to a document's data sources become severed (such as moving the document to a new location) the integrity of the master document becomes affected. Therefore, in the electronic delivery of dynamic compound documents, the referenced data should either accompany the master document or be permanently bound to it.

Distance and Timely Delivery

With the widespread use of the Internet, there are now very few factors which affect the distance that a document has to be sent. However, if physical media are being used, the usual restrictions of weight, volume, packaging and delivery service times apply.

The most powerful method of delivering digital documents is, of course, via a network. As was discussed in Chapter 4, networks virtually eliminate the problem of transferring information over long distances. Successive generations of networking technologies are becoming increasingly faster. Ethernet based networks which are currently capable of transferring data at a rate of 10–100 megabits per second, will eventually be replaced with fibre-optic technologies. Current transmission speeds for fibre-optic networks are rated at about 2.5 gigabits per second – or fast enough to send about one and a half copies of the entire *Oxford English Dictionary* every second.[5] Efficiencies such as these are well recognised and, as a result, networks are unlikely to be surpassed as being the most effective method of document delivery.

Number of Recipients and Media Compatibility

The number of recipients that a document has to be distributed to, often effects the distribution media that is used. When a document has to be distributed to unknown recipients using any possible type of computing system, the lowest common denominator usually has to be catered for. That will usually mean choosing the distribution medium that can be used by the greatest number of recipients. For example, although CD-ROM offers a superior storage capacity, there may not be a sufficient user base of CD-ROM users to warrant this as a distribution medium in some cases. Similarly, recipients may not all be connected to the same network, or might be using an incompatible operating system that formats media differently.

Distribution Methods

In Table 7.1 a number of distribution methods are listed which give an overview of the different methods of document distribution that are currently available.

Table 7.1 Examples of some common document distribution methods

Method	Description
Fixed Media	These involve the use of physical media for the exchange of data and documents. The main criteria for these methods is that both the author and recipient are using compatible systems. Some media types include floppy disk, magneto-optical drive, cartridge, QIC tape, CD-ROM, DVD, DAT tape.
LANs	These involve the use of local area networks based on peer-to-peer or client-server configurations. Transfer of documents is usually very simple, involving a limited number of standards. Delivery is practically instantaneous.
WANs	On a larger scale, wide area networks can be used to transfer documents over larger distances and at high speed depending on the protocols used.
Internet Services	The Internet can be used very effectively for distribution of documents. This network extends to the greatest number of users, however, there are a large number of different protocols to choose from for this purpose, such as: telnet, gopher, WWW, FTP, WAIS and SMTP. Fortunately, the use of these protocols are application driven and transparent to the end-user.
Electronic Messaging	Messaging protocols such as electronic data interchange (EDI) and email, can not only be used as a method of exchanging messages, but can also be used as a transport mechanism for attaching and sending other types of digital documents
DMS and Workflow	Document management and workflow systems are purpose built databases that are used for workgroup storage, access and distribution of documents and the information contained within those documents.

DOCUMENT MANAGEMENT

A document management system is a set of software tools which enables an organisation to create electronic document libraries, search for information across network databases, identify information changes in different versions of documents, provide secure document access and manage workflow processes in the creation, assembling and production of documents.[6]

The Need for Document Management Systems

With the increasing proliferation of digital data, there has been a growing realisation that many computer systems are becoming as cluttered and unorganised as the paper-based offices which preceded them. Without some form of management system to organise digital documents, there is a danger that the advantages of their use could be lost.[7]

The need for document management systems (DMS) is evidenced by statistics relating to the problems associated with traditional paper-based systems. For example, it is estimated that documents claim 40–60 per cent of the average office workers time, 20–25 per cent of a company's labour cost, and 12–15 per cent of corporate revenues.[6,8,9,10] In dollar terms it is estimated that $US600–800 billion dollars a year is spent by Fortune 1000 companies on document management alone.[10] Considering that 90 per cent of the information related to an organisations business is contained within documents, and that only 10 per cent of an organisation's information is traditionally stored in centrally managed databases, a very significant problem exists.[6]

When computer systems are used to create documents, the problem of document management does not go away. Often the gains that are made in productivity, are offset by the cost of trying to manage multiple version of documents and trying to find ways of locating and distributing them efficiently. This problem is often exacerbated by the organisational structure of most operating systems. In many operating systems, files are arranged in rigid hierarchical directories that often use extremely limited naming capabilities, such as the DOS limitation of eight characters and a three character descriptive file extension.

Without additional systems to assist users in the filing and management of digital documents, total disorder can result. Similar to a paper-based system, information can become incredibly difficult to find without the knowledge of the person who originally named or last filed a document. These problems create a need for more powerful and specialised database management tools than those provided by operating systems alone.

An additional incentive for the adoption of a DMS, is that they are being increasingly required as part of quality systems. In the US, the Federal Food and Drug Administration (FDA) has a requirement standard known as OSHA 1910.119. This standard was created to force companies to manage their documents efficiently. Under this standard, companies are required to produce any required document within 15 minutes, otherwise they can be potentially shut down.[11] The ISO 9000 quality control and quality assurance standards are also increasingly favouring the use of a DMS. There is however, little evidence to date that suggests that computer-based management of documents is being widely adopted in the design and construction industries.

Types of Document Management Systems

The idea of a central information database is not a new one. Some of the earliest aims of architects in the use of computers, have always revolved around the idea of a central database that could co-ordinate design and project information.[12,13,14] The systems that were proposed usually revolved around the use of a monolithic, purpose-built database. Today, however, a number of different models exist for the management of documents.

Due to the rapid evolution and improvement of document management systems in recent times, it is difficult to clearly identify distinct classes of systems. There are, however, three predominant approaches which are being used for a number of individual markets. These include:

- text indexing and retrieval systems;
- document image management systems; and
- compound document management systems.

It is anticipated that the distinction between the features of these different systems will gradually disappear over time.

Text Indexing and Retrieval

Text retrieval and indexing systems are based upon the ability to provide fast, accurate and flexible searches through large quantities of text-based data. These systems often provide automatic indexing and powerful document conversion utilities that enable the contents of proprietary document structures to be searched. They are often used in conjunction with document viewing and multimedia technologies, and are also prevalent as search engines on the Internet.

Document Image Management

Document image management systems use hardware scanners to input and convert paper documents into a digital form. Using this type of system, all incoming documents can be scanned in, and then either converted to text using OCR, or left as bitmap images. The resulting digital documents can then be labelled, indexed and stored using a range of different media.

Compound Document Management

Compound document management systems provide a range of modular tools to support library management, document viewing, workflow, revision control, text retrieval, document indexing, document conversion, and automatic document assembly. The principle advantage of these systems, is that they are able to manage documents using a variety of different data types and document structures. These requirements are particularly important in information intensive industries such as architecture, engineering, manufacturing, law, medicine and pharmacy. A large number of specific EDM applications are also available for the engineering segment of the market, which are commonly referred to as Engineering Document Management Systems (EDMS).

The Main Functions of a Document Management System

The best analogy for the principle operation of a document management system, is that of a library. In a library system, two common modes of operation are for the cataloguing and retrieving of information:

Cataloguing
1. Bring in a new or modified book.
2. Generate a card and assign a code number to it, using the details of the book.
3. File the card in a catalogue and place book on a shelf according to its code.

Retrieving
1. Retrieve the card from the catalogue using known details about the subject, title, author, etc.
2. Retrieve the book from the shelf based upon the code number.
3. Check out the book and update the database indicating that it is has been borrowed by a particular user and is no longer available on the shelf.

In a document management system, computing equivalents can be assigned to some of these processes.

- The card catalogue – *a file or a database table.*
- A card – a *database record.*
- Specific descriptors such as title, subject, author etc. – *database fields.*
- Books – *documents or data objects.*

Figure 7.2 illustrates the principle functions of a document management system.

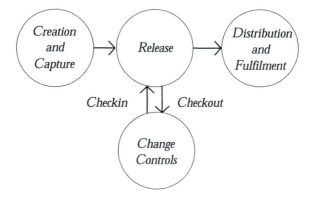

Figure 7.2 The basic document life cycle in a document management system

- At the creation and capture stage, the main activities surround the creation, image capture, or electronic transfer of documents.
- In the release stage, documents are placed in a secure 'vault' area to ensure data integrity and security. It is in this area that methods are developed to enable the distribution and tracking of documents.

- In the change control stage, mechanisms are put into place to prepare, approve and incorporate changes. These mechanisms include practices such as redlining and change authorisation. (Redlining is a form of document mark-up similar to the manual practice of using a red pen to make comments on a proof copy of a document. Many CAD document viewers support this feature.)
- In the final distribution and fulfilment stage, documents are made available for search retrieval and output, via printing, viewing, plotting or faxing.

Availability of Document Management Systems

There are a wide variety of commercially available document management systems available on the market.[15] These systems vary widely in capability to handle different types of documents and their scalability to suit different size companies. Consequently, most DMS systems consist of tool kits for the development of company-specific solutions.

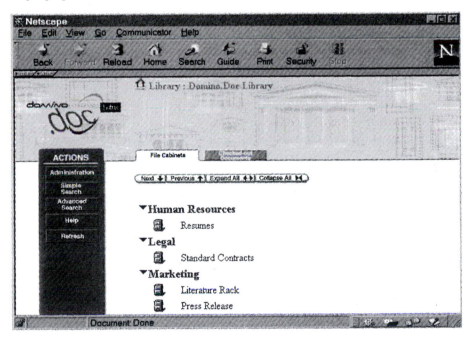

Figure 7.3 The Web based Lotus Domino.Doc document management system

As with many other computing technologies, there are a number of compatibility problems that exist between these systems.[16] For example, many of the LAN-based DMS products available today, are incompatible with each other in the way that they index documents. This increases the difficulty of integrating document management systems between companies.

To overcome some of these incompatibility problems, many document management systems are designed to support neutral document structures such as HTML and SGML, and make use of SQL (Structured Query Language) as a means of querying document databases. Many systems are also available that are entirely Web based and enable functions such as searching, library management, workflow, project management, report management and collaborative application design to be available to users in an intranet environment.[17] Figure 7.3 illustrates a Web-based document management system.

DOCUMENT SECURITY

In the day-to-day management and use of documents, security plays an extremely important role, and relates to:

- *Document authentication* – verification of the identity of the person who generated a document.
- *Document integrity* – assuring that the document that is received is the same as the one that was sent.
- *Document confidentiality* – protecting the information content of a document from those people who are not intended to receive it.
- *Document authorisation* – the determination of whether a document has been created, modified or transferred by an appropriately authorised individual.

In the use of digital documents, many of these areas have yet to be completely resolved. Unlike paper, there are no well-established, industry-wide standards for document security. However, there are a large number of technologies that can be used to provide three basic levels of security, namely:

- Control of document access.
- Protection of document content.
- Verification of document authenticity.

Access Control

While it is generally acknowledged that most designers require access to all project information, it is probably more desirable that access is restricted or controlled to certain types of documents. For example, some members of a design team will require full access to documents for editing and distribution purposes. Other members might only need access for viewing purposes, while other groups might be excluded altogether.

By using a document management system, it is possible to secure documents according to a pre-established plan for access and authorised use. Access in these systems is usually controlled by passwords and individual user privileges.

In addition to stand-alone software solutions, a number of operating systems also incorporate document access and control methods. Networked based operating systems such as Unix, Novell Netware and Windows NT provide built-in security levels using passwords, directory permissions and file permissions.

Facsimile machines can also be used to control access to transmitted documents. By using a special secure mode, a fax can be encrypted and/or stored within a secure 'mailbox' on a recipient's fax machine. Once a facsimile is in a mailbox, it can then only be accessed with the use of a special password.

Protection of Document Content

After the system access control level, documents can also be protected on an individual basis, using password and/or encryption methods.

Document Passwords

The process of verifying a user's identity is called authentication, and one of the most popular methods of achieving this, is with the use of a password. After a password has been authenticated, a user can be assigned access to an entire document or specific subsections of it. They can also be restricted to only being able to perform certain tasks in those areas.

A number of viewer document types such as Hummingbird's *Common Ground* and Adobe System's *Acrobat*, support document password protection. Both systems also supports a feature that can be used to prevent documents from being printed. Other document types have also been developed that support the use of private and public note attachments. This means that notes can be attached to a document and made viewable within an organisation, but made invisible and non-accessible to people externally.[18]

Document types such as SGML and ODA enable restricted access to specific segments of a document.[19,20] Documents protected in this manner, can be marked up according to a number of different security levels. When the document is accessed, it can then be presented according to the security level of the reader. This feature is commonly used in military and other high-security environments.

Document Encryption Basics

The most secure method of protecting any document is to use encryption. Encryption is the transformation of data into a form that is unreadable by anyone without a secret decryption key. Its purpose is to ensure privacy by keeping information hidden from anyone for whom it is not intended.

Cryptography is the art of creating and using cryptosystems for encrypting messages. Its use can be traced back to the time of Julius Caesar. When Caesar sent messages to his trusted acquaintances, but did not trust the messengers, he used to replace every letter 'A' in a message by a 'D', every 'B' by an 'E' and so on, throughout the alphabet. Consequently, only someone who knew the 'shift by 3' rule could decipher his messages.[21]

A *cryptosystem* is a set of algorithms that can be used for encryption purposes. Each algorithm is referred to as a key. In the case of Julius Caesar's cryptosystem of 'shift by *n'*, n can be considered the key. Today of course, encryption systems are far more complex and secure – a need which is necessitated by the existence of powerful cryptanalysis decoding techniques. Some of the most secure and well-recognised encryption standards in use today, include:

- DES (Data Encryption Standard)
- RSA (Rivest-Shamir-Adelman)
- IDEA (International Data Encryption Algorithm)
- MD5 (Message Digest version 5).

Encryption methods are based on two basic models – a public-key method and a private-key method.

Private-Key Encryption

The older of these two, is the private-key method. This system uses a single key that must be used by both the sender and receiver to encrypt and decrypt documents. This is known as a symmetrical method of encryption, and relies entirely on each party existing in a trusted trading relationship. Just like a door with a single lock, any document can be decrypted by someone else who possesses the same key. Figure 7.4 illustrates the principle of private-key encryption.

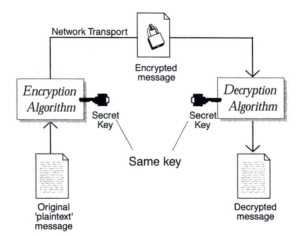

Figure 7.4 The private-key encryption method

One of the most popular systems of private-key encryption is the DES standard. This standard was originally developed by the US government in 1975, and is still used by large numbers of private companies and government departments around the world. The DES standard supports the use of a fixed 56-bit key-size algorithm. Another private-key method is the Kerberos system developed at MIT during the mid-1980s.[22]

The problem with private-key encryption systems is that a new key must be provided whenever a secure link between two entities is required. As the number of possible recipients increases, so does the number of required keys. In a large organisation, the matrix of possible key combinations can be enormous, creating a significant management problem. An obvious flaw in this approach, is that if a key falls into the wrong hands, security is immediately compromised.

One method around the problem of issuing private keys, is to use a secure third-party key distribution centre, or escrow. This distribution centre will issue a key to a pair or group of people wishing to exchange documents in a secure manner. For security reasons, these keys are usually only used once and must be reissued when a new transaction is required. Consequently, this process has been generally regarded as a complex and often inefficient solution to adopt.[23] An alternative is to use a public-key encryption system.

Public-Key Encryption

Public-key encryption involves the use of a pair of keys, one that is published publicly and one that is kept private. The *private key* in this system, is like a personal password and is kept secret to the individual. The *public key* is made available for anyone to use, and can be published as part of a business directory. In order to use the system, *both* parts must be used. A document encoded using the secret key, can only be decoded with the public key and vice versa.

In practice, public-key encryption works in the following way. If two people want to send a confidential document over a network and they have never met or exchanged codes before, the sender would start by looking up and acquiring the recipients public key. The sender would then use the recipients public key to encode a document they are sending to that person. At the other end the recipient's private key is used to unscramble the document. This process is illustrated in Figure 7.5.

The main advantage of the public-key system is that it is asymmetric. Each of the keys are different sizes and the resulting encryption method is extremely secure and requires an immense amount of computing power to break.[24]

The public-key system is also reciprocal in nature. This means that if user A wants to send an encrypted message to user B, they can use user B's public key to encrypt the message. That way, only user B can decrypt the message because only they possess the corresponding secret key. Conversely, if user A uses their private key to encrypt a message, then anyone who has user A's public key will be able to decrypt it. (This latter approach is used more commonly for authenticating messages and will be discussed later). The most common public-key encryption method, is the RSA cryptosystem. Many practical applications exist for the use of public-key encryption including authentication, access control, message integrity, message privacy and digital signatures.

The fact that public-key encryption can be used to send documents in absolute confidentiality, has caused some consternation for US government authorities such as the CIA and FBI. Their concern is that if people use the levels of security that systems like RSA encryption allows, they will not be able to decode messages that might be considered a threat to national security. As a result, the US government has prohibited the export of the RSA cryptosystem outside of the US for encryption purposes, and only allows its use for authentication purposes.[23]

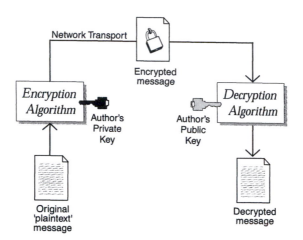

Figure 7.5 The public-key encryption method

Verification of Document Authenticity

A further consideration in the exchange of documents is the use of authentication systems. Authentication is the verification of the identity of a party who generated some data and of the integrity of the data itself. Authentication of a document is generally required as proof of authorship. It can also used be used to establish whether a document was in a particular location at a particular time, and/or whether an authorised person was present at the time it was sent. The three main methods used for these purposes are digital signatures, digital certificates and notary systems.

Digital Signatures

A digital signature can be used as a method of proving the authorship of a document and as a method of verifying that a message was not altered between the time it was sent and the time it was received. A number of different systems are available, and most are associated with the use of messaging documents such as email and EDI.

In a digital signature, a cryptographic hash function (a special security algorithm such as MD5) is used to calculate a fixed-length string of text from a message called a *message digest*.[24] This message digest acts as a digital signature because it has been encrypted with a sender's private key. One of the big advantages of this system is that each signature is unique because it has been generated for a particular document and user and, therefore, cannot be reused.

Whenever a person attaches their digital signature to a message, the signature can be verified by the receiver in the following manner:

- decrypt the signature with the sender's public key;
- generate another message digest from the received message using the same hash function that the sender used; and then
- comparing the newly generated message digest with the one sent.

If both message digests are identical, then the message can be verified as having been sent by the same person who claims to have sent it. If the message digests do not match, it is likely that the sender is not the same person they claim to be, or the message was modified or damaged during transmission. The digital signature process is illustrated in Figure 7.6.

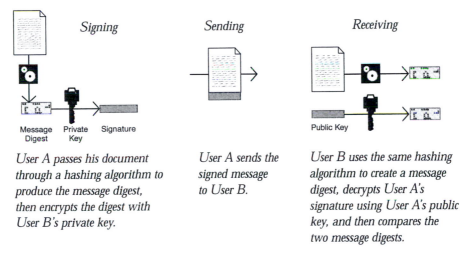

User A passes his document through a hashing algorithm to produce the message digest, then encrypts the digest with User B's private key.

User A sends the signed message to User B.

User B uses the same hashing algorithm to create a message digest, decrypts User A's signature using User A's public key, and then compares the two message digests.

Figure 7.6 The digital signature process of verified message exchange

Fortunately, the underlying process of digital signature creation and verification can be largely shielded from the end-user. One of the most popular applications for the purpose of authenticating email messages, has been PGP (Pretty Good Privacy). PGP was originally released free of charge on the Internet in June 1991, by its author Phil Zimmerman. By May 1994 commercial versions had been licensed to over 4 million users.[25] PGP uses a combination of the RSA, and MD5 encryption algorithms to create a digital signature that assures the receiver that an incoming message is authentic and has not been altered. A typical PGP digital signature is illustrated in Figure 7.7.

When encrypting messages using PGP, different size session keys can be used to yield increasingly complex levels of security, ranging from casual (using 384-bit keys), to commercial (512 bits), and finally to military levels (1024 bits). The latter level is so secure that it is generally regarded as being unbreakable.

Currently, all cryptographic software is classified as export-controlled 'munitions' by the US Department of Commerce. The use of the RSA encryption algorithm in PGP software, for example, is currently illegal in countries outside of the US. The US government has prohibited the exportation of RSA encryption technology because it considers it to be crucial to US security, and does not want it to be exported to countries which might be regarded as a threat to the US The author of PGP, Phil Zimmerman, originally faced a controversial round of litigation in the US to recall the distribution of PGP, because it used the RSA algorithm and was distributed over the

Internet. As a result of this restriction, an international version of PGP has been created which uses the MPILIB encryption method (which is based upon RSA).

Some alternate digital signature technologies, include the 'Haval signature method' based on the use of Hadamard Matrices, and the Digital Signature Standard (DSS) developed by the US National Institute of Standards and Technology (NIST).[23,26] In the US, digital signatures have been given legally binding status in some states.[27]

```
-----BEGIN PGP SIGNATURE-----
Version: 2.7
iQCVAwUBL1ZcUt6pT6nCx/9/AQczQP+P0y0deVy06PGQRCeLuBdSEvI1ajvkP2C
GEFuSBz3y7t+/qitEUbHAvgwS51RfAS2KE2t1daoChPY+7+DapZYE039daouxuz
hbkPQn0Y9tzaLuqpzk0VqAr8m4liAI9ZLui50024mp7Tncm0uict0+)QDPF80An
Pt2BT32+7TM=
=UL89
-----END PGP SIGNATURE-----
```

Figure 7.7 A sample PGP signature

When using EDI messaging, authentication is handled mainly by the VAN provider, and is included as part of the EDIFACT and ANSI X.12 EDI standards. RSA encryption can also be used to improve the security of messages being sent via EDI.

Digital Certificates

The use of digital signatures brings about the question of how to distribute and verify public keys. In order for public-key cryptography to be used effectively, a trusted authority must be used to distribute a type of digital document called a 'certificate' that attests that a public key does in fact belong to a particular person or company. The issuing of certificates (or Digital ID's as they are sometimes called) can be carried out by a trusted third-party vendor certificate authority (CA), a messaging or workflow application, or a certificate server on a LAN or intranet.[28,29]

In their simplest form, a certificate might only contain a public key and a name. However, a more complete record might contain the following fields:

- Owner's public key.
- Owner's name.
- Expiration date of the public key.
- Name of the issuer (the CA that issued the certificate).
- Serial number of the certificate.
- Digital signature of the issuer.

The most widely accepted format for certificates is defined by the CCITT X.509 international standard. This means that any application that conforms to this standard can read or write certificates. This is unlike the type of certificates that are issued by application specific systems such as Lotus Notes, which uses its own proprietary method of certificate generation.

Digital certificates are now widely used for a range of functions such as: email, electronic commerce, groupware, electronic funds transfers, certifying Java applications and applets, certifying ActiveX controls and enabling secure transactions over the Internet using the SSL (Secure Sockets Layer) and S/MIME (Secure MIME) standards. Many of these uses are based around the use of the Internet and are intended to increase consumer confidence in the parties they are dealing with.

When connecting to a Web site that uses digital certificate technology, the server automatically requests a certificate from the end-user's Web browser. Typically a user will have already registered a default certificate for themselves, and the server checks the validity of this certificate. Once the certificate has been validated, the server reads the information contained in the fields that establishes the user's identity and gives them the appropriate access to site resources. This entire process can be undertaken in less than a second. One distinct advantage of this method is that it can circumvent the need for usernames and passwords.

Practical applications for the use of digital certificate authentication in the design and construction industry include:

- the purchase of goods and materials using credit cards;
- distribution of validated information from regulatory bodies (such as standards and building codes);
- submission of planning and building applications to regulatory authorities;
- payment of fees to regulatory authorities;
- distribution of validated mail from authorised individuals or groups (such as a company general manager or Institute President); and
- automatically gaining access to membership controlled web sites (without having to enter a username and password each time).

Digital Notary Systems

For other types of documents which require proof of authorship and evidence of existence at a particular time, a notary system can be used.

A traditional approach to evidencing documents is to use a notary public, such as a Justice of the Peace. A notary verifies a document by signing it, and then countersigning it with the current date and time. They then add details about the document they have just evidenced into their own records. With this system, however, there is no method of proving that the document's contents were not subsequently altered by another party.

A digital notary service is able to provide the same evidentiary services as a paper-based service, but with significantly greater security and verification levels.

A software company called Surety Technologies was the first to develop a publicly accessible notary system that enables any digital document to be digitally date stamped and recorded to prove its existence at a given time. Using their system it is also possible to prove that a document has not been tampered with or backdated in any way.

The Surety *Digital Notary*™ system was developed to reduce exposure to liability from the misuse, tampering or misrepresentation of digital records. Target markets for the use of the system include banking and credit organisations, stock exchange firms, pharmaceutical and medical research firms, law enforcement agencies, judiciary, medical institutions, insurance companies and accounting firms.

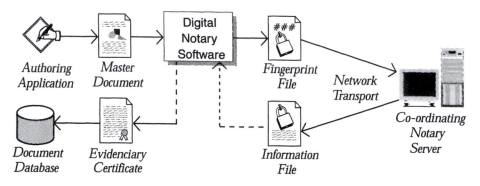

Figure 7.8 The Digital Notary system

The Digital Notary system works by using an application that creates a 'digital fingerprint' of a document (using a similar type of hashing that is used for digital signatures). After creating the fingerprint file, accompanying server software is used to transmit the information (via the Internet, dial-up modem, or other communication methods) to a co-ordinating server using a special synchronisation protocol. Unique identifying information about the document is then transmitted back to the application which sent it. The application then issues a small electronic file that acts as a date-stamped evidentiary certificate as shown in Figures 7.8 and 7.9.

Figure 7.9 A sample Digital Notary signature file

At a future date, (days, months, or even years later) the integrity of a certified digital document can be validated. As further proof that records have been untampered, the server system also creates periodic 'super hash codes', of all the hash codes that were submitted over a specified period of time. These super hash codes are then published weekly in the *New York Times* and various locations on the Internet to prove the integrity of the system at any one time. If any of the records are modified, then the super hash code will also change. Digital Notary certificates have been approved as being admissible in most courts of law in the US.[30]

DOCUMENT STORAGE

In Chapter 2, it was shown how the storage volume of paper-based documents represented a significant problem for many companies. While the use of digital documents represents a significant reduction in the physical volumes that are used, careful consideration should also be made regarding the potential obsolescence of the physical media on which they are stored. For example, classical texts such as the famous Rosetta Stone are still legible twenty-two centuries after it was first created. The physical lifetime of most digital media, however, is only measured in terms of five to thirty years.[31]

A large design and construction office of about 100 staff, may have more than 40,000 drawings and hundreds of thousands of pages of other document types in use at any one time. This can equate to a storage requirement of at least 40 gigabytes or more, just for the documents in current use, and many times more for those in backup storage.

Considering data storage requirements like these, the choice of which media, hardware device or encoding method to use, becomes highly significant. When working in a digital environment, it is important to realise that there is a potential for the accidental erasure of a lifetime's work in seconds, as well as the potential for a more gradual loss through the degradation of storage media, or the obsolescence of certain hardware storage devices.

Storage Media

The choice of which media to store data on is a contentious issue. Two main problems exist in this area. The first is that the permanence of various media types have yet to be firmly established. The second, is that hardware devices to support these media often suffer from a high degree of obsolescence as new storage technologies evolve.

Traditional storage media also suffer from similar problems, with life expectancies of paper ranging anywhere from twenty-five to 2000 years.[32] The actual figure is dependent upon the chemical stability and physical durability of the paper. Generally speaking, the longevity of paper is dependent upon its pH. If it is pH neutral (pH 7), then it stands a greater chance of resisting deterioration by acidic attack. Deterioration can also be affected by the quality of the inks, storage temperature, relative humidity, light, atmospheric pollutants, biological agents, contact with deleterious materials, and various other human causes.[33] Due to changes in paper production techniques, it is generally acknowledged that most modern papers are impermanent, and only have a lifetime expectancy of two or three decades.[32]

Concerns over the longevity of storage media go back as early as Egyptian times 3,000 years ago. In 1145, Roger of Sicily questioned the suitability of paper as an archival material, and decreed that all charters made on paper were to be recopied on to parchment.[32] Today, alternate methods of document conservation include: preservation photocopying, microfilming, preservation photography and the use of various forms of digital media.

Table 7.2 Expected lifetimes and predicted obsolescence of storage media[31,33,34]

Medium	Format/Technology	Life Expectancy (Years)	Obsolescence (Years)
Acid free paper	pH neutral fibre content	100	?
Office copy paper	varies	20–30	?
Newspaper	low-high lignin content	10–20	?
Microfilm	silver-gelatine	100–200	?
Magnetic Tape	3480/3490 cartridge	5–20	5
	Digital Linear Tape	5–20	5
	DD-2	5–15	5
	QIC	2–10	5
	D8 (Data 8mm)	2–10	5
Video Tape	varies	10–30	5
CD-ROM	Yellow Book	5–50	10
CD-R	Gold plated	2–30	10
Magneto-Optical	3.5" or 5.25"	2–30	?
WORM	Pits on bimetallic film	5–100	?
Hard Disk	varies	10	?

Microfilming is still used extensively as a method of document storage and archiving, and is still recommended by a number of preservation experts as a solution for document retention. Its use is advantageous in that life expectancies of more than 100 years are possible. The disadvantages, however, are numerous. Microfilm is not digital; it is not always admissible as evidence in court; it is difficult to use; it requires strict standards for its production, storage and handling; it can be difficult to maintain; it can be easily physically damaged; it is vulnerable to chemical attack; it is monochromatic; it is relatively expensive per page compared to digital storage costs; and it is less suitable for archiving of material where there is a poor contrast between the image and background.

When using digital media for storing documents, there are a large number of technologies to choose from including magnetic tape, CD-ROM, video tape, magneto-optical, WORM (Write Once Read Many), cartridge, magnetic disk, and optical disk. For each technology there are also a large number of industry and commercial standards to choose from. Table 7.2 itemises the expected lifetime and obsolescence of various media technologies. These life expectancies are based upon storage in conditions similar to those in an air-conditioned office environment at 20°C (68°F) and 40 per cent relative humidity.

Hardware Devices

Hardware storage devices and the media that are used in them, have been increasing in storage capacity, increasing in speed and reducing in size for a number of decades. For example, data storage capabilities prior to 1990 were increasing at an annual rate of 25 per cent. To date, this rate has increased to 60 per cent, and industry observers predict that this trend will continue in the foreseeable future.[35] The need for improved storage devices is a result of the increasing size of operating systems, increasing size of application software, and increasing volumes of digital documents.

As storage technologies continue to undergo rapid improvements, it is important to realise that storage media and their associated hardware devices, are inextricably linked. Although a CD-ROM might reliably retain data for up to fifty years, the information on the disk will be unusable, unless a hardware device is also available that can read it.

Encoding Methods

In the storage of digital documents, it is extremely important that the encoding method is well documented and remains relatively neutral. At the time of archiving, it may seem trivial to document the archiving process, file formats or document structures that were used. However, in fifty years time, that information may be invaluable for people trying to decode the contents of a file format that has been obsolete for a decade or more. Even ubiquitous encoding schemes like ASCII are being challenged by alternate international coding schemes such as UNICODE.

The danger of obsolete proprietary encoding schemes, is also one of the reasons that standards like SGML and HTML are being promoted. By using a vendor- and platform-neutral method of structuring and storing documents, the risk of obsolescent encoding schemes are considerably reduced.

Recommended Approaches to Digital Document Storage

Given the susceptible and transient nature of many storage technologies, it is very important to make sure digital documents are continually transferred to storage media which are of a current technology. Digital data is theoretically invulnerable to the ravages of time, however, the physical media on which they reside have proven to be far from eternal, and not even as robust as paper in certain circumstances.[31] To transfer documents from one type of media to another is an extremely easy and relatively inexpensive process to perform when the necessary hardware is available, but can become a prohibitively expensive and tedious act when it is not.

In general, it is recommended that digital archives should be transcribed every five to ten years to ensure that they will not become technologically obsolete. Future access to data relies on an unbroken chain of migrations from technology to technology. If this process is not undertaken, successful recovery of data from obsolete storage media will require the use of the hardware and software that were originally used.[36] In a worse case scenario, the following items will be required to successfully decode data that has been stored in an obsolete format on outdated media:

- information on the recording system;
- the original authoring software;
- the original operating system;
- the original computer hardware;
- operation manuals for the above; and
- ample spare parts.

CALS

One of the most significant examples of the wide-scale adoption and implementation of digital documents, is the CALS project. While this initiative is military based, the principles behind it serve as an example of what can be achieved when a standardised and integrated approach to digital document use is embraced.

The Continuous Acquisition and Lifecycle Support (CALS) initiative was started by the US Department of Defence (DoD) in September 1985.[37] This initiative started out to improve the efficiency and reliability of weapons systems, by mandating that suppliers to the DoD comply with specific document-related standards when delivering technical information.

In the defence forces there were just as many problems associated with the use of paper for documentation purposes, as there were in civilian organisations. Digital alternatives to paper were seen not only as a means of improving efficiency and reducing costs, but as a means of gaining a strategic advantage and saving lives. For example, an Aegis class cruiser in the US Navy has so much paper on board that if it were all removed, the ship would rise 8 cm out of the water.[38] It is estimated that 25 per cent of the technical documents the DoD maintain are out of date or contain errors, and that 5–8 per cent of military fatalities result from these errors.[38] In other areas, it was discovered that 40 per cent of repair times were spent trying to retrieve information from manuals, and that it took 50–60 per cent longer to get documentation into the field when it was in a paper form.[39]

In broad terms, the objectives of CALS are intended to be realised by:

- The provision of a suite of standards which embody an integrated, open systems approach to the creation, exchange and use of technical data.
- Enabling the improvement of the effectiveness and efficiency of systems and processes, through the application of information technology which complies with the CALS standards.[38]

The implementation of CALS is occurring in two distinct phases. In phase one, standards have been defined for the transfer of *all* documents to a digital form. This will allow technical documentation on weapons systems to be stored and exchanged in a vendor-independent (i.e. neutral) form. Originally five principle standards were included, upon which subsequent compatible standards have also been adopted.

- IGES (Initial Graphics Exchange Specification) for engineering drawings.
- CCITT (Consultative Committee for International Telephony and Telegraphy) Group 4 raster format for images such as photographs.
- CGM (Computer Graphics Metafile) for vector illustrations.
- SGML (Standard Generalised Markup Language) for text; and
- MIL-STD-1840 a magnetic tape format for the automated interchange of technical information.

Figure 7.10 illustrates how these standards are intended to be integrated in the CALS environment.

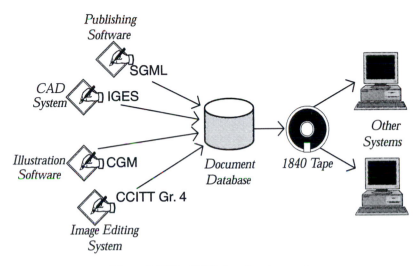

Figure 7.10 The CALS phase 1 environment

Stage two of the CALS project involves building extensive information databases of data and documents. From these databases, concurrent engineering principles can be applied, and contractors can develop sophisticated support systems more quickly and efficiently.

Despite the fact that the CALS standards only appear to address military requirements, they are actually mature implementations of a number of international and national standards that have been developed by many joint government and industry groups. In their development, a lot of input from international commercial companies has been made, to cater for the requirements of technical and business data in those industries. This range of contributors is reflected in the make-up of the CALS Industry Steering Group that now co-ordinates many of the CALS initiatives:[40,41]

- **Industry** (CALS ISG, International Division, Regional Interest Groups, etc.)
- **Professional Societies, Industry Associations, and Consortia** (AIA, ATA, ASME, AIIM, APICS, SME, AFCEA, SOLE, ASE, NSIA, NCGA, PDES Inc., SCAE, EIA, ICA, IEEE, US PRO, SME, ITI, CCIA, etc.)
- **Government** (DoD agencies, NIST, LLNL, ARPA, DOC, DOE, DoT, etc.)
- **International** (CALS Europe, NIAG, SBAC, UK, France, Australia, Japan, Taiwan, Korea, etc.)

Some specific industry sectors that have adopted the CALS strategy, include the automotive, chemicals, aerospace, electronics and computing, construction, road building, and telecommunications industries.

The decision to adopt CALS in the commercial sector, was also encouraged by the huge problems associated with the maintenance of paper-based technical documentation. For example, in 1995 QANTAS airlines were receiving about 300,000 pages of documents (1.5 tonnes) per month.[42] When one of their 747-200 planes was once sold to the US, it had to travel with its complete 10 tonne paper maintenance manual history. This volume of paper was so large that the plane was unable to fly directly to the US in one trip, and had to stop in Honolulu to refuel.[43] QANTAS has now adopted the use of CALS-based standards to manage all of its technical maintenance and reference manuals.

The CALS initiative can be clearly attributed to the need for an environment in which the delivery of timely, accurate and standards-compliant information is critical. Arguably, similar requirements can also be stated for the design and construction industries. The ability to regulate strict compliance to a set of standards like CALS, however, could not be considered to be an option that could be easily implemented – especially considering the industries very fractured and diverse nature. None the less, the CALS initiative demonstrates what can be achieved when there is a standardised, industry-based approach to the creation, exchange and use of digital documents.

REFERENCES

1. Bakos, Y. J. (1995), 'Are computers boosting productivity', *ComputerWorld*, 27 March.

2. Brynjolfson, E. (1994), 'Technology's true payoff - an MIT survey finds that business tends to overlook intangibles when evaluating IT', *Information Week*, 496, p. 34.

3. Robson, W. (1994), *Strategic Management and Information Systems*, London: Pitman Publishing.

4. Tapscott, D. and Caston, A. (1993), *Paradigm Shift – the New Promise of Information Technology*, New York: McGraw-Hill.

5. Voss, D. (1995), 'You say you want more bandwidth? Solitons and the erbium gain factor', *Wired*, vol. 3, no. 7, p. 64.

6. Wood, J. M. (1995), *Desktop Magic: Electronic Publishing, Document Management, and Workgroups*, New York: Van Nostrand Reinhold.

7. May, T. (1994), 'Creative approaches to justifying document management', *EDM '94*, Washington DC.

8. Ames, P. (1993), *Beyond Paper: the Official Guide to Adobe Acrobat*, Mountain View, CA: Adobe Press.

9. Reinhardt, A. (1994), 'Managing the new document', *BYTE*, vol. 19, no. 8, p. 90.

10. Stover, R. N. (1994), 'Document management overview', *EDM '94*, Washington, DC.

11. Maher, K. (1993), 'Document management', *Cadence*, vol. 8, no. 8, p. 33.

12. Bindslev, B. and Burgess, D. (1964), 'CBC: co-ordinated building communication: theory of CBC', *Architects' Journal*, 8 March, p. 795.

13. Mitchell, W. J. (1977), *Computer-Aided Architectural Design*, New York: Van Nostrand.

14. Schilling, T. G. and Schilling, P. M. (1987), *Intelligent Drawings: Managing CAD and Information Systems in the Design Office*, New York: McGraw-Hill.

15. Smallwood, R. (1996), 'Understanding the document management marketplace – a segmented approach', *http://www.infotivity.com/dmmktso.htm*, Document Management.

16. McCusker, T. and Strauss, P. (1993), 'Managing the document management explosion', *Datamation*, July 1, pp. 41–44.

17. Open Text (1997), 'Livelink intranet', *http://www.opentext.com/livelink/*, Open Text Livelink Intranet Web Site.

18. Seybold (1993), 'Adobe Systems' Acrobat', *The Seybold Report on Desktop Publishing*, vol. 8, no. 1, p. 6.

19. Interleaf (1991), *Introduction to SGML*, Waltham, MA: Interleaf.

20. PODA-SAX (1992), *The ODA Brochure*, Project 5320, ESPRIT project 5320.

21. Bach, E., Bellovin, S., Bernstein, D., Bolyard, N., Ellyson, C., Gillogy, J., Gleason, M. and Gwyn, D. (1994), 'sci.crypt FAQ (Part 3): Basic Cryptology', *http://www.cis.ohio-state.edu/hypertext/faq/usenet/cryptography-faq/part03/faq.html*, Usenet newsgroup.

22. Neuman, B. C. and Ts'o, T. (1994), 'Kerberos: an authentication service for computer networks', *IEEE Communications Magazine*, vol. 32, no. 9, pp. 33–38.

23. Wayner, P. (1994), 'Whose authentication systems', *BYTE*, vol. 19, no. 10, p. 128.

24. RSA (1997), 'FAQ 3.0 on cryptography', *http://www.rsa.com/rsalabs/faq/*, RSA Laboratories.

25. Mitchell, W. J. (1995), *City of Bits: Space, Place, and the Infobahn*, Cambridge: MIT Press.

26. Yelland, P. (1995), Electronic signature proves unforgeable, *The Australian: Communications and High Technology section*, November 1994, p. 23.

27. IW (1995), Digital signatures gain legitimacy, *Information Week*, 5th August, p. 24.

28. VeriSign (1997), 'Frequently asked questions about digital IDs', *http://www.verisign.com/repository/digidfaq.html*, VeriSign.

29. Netscape (1997), 'Netscape Certificate Server 1.0 evaluation guide', *http://home.netscape.com/comprod/server_central/query/eval_guide/certificate/index.html*, Netscape Communications.

30. Surety (1997), 'Advanced record authentication for the electronic age', *http://www.surety.com/*, Surety Technologies.

31. Rothenberg, J. (1995), 'Ensuring the longevity of digital documents', *Scientific American*, vol. 272, no. 1, pp. 24–29.

32. Harvey, R. (1990), *Preservation in Australian and New Zealand Libraries: Principles, Strategies and Practices for Librarians*, Wagga Wagga: Centre for Information Studies.

33. Freemantle, R. and Sloggett, R. (1995), 'Preserving the past', *The Conservation of Collections in the University of Melbourne Library*, The University of Melbourne Conservation Service, Melbourne.

34. VanBogart, J. W. C. (1996), 'NML Disposition Chart 48°F (20°C) and 40% RH', *http://www.nta.org/MediaStability/LE/DispositionCharts/20C40RH/*, National Technology Alliance.

35. Merz, J. P. (1994), 'Rigid disk systems', *http://www.nml.org/Publications/TechnicalReports/TechnologyAssessments/TechAssessmentFinalReport1994/6_rigid_disk_syst.html*, National Technology Alliance.

36. VanBogart, J. W. C. (1995), 'Mag tape life expectancy 10–30 years: letter to editor of Scientific American (vol. 272 no. 6)', *http://www.nta.org/MediaStability/LE/LetterToScientificAmerican/*, National Technology Alliance.

37. Frame (1993), *CALS and SGML: a guide to understanding these emerging technologies*, Frame Technologies Pty Ltd.

38. DLD (1992), *Computer-aided acquisition and logistics support: implementation strategy*, Defence Logistics Division, Australian Department of Defence.

39. Walsh, M. (1993), 'Collaborative research in electronic publications', *CALS Australia '93*, Melbourne: EDICA.

40. OSD (1997), 'CALS international standardization initiative', *http://www.acq.osd.mil/cals/cals-isi.html*, Office of the Secretary of Defence.

41. NATO (1997), 'NATO CALS on the Net', *http://www.cals.nato.be/*, NATO CALS Home Page.

42. Godwin, R. (1996), 'Information Management – a Qantas perspective', *STEP Search Conference*, Melbourne: DIST.

43. Bryan, M. (1993), 'QANTAS and Information Management', *CALS Australia '93*, Melbourne: EDICA.

Chapter 8
Professional Opportunities

BENEFITS OF DIGITAL DOCUMENTS

Throughout this book an exposé of work practices, technologies and techniques have been provided to illustrate:

- the definition and purpose of a document;
- how documents are used by the design and construction industry;
- the nature of the digital document environment;
- the data types which make up digital documents;
- a range of available digital document types; and
- a range of practical applications in the use of digital documents.

In an evaluation of the digital document types that have been identified, it is clear that in most cases they not only meet the performance criteria of paper-based documents, but often well exceeded them. In particular, significant gains in the performance of digital documents include:

- **Increased accessibility**. With the use of local area networks and wide area networks such as the Internet, digital documents can be remotely and simultaneously accessed, and shared by multiple readers in geographically distinct locations. Accessibility to information is dramatically increased.
- **Decreased storage size**. Digital documents are far superior to paper in their required amount of physical storage space (by volume).
- **Increased reusability**. When using digital documents, content can be reused, reformatted and presented in a number of different ways that are not possible when using printed documents.
- **Increased delivery speed**. When using large networks such as the Internet, digital documents can be delivered almost instantaneously to any location in the world.
- **Increased search capabilities**. Information content can be easily searched within and across large numbers of documents, enabling information to be located significantly faster than paper-based systems.

- **Increased security**. A number of different security methods can be used to either prevent access to an entire document or control access to specific segments of a document. These security methods are significantly superior to paper-based procedures.
- **Increased verification**. Digital documents can be verified for content, authorship, and existence at a specified time and date. Unlike paper-based procedures, modifications after verification can be more easily detected.

IMPLICATIONS FOR PROFESSIONAL PRACTICE

Since the development of early word-processing and desktop publishing systems, there has been a significant maturation of digital document technologies. Technologies have now developed to the point where it is possible to create, distribute, modify and store documents in a completely digital environment, and for them to be used throughout the entire information life-cycle of projects in the built environment.

More significantly, certain technologies have matured enough to advocate the preferential use of one medium over another – that of digital over paper. The time frame and extent to which a transition between these mediums will occur, is extremely difficult to determine. However, given the speed and extent to which computing technologies such as the Internet are being adopted, there is no question that many industries will almost exclusively use digital environments for the exchange of information.[1,2]

Since the use of documents in the design and construction industry are so ubiquitous and important for the exchange of information, it is extremely important that design professions are able to embrace the changes which are now being undertaken in their use. Those individuals and companies which avoid this issue will place themselves at risk of jeopardising their position in future project teams. In Tapscott and Caston's major study of paradigm shifts in information technology, their main conclusion was that:

> Organisations that cannot understand the new era and navigate a path through the transition are vulnerable and will be bypassed.[1]

On the other hand, significant gains can be made by those professions which adopt the use of digital document technologies and leverage advantages of their use to achieve aims such as increased accessibility to information, improved operational performance, improved quality of product, development of more efficient methods of practice, reduced production and distribution costs, savings in travel and disbursements, and increased value from information repositories and knowledge bases. Practices which adopt these technologies early, and use them as a means of improving the quality and efficiency of their services, stand to gain a significant positional advantage in the industry.

RECOMMENDATIONS FOR THE INDUSTRY

For an industry that is strongly associated with the technology of building, and the co-ordination of information, the cautious adoption of computing technology to assist this process continues to be an anomaly in many regions. Clearly, there still needs to be an increased awareness of the potentials of integrated digital work environments.

In many respects, the use of technology and the many developments it can bring, are still looked upon with fear and trepidation. Characteristically, people are known to instinctively resist any change that will have a marked effect on their daily lives.[1,3] Many professions have used paper for hundreds of years and will be tempted to retain the legacy investments they have made in the techniques, experience, and skills they have developed in the past, no matter how outmoded they may seem.[1]

The main reason for protests against technological change are often based upon ignorance and misconceptions.[3,4,5] Therefore, a way of bringing around a better understanding of technology and to reduce misconceptions about it is to educate and expose people to the way that technology can be used. A number of individual recommendations to achieve this aim can be made:

- **Education of design professionals**. Architects, engineers, and designers need to be made aware of the wider context of digital technologies in addition to the traditional mediums they use. An understanding of the broader context of document use in a digital environment will help to facilitate this process.
- **Education of clients**. Clients need to be made aware of the benefits of using design professionals who are able to communicate using a wide variety of media. There are also a significant number of benefits that can be realised in the capture of information for their own business.
- **Education of manufacturers**. Manufacturers need to be encouraged to provide product information in a digital form. The ease with which such information can be obtained, edited and reused often advocates the use of products which are specified in this manner. The Internet currently provides one of the most extensive distribution methods for this purpose.
- **Education of the design and construction industry**. In general, there needs to be a wider awareness of how digital technologies can be used to assist collaboration among consultants in the construction industry.
- **Demonstration of working systems**. One of the best ways to convince people of the way that new technologies can be used is to demonstrate their use. Independent Institutes such as the AIA, RAIA, AIB, CSIRO and others need to establish regular seminars and workshops which are able to demonstrate integrated digital work environments.
- **Recommendation of appropriate technologies**. Ongoing *vendor-independent* reviews of digital technologies should be on the agenda of many professional institutes. Findings from these reviews need to be passed on to institute members, and the industry in general, to assist in the selection of appropriate technologies.

- **Provision of on-line services**. Professional institutes such as the RAIA, should be increasing the accessibility of information to its members via electronic means. Practice notes, management notes, law notes, reports, contract pro formas and newsletters are just some of the information that can be easily distributed in a digital form.

While it is acknowledged that there are still many complex technical issues that need to be resolved in the use of digital documents, one of the greatest challenges of all will be the universal acceptance and adoption of digital document technologies in a manner that will benefit the entire design and construction industry.

REFERENCES

1.   Tapscott, D. and Caston, A. (1993), *Paradigm Shift – the New Promise of Information Technology*, New York: McGraw-Hill.

2.   Negroponte, N. (1995), *Being Digital*, Rydalmere: Hodder and Stoughton.

3.   Gunston, W. (1971), *Technology for Man's Survival*, E. de Bono (ed.), Technology Today, London: Routledge and Kegan Paul.

4.   de Bono, E. (1971), *Technology Today*, London: Routledge and Kegan Paul.

5.   McLuhan, M. (1964), *Understanding Media*, London: Abacus.

ABBREVIATIONS

AEC	Architecture, engineering, construction
AIA	American Institute of Architects
AIB	Australian Institute of Builders
ANSI	American National Standards Institute
AP	Application Protocol
API	Application Program Interface
ASCII	American Standard Code for Information Interchange
ATM	Asynchronous Transfer Mode
B-ISDN	Broadband Integrated Services Digital Networks
BCA	Building Code of Australia
BCD	Binary Coded Decimal
BMP	Microsoft Windows Bitmap format
CA	certificate authority
CAD	computer-aided design
CALS	Continuous Acquisition and Lifecycle Support
CBC	Co-ordinated Building Communication
CCITT	Consultative Committee for International Telephony and Telegraphy
CD-I	Compact Disk Interactive
CD-ROM	Compact Disk Read-Only Memory
CD-R	Compact Disk Recordable
CDA	Compound Document Architecture
CGM	Computer Graphics Metafile
CICA	Construction Industry Computing Association
CIL	Computer Integration Laboratories
CISC	complex instruction set computer
CMCD	computer-mediated collaborative design
CORBA	Common Object Request Broker Architecture
COM	Component Object Model
CPU	central processing unit
CRT	cathode ray tube
CSC	Cascading Style Sheet
CSIRO	Commonwealth Scientific and Industrial Research Organisation
CSV	comma separated values
CTI	Computer/Telephone Integration
DAT	Digital Audio Tape
DES	Data Encryption Standard
DIF	Lotus Data Interchange File format
DMS	document management system
DoD	Department of Defence
DOS	Disk Operating System
DSOM	Distributed Systems Object Model
DSS	Digital Signature Standard
DSSSL	Document Style Semantics Specification Language

DTD	Document Type Definition
DTP	Desktop Publishing
DVD	Digital Versatile Disk
DWG	AutoCAD drawing file format
DXF	Drawing Interchange Format
EBCDIC	Extended Binary Coded Data Interchange Code
ECI	Electronic CAD Interworking
EDI	Electronic data interchange
EDMS	Electronic or Engineering Document Management System
EDP	electronic data processing
EFT	electronic funds transfer
EPS	Encapsulated PostScript
ERD	Electronic reference document
FAX	facsimile
FOSI	Formatting Output Specification Instance
FTP	File Transfer Protocol
GIF	Graphics Interchange Format
GUI	Graphical User Interface
HPGL	Hewlett-Packard Graphics Language
HTML	Hypertext Markup Language
HTTP	Hypertext Transfer Protocol
IAC	inter-application communication
IAI	Industry Alliance for Interoperability
IDEA	International Data Encryption Algorithm
IFC	Industry Foundation Classes
IGES	Initial Graphics Exchange System
ISBN	International Standard Book Number
ISDN	Integrated Services Digital Network
ISO	International Standards Organisation
ISSN	International Standard Serial Number
IT	information technology
JFIF	JPEG File Interchange Format
JPEG	Joint Photographic Expert Group
LAN	local area network
LCD	liquid crystal display
LZW	Lempel-Ziv Welch
MAN	metropolitan area network
MD5	Message Digest version 5
MDA	Mail Delivery Agent
MHS	Mail Handling System
MTA	Mail Transfer Agent
MIDI	Musical Instrument Digital Interface
MIME	Multipurpose Internet Mail Extension
NC	network computer
NIST	National Institute of Standards and Technology
NPWC	National Public Works Council

OCR	optical character recognition
ODA	Open Document Architecture
ODL	Output Description Language
OLE	Object Linking and Embedding
OEM	Original Equipment Manufacturer
OPAC	On-line Public Access Catalogue
OPR	optical page recognition
OS	operating system
OSIRM	Open Systems Integration Reference Model
PBM	Portable Bitmap
PC	Personal Computer
PCD	Kodak PhotoCD
PCL	page control language
PCX	PC Paintbrush File Format
PDA	personal digital assistant
PDF	Portable Document Format
PDL	page description language
PDO	Portable Distributed Objects
PGP	Pretty Good Privacy
POV	Persistence of Vision
QA	quality assurance
QMS	quality management system
RAIA	Royal Australian Institute of Architects
RAM	random access memory
RF	radio frequency
RISC	reduced instruction set computer
RLE	Run Length Encoding
RSA	Rivest-Shamir-Adelman (compression)
RTF	Rich Text Format
SGML	Standard Generalised Markup Language
S/MIME	Secure Multipurpose Internet Mail Extension
SMTP	Simple Mail Transfer Protocol
SSL	Secure Sockets Layer
STEP	Standard for the Exchange of Product data
STICI	Self-Teaching and Interpretive Communicating Interface
SQL	Structured Query Language
SYLK	Microsoft Symbolic Link Format
TGA	Targa file format
TIFF	Tagged Image File Format
UNICODE	Universal Code
VAN	Value Added Network
VM	virtual machine
VPN	virtual private network
VR	virtual reality
VRML	Virtual Reality Modelling Language
WAIS	Wide Area Information System

WAN	wide area network
WYSIWYG	what you see is what you get
WORM	Write Once Read Many
WP	word-processing
W3	World Wide Web
WWW	World Wide Web
XML	Extensible Markup Language

INTERNET RESOURCES

The following titles and information sources were found to be particularly helpful in the research of this book. They are listed for general interest, and as a starting-point for further reading on the various topics covered by this book. Additional Web sites can also be found in the references at the end of each chapter. As with many Internet references, actual site addresses are often subject to change.

Newsgroups (Usenet)

Usenet (short for user's network) is made up of all of the computers on the Internet and other associated networks that receive network newsgroups. Over 20,000 newsgroups on almost every conceivable topic exist. The following newsgroups have been found to be particularly useful.

news://comp.mail.misc
Discussion on the use of e-mail.

news://comp.multimedia
Discussion of interactive multimedia technologies of all kinds.

news://comp.text
Discussion of text-processing issues and methods.

news://comp.text.desktop
Discussion of the technologies and techniques of desktop publishing.

news://comp.text.pdf
Discussion on the use of Adobe Acrobat.

news://comp.text.sgml
Discussion on SGML and other mark-up languages.

news://comp.theory.info-retrieval
Discussion of information retrieval topics.

news://sci.crypt
Discussion on various data encryption and decryption issues.

Web Sites

The following list of URLs (Uniform Resource Locators) are a selected list of addresses relating to the use of digital documents and other related areas of interest.

Adobe Systems
http://www.adobe.com/
Adobe create some of the industry leading software products for the design and production of documents. Also includes many references to the PDF format. The Acrobat Reader software can be downloaded free from this site.

AEC Information Centre

http://www.aecinfo.com/

The AEC Information Centre provides a comprehensive electronic forum for the delivery of information to the architectural, engineering, construction and home building industry.

American Institute of Architects

http://www.aia.org/

The AIA provides an excellent range of services for the public and its members via the Web. A good example of how a professional institute can represent itself in a digital environment.

Architectural Engineering Virtual Library

http://energy.arce.ukans.edu/wwwvl/wwwarce.htm

The architectural engineering virtual library contains links to sites relating to the application of engineering principles to the design, construction and operation of technical systems for buildings.

Architectural Virtual Library

http://www.clr.toronto.edu:1080/VIRTUALLIB/arch.html

The architectural virtual library contains a large number of links to sites around the world containing information relevant to architecture. There are also many links to architectural firms, institutes, organisations and building product suppliers.

Digital Libraries

http://www.parc.xerox.com/istl/projects/dlib/

The start of joint initiative of the US National Science Foundation (NSF), DARPA, XEROX and NASA for research on digital libraries.

Digital Notary System

http://www.surety.com/

Developers of the Digital Notary System as discussed in Chapter 7. Surety provide a unique record authentication service for electronic record certification and authentication of digital documents.

Electronic Text Archive

http://www.etext.org/

An electronic archive of books, magazines, zines, mailing lists and other resources.

Engineering Virtual Library

http://arioch.gsfc.nasa.gov/wwwvl/engineering.html

The engineering virtual library contains a large number of links to sites around the world containing information relevant to engineers.

FX Palo Alto Laboratory

http://www.fxpal.xerox.com/

A research laboratory for Fuji Xerox that is researching the 'office of the future' and the 'document of the future'.

Interleaf Corporation

http://www.ileaf.com/

Developer of integrated document creation and management solutions.

IT2000

http://www.ncb.gov.sg/ncb/it2000.asp

'IT2000 – a vision of an intelligent island' is a statement from the Singapore government on achieving international competitiveness through the sharing of various forms of digital media, across a high-capacity, high speed information infrastructure.

Lend Lease

http://www.lendlease.com.au/property/

The home page for Lend Lease Corporation.

Netscape Communications

http://home.netscape.com/

Developers of Web technology, servers and browsers. Netscape Navigator is currently the most popular browser used on the Web.

Palo Alto Research Center (PARC)

http://www.parc.xerox.com/

A very highly regarded research laboratory, founded in 1970, that does a considerable amount of work on the use of documents.

PGP

http://www.ifi.uio.no/pgp/
http://www.pgp.com/

Home pages of the International and US versions of PGP authentication.

Rank Xerox Research Centre

http://www.rxrc.xerox.com/

Specialises in the development of digital, paper and other document technologies. A particular area of focus is multilingual document use.

Royal Australian Institute of Architects

http://www.raia.com.au/

Home page of the RAIA.

RSA Security

http://www.rsa.com/

The RSA Security Inc. home page. Information on a large range of security and encryption issues.

SGML Home Page

http://www.sil.org/sgml/

A site established to assist developers and users of SGML related products and document mark-up.

University of Melbourne
http://www.arbld.unimelb.edu.au/
Faculty of Architecture, Building and Planning home page.

US Library of Congress
http://lcweb.loc.gov/
Home page of one of the largest libraries in the world.

Verity Text Search Engine
http://www.verity.com/
Developers of full-text search engines that are being incorporated into many document management systems.

Web Search Engines
http://www.altavista.digital.com/
http://www.hotbot.com/
http://www.excite.com/
These sites are well renowned for their extensive search capabilities across the Web.

World Wide Web Consortium
http://www.w3.org/
The World Wide Web Consortium (W3C) was established in 1994 to develop common protocols for the evolution of the World Wide Web.

Xerox
http://www.xerox.com/
Renowned for its photocopiers, Xerox has now re-badged itself as 'The Document Company'. Xerox now focuses heavily on both digital and paper-based document solutions.

INDEX

A

Acid free paper, 192
ActiveX, 74, 76–7, 136, 166, 167, 189 *see also* OLE
Adobe Acrobat, 47, 154–60, 207
AEC, 203, 208
AIA, 195, 203, 208
AIFF, 99
Alberti, 2
Analogue device, 44
Animation, 70, 89, 91, 97, 98, 106, 144, 145, 148, 160, 161, 163
Animation formats, 97
ANSI, 203
ANSI X.12, 130, 188
Application-centric, 72, 112–3
Applications, 69–7
    for the construction industry, 69
    Internet based, 74–77
    Java, 75–6
    scripting of, 74
    text based, 71
Architects, 1–2, 4, 7, 8, 23, 26, 40, 46, 54, 63, 111, 122, 145, 179
    change in the industry, 23–24
    in the construction industry, 23–6
    services, 26–8
Archive, 18, 30, 40, 105, 193, 208
ASCII, 83, 84–5, 88, 95–7, 106, 119–20, 123, 125, 128–9, 134, 136–7, 147, 154, 193, 203
ATM, 64, 203
Audio data, 98–9
Augmented reality, 52–3
Authentication, 129, 142, 182–6, 188–9, 208–9
Authorisation, 36
Authorship, 126, 186, 189, 200
AutoCAD, 85, 95, 111, 113, 115, 123, 204
Auto-ID, 48–9

B

Bar codes, 48
Base64 encoding, 128
BCAider, 151–2
BHP, 130
BinHex, 128

Bitmap(s), 13, 47, 51, 70, 89–94, 96–7, 100, 102, 104, 106, 111, 132, 135, 157, 179
    benefits of, 94
    limitations of, 94
Bits, 1, 65, 81–3, 91, 98, 132, 176, 187
Boeing, 142
Bookmarks, 156
Browser plug-ins *see* plug-ins
Brunelleschi, Filipo, 4
Building Code of Australia (BCA), 151
Bush, Dr. Vannevar, 143

C

CAD, 4, 10, 29, 38, 45, 47, 51, 57, 63, 65, 69–70, 73, 85, 88–9, 91, 94–5, 97–8, 105, 111, 113, 115, 121–3, 125, 128, 135, 142, 148–9, 154, 163–4, 176, 181, 203–4
Caesar, Julius, 183
CALS, 93, 103, 131, 142, 157, 194–6, 195, 203
Case Studies
    Adobe Acrobat, 157–60
    BCAider, 151–2
    IETMS, 152
CCITT, 93, 97, 102–3, 155, 188, 194, 203
CDA, 137, 142–3, 203
CD-ROM, 16, 52, 93, 105, 145, 151, 161, 164, 175–7, 192–3, 203
CERN, 146
Certificates *see* digital certificates
CGI, 74–5
CGM, 194, 203
Colour, 92, 123
Common Ground, 153
Compatibility, 174, 177
Compatibility,
    problems with 111, 122, 181–2
Component editors, 72
Component-based applications
    Component based, 71–74
Components, 72
Compound documents, 72, 74, 91, 98, 113, 135–7, 149, 155, 176, 179
Compound document management, 179

Compression, 92–3, 95, 97–8, 101–6, 155, 161, 167, 205
Compression file formats, 105–6
Compression of data, 101–6
Computing fundamentals, 44–5
Concurrent engineering, 40, 195
Confidentiality, 129
Construction industry
    current model, 25–26
Copyright, 36
CORBA, 73, 136, 203
Cost of Implementation, 174–5
CPU, 44
CRT, 50, 51, 203
Cryptography, 183
Cryptosystem, 183
CSIRO, 151, 201
Cut and paste, 136

D
DAT, 203
Data integrity, 186
Data retrieval, 106–7
Data storage, 191
Data types, 28
    basic principles, 81–2
    numerical, 82–3
    text, 83–88
Database, 18, 37–8, 48–9, 56, 62, 70, 75–6, 106–7, 115, 123–4, 133–6, 140, 149, 163–4, 177–80, 182, 195
Department of Defence (DoD), 194
DES, 184, 203
Desktop publishing, 45, 71, 89, 93, 97, 121, 133, 154, 168, 200, 207
DIF, 203
Digital
    definition of, 44
Digital camera, 46, 92
Digital certificates, 188–9
Digital ink data, 99–101
Digital notary system, 189–90, 208
Digital Signature Standard (DSS), 188
Digital signatures, 186–8
Digital storage, 15
Digital vs electronic, 44–5
Display devices, 50
    future developments, 52–3
    portability of, 50–1
    resolution, 51
    size, 51

DMS, 56, 177–9, 181, 203–4
Document authentication, 182
Document authorisation, 182
Document confidentiality, 182
Document image management, 179
Document integrity, 182
Document interchange, 114, 119, 121, 123, 142–3
Document management, 177–82
    main functions of, 180–1
    types of, 179
Document passwords, 183
Document presentation and rendering, 12–13
Document structures, 110, 112–3, 136, 167–8, 179, 182, 193
    need for, 110
    traditional methods, 110
Document Style Semantics Specification Language (DSSSL), 141
Document technologies
    selecting appropriate, 173–5
Document Type Definition (DTD), 138
Document-centric, 72, 74, 110
Documents, 7
    a comparison of, 165–7
    a paradigm shift in the use of, 1
    accessibility, 199
    archival, 30
    as a container, 9
    as a valuable asset, 35
    benefits of digital, 199–200
    classification of, 112
    complexity of, 176
    components of, 9
    for contract administration, 31
    for contract documentation, 31
    definition of, 7
    delivery of, 199
    design, 31
    distribution methods, 175–7
    distribution of, 177
    duplication of, 14
    dynamic compound, 135–6
    electronic reference and hypermedia, 143–52
    filing of, 18
    float, 18
    formatting, 12
    general office, 30
    interchange, 117–25

known problems with use of, 35–7
labour cost, 178
legal requirements, 7
messaging, 33, 125
multimedia, 160–5
office documents, 28–33
office management documents, 29
output, 115–7
performance criteria of, summary, 40–1
pre-design, 30
processable compound, 136–43
project, 30
proprietary, 113–5
quality management, 29
reference, 32
retaining, 16
reusability, 199
size of, 176
storage size, 199
summary of benefits for digital, 19–20
trading, 32
transfer of, 193
types of, 9–11
viewer, 153–60
volume of project related, 33–5
DOS, 61, 65–6, 68, 105, 153, 155, 157, 173, 178
Drawings, 31, 33, 122–3
DSSSL, 141, 150, 203
DTD, 138–42, 147, 149, 204
Du Pont, 125
DVD, 15, 204
DVI, 98
DWG, 115, 204
DXF, 121, 204
Dynamic compound documents, 113, 166
    see also documents, dynamic compound

E
EDI, 56, 126, 129–31, 166–7, 177, 186, 188, 204
EDIFACT, 130, 188
EDMS, 56, 179, 204
EFT, 204
Electronic
    definition of, 44
Electronic book, 52
Electronic forms, 126, 133–4
Electronic funds transfer (EFT), 130
Electronic reference documents, 113, 143–52

Electronic mail, 55, 56, 60, 62, 75, 85, 98, 100, 126–34, 155, 158, 177, 186–8, 207
    attachments, 128
    encoding, 128
    gateways, 128
Encryption, 36, 61, 62, 64, 129, 167, 183–8, 207, 209
    Private key, 184–5
    Public key, 185–6
Engineers, 1, 2, 4, 7, 14, 40, 46, 54, 56, 63, 111, 122, 145, 201, 208
Enhanced customer service, 159
Envoy, 153
EPS, 204
Extensible structure, 167
Extranet, 61

F
Facsimile, 15, 19, 103, 126, 131–2, 183, 204
Fast-track construction, 39
Fax, 18, 50, 93, 126, 131–2, 181, 183, 204
FIF, 93
File encryption, 64
File locking, 63
Firewalls, 63
Fixed media, 177
FLI, 97
Fonts, 86–8, 120, 122, 137, 155, 168
Ford Motors Company, 37
Forgery, 36, 129–30
Formatting, 13
Fractal, 93, 102, 104
Frame relay, 54, 57, 64
FTP, 56, 60, 63, 128, 146, 148, 177, 204
Full-text searching, 146

G
Gateways, 59, 127–8
GhostView, 117, 153
GIF, 93, 97, 103, 129, 148, 204
Gopher, 148
Graham Bell, Alexander, 126
Graphics data, 74, 88–91, 97–9, 107
    an introduction, 89
    basic terminology, 89–91
Graphics file format, 88–9, 91, 93, 96, 103, 131, 149
Great Fire of London, 23
GUI, 45, 66–8, 135, 204

H

HCOM, 99
Heterogeneous networks, 59
HPGL, 116
HTML, 85, 135, 137, 141, 146–50, 157,
    162, 166–8, 174, 182, 193, 204
    style sheets, 150
Hypercard, 161
Hypermedia, 60, 70, 113, 134–5, 141,
    143–52, 143–6, 147, 151–2, 160
Hypermedia documents, 113

I

IAC, 204
IAI, 204
IBM, 3
IconAuthor, 161
IDEA, 184, 204
IETMS, 152
IFC, 204
IGES, 121, 123–4, 194, 204
Index, 145
Industry Alliance for Interoperability
    (IAI), 125
Industry Foundation Classes (IFC), 125
Information life-cycle, 200
Information repository, 20, 110
Infrared, 52, 56
Ink data, 100
Input Devices, 45–9
Intangible benefits, 175
Integrated computing environment, 43
Intel, 66, 93, 98
Intellectual Property and Copyright, 36–7
Interchange, 166–7
    CAD, 122–5
    database and spreadsheet, 120
    retaining formatting, 120–1
    text based, 119–20
    word-processing, 121–22
Interchange documents, 113
Interchange formats, 118–9, 121–3
Internet, 1, 3, 43, 54–8, 60–1, 63, 65,
    67–8, 73–4, 75–7, 93, 98, 105–6, 126–
    30, 136, 141, 146–7, 149, 155, 157, 161–
    63, 168, 174, 176–7, 179, 187–9, 190,
    199, 200–1, 204–5, 207
Intranet, 58, 60, 161, 181
ISBN, 204–5
ISDN, 54, 57, 64, 203
ISO, 204

J

Jaggies, 51
Japan, 132, 195
Java, 58, 73–6, 136, 153–4, 161, 188
JFIF, 204
Jot, 100
JPEG, 93, 97–8, 102–4, 148, 155, 204

K

Kanji, 132
Kerning, 150
Keyboard, 45
Keyword searches, 152
Keyword searching, 146
KPMG, 157

L

LAN, 54, 57–8, 126, 177, 181, 188, 204
LCD, 204
Le Corbusier, 2
Legacy data, 47, 110
Library, 11, 122, 179–80, 182, 208
Linking, 144
Lotus DIF, 95
LZW, 93, 97, 102–3, 155, 204

M

Macintosh, 66, 75, 89, 93, 97–9, 105, 154,
    157
MacroMedia, 161
Magnetic disk, 192
Magnetic stripe, 49
Magneto-optical, 192
Mail systems, 126–7
MAN, 54, 204
MAPI, 127, 134
Margins, 150
Mark-up, 12
    procedural, 12
    structural, 12
MD5, 184, 186–7, 203–5
Media life expectancies, 191–2
Media obsolescence, 191
Memex, 143–4
Messaging, 166
Messaging documents, 113
MetaCard, 161
Metafiles, 96–7
MHS, 127
Microfilm, 16, 30, 192
Microkernels, 67

Microphones, 46
Microsoft Windows, 75, 93, 97, 135, 146
Microstation, 95, 115
MIDI, 98–100
Military, 47, 53, 183, 187, 194–5
MIME, 129, 204
M-JPEG, 97
Monge, Gaspard, 4
Mouse, 45
MPEG, 97
MPILIB, 188
Multifunction devices, 50
Multimedia, 11, 43, 46, 56, 70, 91, 98,
    106–7, 112–3, 141, 144, 149, 160–6,
    168, 179, 207
    for design, 163
    for education and reference, 164–5
    for product information, 163–4
    in the construction industry, 163–5
Multimedia devices, 46
Multimedia documents, 113
Multimedia formats, 98

N
Native document formats, 113–5, 118
Navigable interface, 167
Navigation, 144, 166
NCSA Mosaic, 146
Negroponte, Nicholas, 2, 126, 132
Nelson, Ted, 144
Netscape, 147, 209
Network
    security, 61–4
Network computer, 58, 76
Network computing, 53, 58, 76
Networks, 53–65
    and file encryption, 64
    and file locking, 63–4
    file Permissions on, 62–3
    firewalls, 63
    future of, 64–5
    heterogeneous, 59, 110, 157
    interconnectivity between, 59–61
    Internet technologies, 60
    logins, 61–62
    principal functions, 55–6
    sharing and transfer of data, 56–7
    sharing of peripherals, 57
    sharing of processing, 58–9
Neutral structure, 167
News, 148

Newspaper, 192
Newton, 101
Notary Systems *see* Digital Notary
    Systems
Numerical Data, 82
NURB, 96

O
Object-orientation, 67
Object-oriented, 66–7, 71, 125, 135–6
OCR, 47, 70, 132, 157, 179, 205
ODA, 137, 142–3, 183, 205
ODL, 205
Office document types
    methods of classifying, 28
Office management documents, 26
OLE, 73, 76, 136, 166, 167, 205
OPAC, 205
Open Media Framework (OMF), 161
OpenDoc, 73–4
Operating Systems, 65–9
    basics of, 65–6
    microkernels, 67
    new generation, 66
    object-orientation, 67
    user interface, 67–8
OPR, 205
Optical disk., 192
OSI, 59, 60, 204–5
Output description languages, 115
Output devices, 49
Output documents, 112

P
Page description languages, 13, 115–6
Paper, 13
    as a document substrate, 13–9
    consumption, 17
    consumption of resources, 17
    delivery methods, 18
    management issues, 18–9
    reproduction of, 14–5
    storage of, 15–6, 18
Paper-based documents, 145
Paper-based system, 37, 178, 199
Paper versus digital, 13
Paperless office, 14
Papyrus, 2
Participants in the design process, 24
Password, 61–2, 64, 182–3, 185, 189
Pattern recognition, 107

PBM, 93
PCD, 205
PCL, 85, 115–6, 166, 205
PCX, 93
PDA, 68, 76, 100, 205
PDF, 153, 154–8, 166–8, 205, 207
PDL, 13, 88, 97, 115–6, 205
Pen based input device, 52
Pens, 46
PGP, 129, 187–8, 205, 209
PhotoCD, 93
Photocopiers, 14, 50, 210
Photocopies, 14
Photography, 89, 191
PICT, 97
Pixels, 9, 51, 90–2, 94, 97–8, 102, 104, 106
PKZIP, 103
Plotters, 49
Plug-ins, 99, 149, 154, 157, 161, 162, 174
PNG, 93
Portability, 166
Portable Digital Document (PDD), 153
PostScript, 13, 85, 88, 97, 116–7, 153–5, 166, 204
Print merge, 136
Printer, 10, 13, 15, 18, 44, 47, 49, 50, 57, 86, 88, 91, 94, 96, 112, 115–7, 153
Printers, 49
Process reengineering, 37–8
Processable compound, 166
Processable compound documents, 113
    see documents, processable compound
Professional practice
    implications for, 200
Project documents, 26
Proprietary document formats, 111–4, 117–8, 168
Publish and subscribe, 136
Publishing, 13, 16, 45, 70–1, 93, 97, 115, 133, 140, 149, 154, 166, 168, 200, 207

Q
QA, 205
QANTAS, 195
Quality management systems, 38–9
Quicktime, 98, 162, 165

R
Radio, 48, 52, 133, 135
Radio frequency tagging, 48
RAIA, 205, 209

RAM, 44
Raster, 13, 51, 90, 93, 102, 194
Reference documents, 27
Relevance-ranked searches, 106
Rendering, 12
RIFF, 98
RLE, 93, 97–8, 102, 106, 155
Roger of Sicily, 191
Rolls Royce, 142
RSA, 184–5, 187–8, 205, 209
RTF, 85, 97, 121, 166, 205

S
S/MIME, 129, 189, 205
Scanners, 47
Searchable content, 167
Security, 11, 15, 35–7, 49, 60–2, 64, 76–7, 125, 129, 140, 180, 182–90, 200, 209
Security and privacy issues, 35–6
SGI, 93
SGML, 70, 85, 137–42, 147, 149–50, 152, 157, 166–8, 182–83, 193–4, 205, 207, 209
    application of, 141–2
    HyTime, 141
SGO, 95
Shell, 125
SIF, 121
Signature, 28, 33, 36, 64, 100, 126–7, 129–30, 142, 186–88, 190
Signatures see digital signatures
Simple Mail Transfer Protocol (SMTP), 127
Smart Cards, 49
SMTP, 60, 85, 127–9, 134, 177
SND, 99
Software, 109
Sound, 46, 82–3, 97–9, 106–7, 137, 141, 145, 160, 162–3
Special Data Capture Devices, 48–9
SQL, 205
SSL, 205
STEP, 121, 123–5, 131, 142, 205
STICI, 205
Storage, 191–3
    encoding methods, 193
    hardware devices, 192
    recommended approaches to, 193
    suitablity of media types, 191–3
Storage devices, 193
Storage of digital documents, 193

Style Sheets, 150, 168
SuperCard, 161
Surety Technologies, 189
SYLK, 205

T
Table of contents, 145–6
Tagging, 48, 137, 157
Tapscott and Caston, 200
Tar, 105
TCP/IP, 60, 130, 147
Telnet, 148
Text indexing and retrieval, 179
TGA, 93, 205
TIFF, 93, 205
Translators, 118, 119
Truecolour, 92
Types of documents
    actual documents, 10
    virtual documents, 10
Typographic issues, 115

U
UNICODE, 83, 85–6, 193, 205
United Airlines, 142
User interface, 67–8
UUencoding, 128

V
Value added networks (VANs), 130
Vector, 45, 47, 51, 88–91, 94–7, 106, 111,
    118, 123–4, 194
Vector files
    benefits of, 95
    limitations, 96
Vectorisation, 47, 94
Vectors, 94–6
Verification levels, 28
Verification of document authenticity, 186
Verne, Jules, 126
Video camera, 46
Video conferencing, 46, 56–7
Video tape, 192
Viewer, 166
Viewer documents, 113
Virtual private networks (VPN), 54–5, 61,
    205
Virtual Reality Modelling Language
    (VRML), 98, 162–3, 205
Vision Systems, 48
Visualisation, 70

Voice recognitionsystems, 48
VR, 205

W
WAIS, 146, 205
WAN, 54, 58, 177, 206
WAV, 99
Wavefront OBJ, 95
Wavelet, 104
Web browser
    plug-ins, 99, 149, 154, 161, 174
Web browsers, 60, 68, 147
Windows, 173
WMF, 97
Word-processing, 15, 71, 76, 84
Workflow, 177
World Wide Web, 56, 63, 110, 135, 141,
    146–50, 163, 168, 177, 206, 210
WorldView, 153
WORM, 192, 206
WWW *see* World Wide Web
WYSIWYG, 206

X
Xanadu, 144
Xerox, 209
XLS, 115
XML, 149–50, 206

Z
Zimmerman, Phil, 187
Zip, 105

COLOPHON

This book was designed and produced digitally. Apart from one introductory phone call between the author in Australia and the publisher in England, all communications, correspondence, proofing and production was performed digitally.

Hardware
Pentium 90Mhz 32Mb RAM 1.6Gb HDD, NEC 17" *MultiSync 5FGp* monitor, Hewlett-Packard *LaserJet 6L* (for proofs), Netcomm *Smartmodem M34F*, Conner 4mm *DAT backup* drive.

Communications
Netscape *Communicator* 4.02.

Page composition and layout
Microsoft *Word* 95.

Typeface
Body text: *Bembo.* Titles: *Franklin Gothic.*

Digital Proofing
Adobe Acrobat PDF v3.0.

Digital Reproduction
Adobe Acrobat Distiller v.3.0, Adobe Acrobat Exchange v.3.0.

Graphics Illustration
Claris *Draw* 1.0, Corel *Draw* 7, Adobe *Photoshop* v4.0,

Reference database and bibliography
Niles and Associates *Endnote Plus* v2.3.

Backup
Cheyenne Backup for Windows 95.

OCT 24 2013	DATE DUE	
OCT 25 2013